The texts of Paulo Freire

PAUL V. TAYLOR

Open University Press
Buckingham · Philadelphia

Open University Press
Celtic Court
22 Ballmoor
Buckingham
MK18 1XW

and
1900 Frost Road, Suite 101
Bristol, PA 19007, USA

First Published 1993

A catalogue record of this book is available from the British Library

Library of Congress Cataloging-in-Publication Data

Taylor, Paul V., 1946–
    The texts of Paulo Freire/Paul V. Taylor.
        p.   cm.
    Includes bibliographical references (p.   ) and index.
    ISBN 0–335–19020–0. – ISBN 0–335–19019–7 (pbk.)
        1. Freire, Paulo, 1921–   . 2. Education–Philosophy.
    3. Critical theory.   4. Critical pedagogy.   5. Popular education.
    I. Title.
    LB880.F732T39   1993
    370.11'5–dc20   92–27643
                                                                                     CIP

Typeset by Type Study, Scarborough
Printed in Great Britain by Biddles Ltd, Guildford and Kings Lynn

Contents

Note on language and sexism

It is regrettable that so much of the vigour and commitment of those who write and teach against oppression is vitiated by sexist language. Sadly, if we construct the struggle for freedom as an engagement for 'man's liberation', we may be contributing to the suppression, invisibility or powerlessness of women. We can no longer inhabit a world where 'men are oppressed' and where we try to educate people that a man can 'liberate himself' and can achieve 'his ontological vocation through his own efforts'.

I have discussed this problem of sexist language in my correspondence with Professor Freire. He has indeed confirmed that it was certainly not his intention to cause offence by the apparently sexist translations of his work, and he agreed wholeheartedly that such 'old forms of writing' should be avoided.

Professor Freire willingly agreed that I should retranslate his early works, avoiding sexist language and in keeping with his own efforts, since 1975, to find more acceptable linguistic expressions. This I have tried to do where I have had the original text to hand. In other cases, I have reworked or reworded the available translations.

Equally, I have rephrased other texts used in this study, albeit without permission. I have tended to use *person* or *humankind*, *she/he* and *their*, but I have also circumvented the linguistic problems of certain texts by using the formula of *we*, *us*, and *our*. The essential meaning of the texts has not been altered, but there may be a nuance of direct, personal expression which is more evident here than in the original sources.

The task of trying to create a discourse on liberating education that is anti-sexist has been difficult. It is hoped that any strain experienced by the reader because of unfamiliar linguistic forms will be tolerated in the light of my underlying intention to engage all those who wish, as Subjects, to enter an authentic and authenticating dialogue.

Acknowledgements

Many people have contributed to the constructive dialogue on which this book is based. I am grateful to my students and colleagues at De Montfort University, Leicester and at the Université de Tours who have helped me to convert theory into practice. I would particularly like to thank Theresa Purcell, Biant Suwali Singh, Elke Mathes and Numa Murard for their comments, criticisms and constant encouragement.

In large part, this book could not have been completed without the counsel and help of Keith Hoskin, at Warwick University, whose insights into the power of literacy I have relished, just as I have enjoyed his enthusiasm for the debate. In addition, I have had the enormous advantage of working with a careful and supportive publisher whose efficiency and guidance I have greatly appreciated.

We have tried to ensure that all our responsibilities towards other copyrights have been honoured. The pictures of the codified themes which I have used here have been circulating in various 'Freirean' groups and courses for many years. As I am uncertain of the source of the pictures in my possession, I have taken the liberty of referring the reader to the most accessible sources: Freire's *Education: the Practice of Freedom* (1976) and Brown's *Literacy in Thirty Hours* (1974). Despite the demise of the Writers and Readers Co-operative, who held the copyright of both these editions, every possible attempt has been made to seek the permission of previous copyright holders on whose amicable consideration and understanding I hope I can rely.

Finally, my love and fullest thanks go to the family, Sally, Luke and Ruth who have supported me in every possible way through the highs and the lows of researching and writing.

My thanks to these special people does not implicate them in the faults and shortcomings of the book. Despite all, should the book fail in any way to meet the ideals of engaging in real dialogue, the responsibility will be wholly mine.

Introduction: The textualizing and contextualizing of Freire

Paulo Freire, educator, philosopher and political activator, has the capacity to excite and frustrate friends and critics alike. He is not, apparently, a man about whom one remains neutral. With almost cultic status, he has been called the greatest living educator, a master and teacher, first among a dying class of modern revolutionaries who fight for social justice and transformation. His pedagogy is epoch making: he is a legend in his own time.[1]

But is he a living legend, still relevant today? For some he represents the period of youth, idealism and enthusiasm which was fashionable in the late 1960s and early 1970s but which since has been tainted with disillusion and middle age. For others his philosophy was and is much more than a passing, opportunist discourse on liberating education. It has provided the basis for radical experimentation in education and for asserting that the kind of dialogic education which Freire proposed is the only viable means, other than that of the bullet and the bomb, for attaining social change and freedom.

The two ideas of education and freedom have always been intertwined: 'As an educator, Freire is mainly concerned with the educational means of freeing people from the bondage of the culture of silence' (Reimer 1970: 69). This view is illustrated by the report that

> The direct outcome of his work in Brazil and Chile has been that various groups of oppressed people, who have lived for years in a world where they have been imprisoned by mental and physical poverty, now have a new hope, a renewed desire to live a life as full human beings, a belief that they can affect their own destinies and a desire to become educated. He has provided them with the tools to liberate and educate themselves. (Haviland 1973: 281)

Yet is this, was this ever, really the case? In what sense can education be linked causally to the complex processes of liberation? Does education combat 'mental poverty' as it might do 'physical poverty', even supposing that the former denotes a meaningful, social or individual deprivation? One response frequently offered is that the so-called Freirean method is not primarily concerned with education but with a much greater human need, namely the development of a just society.

This may sound a grandiose claim, but it is one that underlies the suggestion made by many commentators that the *Pedagogy of the Oppressed*, for example, should not be read as a 'revolutionary pedagogy' but as a 'pedagogy *for* revolution' (Harman 1971).

What is surprising is that there should be need at all for any discussion about the central tenet of Freire's philosophy. But discussion there certainly is. There is no shortage of critics who blame Freire himself for this lack of clarity and for creating a magma of texts, analyses and reflections beneath the apparently solid crust of his literacy method. They point to the contorted manner of his writing; his lack of human experience; his circular logic and confusing repetitiveness. He is obscurantist, too mystifying, too abstract, too psychological, too utopian. His method requires a high level of social manipulation and can be used equally to domesticate as to liberate.[2]

It is these contiguous elements of confusion, criticism, contradiction and commendation that make any study of Freire fascinating but difficult. Yet we cannot allow his appeal: 'Many people say I am a contradictory man, and I say I have the right to be contradictory. Let me be in peace with my contradictions' (1979: 11). This may have been a felt need on his part, but it is inconsistent with that process of conscientization in which he otherwise actively encourages people to 'refuse to be inactive readers and to become agents of their own learning' (1976c). Dialogic education must also be dialectic education, and we have to reject the homogenization of knowledge and seek to 'problematize', to bring into question what is given by exploiting the contradictions, by finding those *contra-dicta* that mean that something can be 'said against' the *status quo*.

In refusing Freire his contradictions, however, we are not simply attempting to rationalize his system. We cannot demythologize Freire by imposing an illusion of coherence on his inconsistencies. The critical reader is not condemned to find a coherent Freire inside the disparate texts which are available. On the one hand, there is a danger in any review of ideas, particularly when the period under review spans half a century, of making earlier texts anachronistic by imposing on them the author's later understandings. On the other hand, there is the temptation to 'read between the lines' and so find or implant that inner thread of consistency and logic which the reader thinks she or he has perceived.[3] We may have to accept as inevitable, even desirable, that a method founded on the principles of dialogue should be exposed by the evidence of incomplete premises and even downright contradiction.

A chronology of ideas will take account of the fact that key terms and core principles may have changed and developed with time. The reader, in that case, can fall back only upon the internal evidence of a date-marked text to speculate on what the author was trying to say at that time. Some of those ideas will be situation specific (for example, Freire's work in 1961–3, or his activities in Guinea-Bissau) so that there may be corroborating evidence of other external texts or con-texts which 'explain' the texts.

With Freire, this textualizing is no easy task. His sincerity is not in doubt; not even a casual reader could miss the passion and strength of this commitment. The difficulties lie rather in establishing a proper image of the man himself and a clear catalogue of his work. What do we know of Freire's life, what has he said and written, in what context and to whom was he speaking and writing?

It is important to note that there is as yet no accredited biography of Freire. I have formed only an incomplete jigsaw picture, using pieces gleaned from his writings and interviews and from people who knew him. Although he often asserts that 'any statement on education implies a statement about a person's relationship with the world', he has been less than expansive in dealing with his own biography.

Here I have preferred to use the term 'bio-text' rather than biography. First, because Freire has always insisted on writing his own life in his own script. The kind of popular biography that many seek, he would regard as necrophilic: it would be a 'treacherous memorial because it is logical and necessarily centripetal, and that means life-denying' (Sturrock 1974).

Second, 'bio-text' draws attention to the fact that this study is a *reading* of Freire, in the fullest sense of the word. It is an attempt to read what he has written and to read his world, to understand what he has done and how he has done it, allowing actions to speak at least as loudly as words. Biography is strictly a writing of a life: bio-text reads a life, critically always, but with humility, enabling us to analyse the content of the text, 'keeping in mind what comes before and after it, in order not to betray the author's total thinking' (1985a: 3).

We shall therefore be able to feel how the centrifugal force of Freire's pedagogy flies outwards in search of dialogue and the possibility of change, how he harnesses Aristotle's dictum that each person is capable of being 'other' to a method that is more focused on what we can become than on what we are. However, reading Freire is also a process of listening to Freire for, ever provincial despite his international acclaim, he often prefers to talk his 'texts' rather than write them.

He has always admitted that he is 'more used to talking than to writing' (1975d), but he values this in a very positive way. For him, speaking, even with a provincial accent, is the prerequisite of literacy. His method demands that one learns to speak before one can write and read, not least because speaking is the essential mode of dialogue: 'In the last analysis, you are recreating yourself in dialogue to a greater extent than when you are solitarily writing, seated in your office, or in a small library' (1987a).

His preference for speaking a text, rather than writing a text, is marked in the reprint of dialogues and conversations (1985a), in his 'talked book' with Shor (1987a), in the further dialogues and reflections with Macedo (1987b), in *Learning to Question* with Faundez (1989), and in his collection of interviews and discussions (1991). This raises the technical question of the authorship and ownership of the text: whose text are we actually reading? The fact that a 'book' is largely spoken, makes the *writer* more a *dictator*, and it takes less than a Derridean twist of language to expose the relationship between power and knowledge which that evokes.

To whom, then, belongs the 'author-ship', the author-ity, of Freire's books? McLaren (1988) suggests, for example, that

> Macedo brings a complementary and critical voice both to the theoretical and the practical aspects of Freirean pedagogy. He helps to clarify some of Freire's positions on the pedagogical implications and applications of his work. (McLaren 1988: 219)

It is perhaps significant that Freire's early work was 'authored' alone (*Education as the Practice of Freedom, Pedagogy of the Oppressed*, and *Letters to Guinea Bissau*), while nearly all his work published since his return to Brazil is 'co-authored' (with Guimaroes, 1983b; with Betto, 1985b; with Shor, 1987a; with Macedo, 1987b; and with Faundez, 1989).

Is it possible now to hear the voice of Freire without listening also to his acolytes? When he works and reworks the core of his ideas and publications, often through dialogue and discussion, who is the real author: Freire when he answers a particular question or his interviewer for drawing him out or leading him on? We might even ask: Is Freire's pedagogy the work of one man, or does it now represent a 'school of thought' in which Freire is but the principal partner? That is a problem which we shall have to consider, but it is not the only one if we want to trace the development of his ideas. Somehow, we shall need to establish a proper chronology of his 'grapho-texts', that is, all that he has actually written and published. Again I prefer the term 'grapho-texts' to that of 'bibliography' because it can include, with the long list of books, articles and interviews, recorded speeches, transcripts of conferences, reviews in journals, notes and letters, while stressing the role of the author as a writer, as someone who is in the process of writing a word and a world.

Freire's work, which has been published in seventeen languages, appears, in the main, in Portuguese, Spanish, English, French and German. Not only does that create a mixed vocabulary (for example: Educaçåo, Educacíon, Education; Conscientizaçåo, Conscientizacíon, Conscientization; Culture Circle, Circulo de Cultura) where the apparently similar words are nuanced and do *not* necessarily mean the same, but also it frequently causes his work to suffer either from cross-translation (for example, does 'Bewußtseinsbildung' convey the meaning of 'education for critical consciousness'?) or from repeated publication, or from both.

Some work has even been translated back into Portuguese by Freire: 'My best writing on the "culture of silence" is the Portuguese edition of *Education as the Practice of Freedom* of which I have lost the original and so had to translate it back from the English edition' (Costigan 1983). Some has been cross-translated: one finds, for example, that the article 'Conscientization and Liberation' which appeared in *Communio Viatorum* is a 1974 English translation of a Spanish version of a discussion originally conducted in Portuguese.

Even material in the same language can appear at first glance to be two

4

different texts but which, in the event, prove to be the same substantive material translated by different people with differing perspectives. For example, 'Notes on Humanisation and its Educational Implications' from the seminar *Tomorrow Began Yesterday* (Rome, November 1970) was translated from the Portuguese original by Louise Bigwood. This was retranslated by Donaldo Macedo in Freire (1985a: 111–19) as 'Humanistic Education' but with an appreciable difference of emphasis and of interpretation.

Finally, editorial presentation can result in noticeable differences even between two translations of major texts. One of the most significant examples is that of the English and French versions of *Pedagogy of the Oppressed*. A number of paragraphs of the original Portuguese do not appear in the same place in either of the two translations. Critically, the English version sometimes includes quotations in the body of the text, where the French uses footnotes. Equally, where the English merely cites the author, the French text often provides a detailed reference with the title, date and page. A comparison of the three texts clearly shows how the editor has become a co-author.

In referring the reader constantly back to the text, I have quoted the most accessible versions. The reader will therefore need to note that the date given for the reference is often a poor guide to the date when the work was actually written. Throughout this book, I have given references to Freire's own work simply by date, indicating where appropriate a particular page reference. References to other authors are clearly indicated with the name of the author.

These difficulties in establishing the authentic texts of Freire's works serve to provide an important caveat. It needs to be noted that the use of phrases like 'Freire's philosophy' or 'the Freirean method' are somewhat misleading. They should be better seen as a shorthand, a way of referring to what is a complex package of ideas and techniques the authorship of which is not always clear. On the contrary, what becomes increasingly obvious to the reader of Freire is that his words are not only his own. He is highly eclectic:

> He has reached out to the thought and experience of those in many different situations and of diverse philosophical positions: in his words, to 'Sartre, Mounier, Eric Fromm and Louis Althusser, Ortega y Gasset and Mao, Martin Luther King and Che Guevara, Unamuno and Marcuse'.
> (Shaull 1982: 10)

The list is impressive, but again misleading. Nowhere in his writing does Freire make an explicit reference to Unamuno, while two of the most important influences on him, Karel Kosik and Lucien Febvre, are not mentioned here. Of course it is not always necessary to seek 'cause and effect' in the inter-textuality of two or more authors, so that one can clearly be seen to have influenced the other. Although Unamuno, in his *The Tragic Sense of Life* provides a framework of ideas and understandings that greatly illumine the reasoning and culture of Freire (in that it is obviously Catholic, Aristotelian and Manichean, where the boundaries and causes of pain and loving are often intertwined), what we find is more an affinity of ideas and interpretation than a direct influence. Perhaps what Freire found most in Unamuno, as in many other authors, was the sympathetic echo of his own voice, and therefore he did not feel the need to acknowledge that by direct quotation.

What this degree of eclecticism means is that we cannot find or study Freire without also exploring the genealogy of his ideas. He is not a pedagogic Copernicus who, alone, found a new way of looking at the universe of education. He is rather a syndicate of theories and insights. His particular genius lies in his ability to construct out of all these disparate ingredients a recipe that produces both a philosophy and a practice of literacy. His achievement, more Newtonian than Copernican, was to analyse the gravitational pull between power and literacy and to suggest that it would be possible to create a new dynamic of educating. This would create a changed interaction, the process of which is dialogue (speaking the word) and the product of which is liberation (writing and righting the world).

The 'reading' of Freire therefore requires a triple redaction: the auto-text or bio-text which interlinks biographical details; the grapho-text, penned or dictated, of his books, articles and interviews; and the altero-text or con-text which is supplied by other co-'writers', the acknowledged or unacknowledged sources on which he relied, and the historical circumstances through which he lived. This is an extremely complex process. Leach (1982) suggests that

> The pattern of his work, which can be traced through from the early essays to *Pedagogy in Process*, contains a central core of beliefs or 'principles'. In each successive work these fundamental principles are repeatedly restated in different ways. (Leach 1982: 185)

None the less, Freire's work is not neatly stratified: there is no simple, evolutionary logic that provides the infrastructure to his life and works. What we are required to do is to interweave this triple helix of textuality (bio-, grapho-, and altero-) into a critical study that will expose the coherence of Freire's insight and the warp of contradiction which his texts expose. We shall need to consider the enigma posed by Freire: that an upper-class Brazilian lawyer should become the pedagogue of the oppressed masses, not just in his own country but throughout the Third and First Worlds; that his successful literacy method is based on flawed theorizing; that Dialogic Education may only be a benign form of Banking Education; that this very South American approach to education can be placed firmly within mainstream European traditions; and that, despite all the contradictions and inadequacies, Freire offers a unique insight into the way Literacy presents and manages the fundamental relationship of Power and Knowledge.

'Reflection', says Freire (1973b: 6), 'is only legitimate when it sends us back to the concrete context where it seeks to clarify the facts'. That is why he was so committed to the deconstructive methodology of *Codification* and *Decodification* which are the strategies by which he seeks to conscientize and to achieve that praxis which is based on naming, reflecting and acting. It is, therefore, wholly appropriate to attempt to place Freire in his own intellectual, political and social context, allowing him to speak for himself, to 'name his own world'. This demands, on the part of the reader or investigator, an ability to go beyond philosophical voyeurism in search of a holistic archaeology to discover the personality and pedagogy of Freire, with all his complexities and contradictions.

Conventionally, a 'history of ideas' tries to understand its Subject/subject by identifying with the person and their way of thinking, to come inside that person and so explain their view of the world.[4] However, this essentially *emic* perspective tends to provide a lens that either magnifies or reduces the subject. This distortion, as Brookfield (1984: 6) indicates, arises because the study of learning and pedagogy does not yield easily, if at all, to the discipline or methodology of scientific research.

What is therefore needed as a methodology is the prism of an *etic* analysis which will ensure a more objective view of the subject by exposing its component parts but without destroying its integrality. First, the value of this approach is that it enables me, the reader, to engage in a cross-cultural discussion with Freire, given that we are not of the same age, culture or language background. Second, an *etic* analysis allows me to view Freire from the outside, thus finding his relevance to me and to education in a non-Third World, non-South American environment. Third, it helps me to deal with contradiction and inconsistency, whereas an *emic* view would seek the integration of all the disparate elements, biographic, intellectual and historical into some coherent whole. An *etic* methodology provides a legitimate entrée into the hyper-complexity of Freire's thinking and practice. It does so because it can accept that this is not an exhaustive study of the total Freire but rather a partial (in both senses), empathetic but critical rewriting of an extra-ordinary pedagogy.[5]

Chapter 1 concentrates on Freire's bio-text and on some of his grapho-texts. It is not intended as an intellectual biography, an historical review of the development of his ideas but rather as a biography of an intellectual. It serves, for the reader new to Freire, as an introduction to a very complex person who grew up in a world perhaps very distant from that of the reader. It gives some details of his early life, the context in which he developed his teaching method, his first steps into literacy and his progress on to the international, educational stage. Against the backdrop of the various texts which he wrote during this period and into the 1980s, for which a brief thumbnail sketch is given, the bio-text concludes with Freire's return to Brazil, his new life there and his return to his professional origins as director of his own literacy programme in his post as Secretary for Education in São Paulo.

Freire has only ever been truly Brazilian, spiritually and culturally. Chapter 2 takes that as given, but looks in detail at the evidence that Freire cannot be dismissed as some bizarre, South American educator who invented a high-speed method of teaching illiterate peasants to read. The conclusion is that Freire is, in reality, an educator within the mainstream of traditional, European pedagogy, who is fluent in applying Aristotle, modern Existentialism, Marxist Humanism, and all the liberalism of *éducation nouvelle* to a method which has a long pedigree in many, different social and labour reform movements.

Chapter 2, therefore, looks at this spider's web of influences, sources and borrowings. It is less a detailed analysis of these diverse philosophies and traditions than an attempt to see Freire afresh through the perspective of these differing traditions. The reader can imagine a dialogue or 'talking book' between, for example, Freire and Aristotle, or Freinet, and can ask: What do they have in common? How would they understand each other? Would Freire make as much sense to Hegel, for example, as Hegel makes to Freire?

The extended essay on Dialogue and Conscientization in Chapter 3 continues this 'Pedagogy of Questioning'. It would have been easy just to describe Freire's understanding of these two key ideas, but I have preferred to link the main elements together by 'problematizing' them, offering some of the questions which have arisen in my use of Freire or in student discussion groups. I am not offering easy, prepackaged solutions: the debate is too important and too interesting for that. Ideally, the reader will be encouraged to go back to the Texts, to read and reread Freire and so formulate his or her own response. One of the principles of Freirean pedagogy is that the reader should not enthusiastically agree with what an author says, nor dismiss an argument out of hand, without actively rewriting his or her own interpretation of the original Texts. To that end, and so that the reader can read Freire himself in parallel, I have tried to give sufficient references to the essential source material without, it is to be hoped, being too disjointed or pedantic.

Chapters 4 and 5 constitute the second stage of Freire's method, the decodifications. First, I have considered certain questions which arise from Freire's theory of linguistics and communication, in particular, drawing attention to his Nominalism and exploring whether there is a fundamental contradiction between the use of this syllabic parsing of key nouns and the aims of dialogue and what Freire calls 'annunciation'.

Second, I have made a detailed textual analysis of the content of Freire's teaching material, the generative themes and codified situations which he published in *Education: The Practice of Freedom*. I have tried to expose and then exploit the 'Pedagogy of Contradiction' which is implicit in Freire's own account of these codifications. It is a critical reading that tries to cut through the language of mysticism and idealism in which Freire so often expresses himself. I have tried to look objectively, as an educational agnostic, at this sequence of learning and teaching, in order to appreciate the consequences, for better or for worse, of Freire's remarkably *bibliocentric* pedagogy.

The final chapter turns this last point again into a question. If Literacy is not about reading, what is it about? The discussion explores the power of Literacy in the light of the literacy or literateness of Power. Using the framework provided by Freire, we can then look at the underlying definition of literacy and why it is so often valued only because it is patriarchal and functional. That question is essential for, without an answer, a literacy of liberation is a contradiction in terms. It is a discussion which reflects the third stage of Freire's method: reflection turning to action. What does this pedagogy help us to do or to see which we could not do and could not see before?

The words *pedagogy* or *pedagogue* may sound strange, even pretentious, to some English speakers, but I have used them throughout the book, often in preference to *educator* or *teacher*. First, because they are the terms that Freire himself uses, they mark off an approach to teaching and learning which is quite particularly identified with him. Second, although the terms can be used quite easily in most other European languages, I wanted to stress their classical connotation. Traditionally, the pedagogue was the servant who accompanied the learner to his or her place of learning. It is a wonderful image with which to invert, or subvert, the image of the teacher in the Banking System of education where it is the teacher who leads and the learner who follows, the teacher who controls, who imposes, who is superior in every way to the learner. The essential challenge to the Freirean educator is to become a companion to the learner, to 'get alongside' them, to encourage, to help them to be creators and not consumers of their own learning: to be, in short, a pedagogue.

The *pedagogy of the oppressed* is not a pedagogy for the oppressed or simply with the oppressed. It is a pedagogy that belongs to the oppressed: it is *The Oppressed's Pedagogy*. The title of Freire's most famous book, *Pedagogy of the Oppressed*, is grammatically both a subjective and an objective genitive. However, for the oppressed's pedagogues, there is no confusion. One cannot be a pedagogue of the oppressed and a pedagogue of the Banking System at one and the same time.

There is no safe haven of neutrality in pedagogy. I discovered that through hard experience the first time I used Freire's method. I was working in the mid-1970s in French West Africa as a fieldworker and as a consultant to a number of aid agencies – the International Red Cross, The United States Agency for International Development (USAID) and the American Lutheran Church. The aim was to negotiate with the Tuareg and Bororo nomads of the Sahel ways in which they could 'break out of the drought' which had devastated the region over several years, combat the cyclical precariousness of their life, and radically alter a situation in which they were 'objects' of oppression. The Sahel is the fringe, the margins of the desert. It is a word that both represents a geographic fact and provides a powerfully evocative symbol of social marginalization and cultural domination.

In researching the urgent vocabulary of those communities, in identifying with them the generative themes which were then discussed in small groups, from which came proposals for action, community development and change, I experienced Freire's method in action. I know that it works.

What did not work for me was the discovery, naive perhaps, that the politics of aid is not interested in independent, critically aware 'recipients'. I lived through exactly what Freire analyses with such jarring exactitude in *Extension or Communication*: the educator has become (or always was) an agent of cultural invasion and political extensionism. I learnt, as Freire had, that Memmi's *Portrait of the Colonizer* could have been written just for me.

I had first read *Pedagogy of the Oppressed* in 1974, after a fortuitous encounter with Bill Cave, a Visiting Professor at Edinburgh who had come from Michigan State University. I still remember the discussion (good pedagogues have that kind of effect) when he asked, 'Have you read Freire . . . ?' I hadn't, but I recall the excitement, the frustration, the completely destabilizing impact of that first reading. It is the same today: each time I read Freire, I react at the extremes.

Sometimes, I think I get an insight, a glimpse of what he is really trying to say, and it is profound, exact, stimulating and genuine. Other times, I am submerged under mystical nuances, Easter experiences, all kinds of -izations, and a sense of unreality tinged with piety.

My experience in Africa left me knowing two Freires, and never the two did meet. One was theoretical and philosophical, the other was practical and effective. This remained so until the mid-1980s when several circumstances converged to change that. The first was the British publication of *Pedagogy in Process*, Freire's work in Guinea-Bissau. There seemed here to be a greater confidence in his thinking, a sharper analysis of social or socialist pedagogy, and a real effort to confront the question of cultural invasion. I felt encouraged to reread and rediscover the *Pedagogy of the Oppressed*.

The second 'moment of learning' came about because I was responsible, at Leicester Polytechnic where I was a tutor on the Youth and Community Development Course, for a module on 'Community Education and Non-Formal Education'. Obviously the content of the course was going to treat Freire's philosophy and techniques of creating learning, but we were enabled, through challenging discussion in the group, to experiment with putting theory into practice, effectively creating our own Cultural Circle. At the beginning, as Elizabeth Ellsworth (1989) recalls of her own experience, this 'did not feel empowering'. Yet, gradually, as we, and the Institution, grew more accustomed to the dialogue, we came to realize its possibilities. Some people, says Alinsky (1973), believe it when they see it: others see it only when they believe it.

I think we came to believe that liberating education was possible and we began to look again at our field practice as educators and community workers. We were greatly helped by a visit to the ever inspiring *Adult Learning Project* in Edinburgh,[6] and other visits, other researchings and many discussions confirmed our view that, despite the difficulties of the text, despite the contradictions, Freire's approach made possible genuine personal learning and authentic community work. As a teacher, it was a great privilege for me to be associated with this *cru* or crew of 1985–7 and this book is, in many ways, the fruits of their risks, their commitment and their discoveries.

It was then Augusto Boal who opened up new insights for me into the working of Freire's mind and method. His *Theatre of the Oppressed* (1980a) moves Freire out of the classroom and into the theatre of life. It is a new way of looking at the world: that is the root of the word *theatros* – a place for viewing, for observing.[7] But the techniques of theatre, the importance of declaiming and communicating, the playing of roles, the imagination to be other, the literacies of culture other than those which are bibliocentric, all contributed to enlarging my understanding of pedagogy. It is not just a method of teaching or a way of learning: it is a way of life. It was only when I had found that out for myself, did I find it written large across every page in Freire.

Now that I find myself in the very non-Freirean world of French education which is hyper-Cartesian in Thought and ultra-hierarchical in Form, I am trying to find the confidence to open up my classroom again to let in Boal's invisible theatre. I understand better now what Freire means when he says that pedagogy has to be reinvented, restlessly, earnestly. It is a sad compliment to the efficacy of this refined Banking Education that none of Freire's major works is currently available in French. Freire is dismissed, it seems, because he has no theoretical underpinning, because he is Brazilian, because in France there is social inequality but not oppression. So my students and colleagues, who have not been educated to imagine a pedagogy of liberation, ask: But who is Freire? What does he stand for? Does it make sense?

Yes, it does, that is if you understand how the same person can receive the Unesco Prize for Peace Education, as Freire did in 1986, and be the author of one of the most subversive and revolutionable pedagogies of modern times. His preferred epitaph is: 'Paulo Freire was a man who loved, who could not conceive of life or human existence without love and without the quest for knowledge. Paulo Freire lived, loved and tried to understand' (1991: 128).

That epitaph he wrote himself, but it is not his last word. It does, however, serve as a summary of all the other Texts that he has written, spoken and lived. He is that kind of person because he is that kind of pedagogue.

ONE

A biographical sketch

Introduction

The life and work of Paulo Freire has many phases and many facets as befits a man who has always been physically and mentally 'in transit'. He has lived through anonymity and fame in Brazil, acclamation and success in the wider world of Africa and Europe, and is now back in South America, living perhaps more on remembrances and mature reflection rather than on the impulsiveness and vigour of the creativity which drove him in the early years.

He was born into a comfortable, middle-class family – an unlikely setting, culturally, economically and socially, for someone who was to become one of the great champions of the oppressed poor. Indeed, even up to the time when he started work as a trade union lawyer, Freire's only exposure to the working and the non-working classes had been when the family suffered severe, but temporary, financial difficulties during the Depression.

That setback almost prejudiced his schooling. Although he could read before he went to school, poverty or hunger, or lack of application, caused him to repeat two years of education, resulting in a delayed entry into university. But when the family was financially and socially back on course, it went without question that Freire should go to university to study Law. What is interesting, however, is that the local university was in many ways a French academic institution. The Brazilian tertiary system of education, in its choice of disciplines and in its structuring of examinations and degrees, had been modelled on that of the French. The content and style of courses had been strongly influenced by the core group of French intellectuals who were a major influence in the development and expansion of the universities in Brazil and who enabled the Faculty of Social Science, which included Law, to be the elite cornerstone of that expansion.[1] It was through the resources of their libraries and teaching that Freire was introduced to the works of Althusser, Foucault, Fromm, Lévi-Strauss, Maritain, Mounier and Sartre, all of whom were to have such a formative influence on the development of his pedagogy.[2]

The groves of academe clearly suited Freire the intellectual, but it gave him little sense of direction as he left university. He was quickly a lawyer, high school teacher of Portuguese, and then adult educator, married but unsure whether his career options would be curtailed by family responsibility.

Looking back, one has the impression that those experiences between 1944 and 1959, about which little has ever been said, are almost 'lost years' for Freire. In the event, a career was thrust upon him. By the genius of fate, Freire was the right man in the right place at the right time, qualified by the rare mix of his experiences and skills to accept the invitation to direct the government's literacy programme in the North-east State, Brazil.

From there, the details of his life are better known. Regional success led to national recognition as his programme expanded. As educator and government consultant, he created the base for radical reform in both the education and the electoral systems. It was this success that first led to his downfall and exile in 1964, and then later to his rehabilitation as an international figure. He worked first in Chile, next in Harvard, and then in Geneva as consultant to the World Council of Churches, through a period of upheaval and transition, from 1964 to 1970, that produced his most important writings.

For some, this represents the height of his career. He was recognized world-wide, speaking at conferences and maintaining consultancies throughout the Third and the First World, a government adviser and fêted academic. He was one of the central figures of the 1970s.

This is still how Freire is most widely remembered, but he is, in fact, an exile returned. In June 1980 he left Geneva to take up a post at the Catholic University of São Paulo. He returned to his two confirmed loves: Brazil and teaching. Except for a short but effective sortie into local politics as Secretary for Education (1989–91) in the city of São Paulo, he has remained a university professor, continuing to write and to lecture in Brazil and on the international circuit.

None the less, a criticism which Youngman (1986: 152) made in the mid-1980s, that Freire has not produced a significant new work on his pedagogy and practice, is all the more true in the early 1990s. True, that is, only if we are looking for the renovation of an idea which we feel is worn or unfashionable, or if we are insisting that ideas, somewhat like fashions, must change with the times. Freire himself says (1991: 118) that a writer is not obliged to dress up an idea just to be modern. We might also have to allow for the fact that Freire, at the age of 72, can simply point to the *Pedagogy of the Oppressed* and argue that it is still as valid now, although it has become a 'classic text' as it was when it was first 'revolutionary' and just published.[2]

There is no doubt that Freire's work is not finished. He has remarried and has resigned from his local government post. The renewed experience of literacy teaching and management will most certainly result in a new book in the near future. How different might that be from his early work? Has Freire yet to write the definitive version of his pedagogy? To answer that and, at the same time, to identify the main elements of his philosophy and educational practice, we need to review his bio-text in more detail and so follow the life cycle of a complex idea and of an even more complex personality.

Early life

Paulo Freire was born in Recifé, North-east Brazil, on 19 September 1921. He was one of several children in an established middle-class family which, according to Freire's later reflection, was but average for Recifé at the time. What did he mean by that? His description of 'the average house in Recifé where I was born' is instructive (1987b: 30): it was an old house, with bedrooms, an attic, hall, terrace and back yard, with the family's cats, father's dog, and grandmother's fat chickens, all surrounded by roses, jasmine and mango trees in a street where the lamplighter passed to light the elegant gas lamps each evening.

His parents were bourgeois and of liberal attitudes (Jerez and Hernandez-Pico 1971: 498). The father, Joaquim Temistocles, held an officer's post in the military police, and he tolerated, rather than approved of, the fact that Edeltrudis, his wife, held strongly Catholic convictions. He himself frequented a local spiritualist circle (Gerhardt 1979: 40).

Joaquim Freire was concerned that his son should have a good education. Freire (1978: 132) called his father his 'first teacher', remembering how he wrote words with a stick in the sand in the shade of a wonderful mango tree in the back yard and how he helped his children to make new words out of the parsed syllables. The method Freire would use himself later with non-literate adults, but its efficacy was even then proven because, by the time he went to Eunice Vascancello's private school, the young Freire was already literate (1987b: 32).

That early progress, however, was impeded by the severe financial reverses which the family suffered during the Great Depression of 1928–32. Freire experienced real hunger, a fact by which he explained his poor showing at school. Twice he had to retake a complete school year (Collins 1977: 5), finally entering secondary school two years behind his age group. A number of informed commentators, notably O'Neill (1973) and Jerez and Hernandez-Pico (1971), report that he was considered by some of his teachers to be mentally retarded.

'We shared the hunger', says Freire (Mackie 1980: 3), 'but not the class', an important distinction which Freire later recognized as one of the reasons which had enabled him to continue his schooling. His father had insisted, despite the setbacks, on keeping up the appearances of respectability. He continued to wear a tie, and he kept on the house in Recifé, although the family moved briefly to Jaboatao. He dispensed with all non-essential furniture but not with the German piano (Jerez and Hernandez-Pico 1971). He died in 1934, fatigued prematurely perhaps by the stress of this period.

Freire was only 13: the loss of his father and the increased difficulties for the family proved a very traumatic experience. Despite his efforts and those of his sister and elder brothers, Stella, Armando and Temistocles, the plight of the family did not improve. So Freire starting 'teaching', giving supplementary lessons in Portuguese to children of his own age at the private high school which he attended. He found it a gratifying experience, and decided then that his particular ambitions lay in becoming a teacher.

His tutoring was also some recompense to the high school for, after the death of his father and given the financial insecurity of the family, Freire was allowed by the director, Aluizo Aruajo, to have a free place at his school. Without this free place, Freire would probably never have completed his secondary schooling.

Success even to this level, and then a passage through university, was not intended, however, for all Edeltrudis's children. Even within the family, Freire was privileged: 'Because of my problems, the eldest in my family began to work and help our condition, and I began to eat more' (1987a: 29). He was, at the time, in the second or third year of high school so the improved financial position of the family was certainly a critical factor in his continuing through to his high school graduation-baccalaureate. 'To the extent I began to eat better, I began to understand better what I was reading'.

He entered Recifé University to study Law and Philosophy but he also read Linguistics. It was a standard route for the intellectual middle classes (Gerhardt 1979: 42), and it gave Freire his first university degree. It was also the fruit of privilege which Freire later came to see as 'my university training – perhaps, to be more accurate, I should say my elitist university training', access to which had been facilitated by his class position (1978: 117).

In his detailed appraisal of Freire and of his early work, Mashayekh (1974) also formed the view that schooling in Recifé was a privilege enjoyed only by the minority.

> That Freire's mind and future vocation was shaped by the social situation into which he was born and in which he grew into manhood seems evident. It was this schooled minority which dominated the social and economic institutions of society and enjoyed the benefits they produced. The majority lived in circumstances of grinding poverty and oppression. They were to be seen in the streets and served in the shops and homes, but were not 'heard'. They lived in what Freire called a 'culture of silence', condemned to passivity. (Mashayekh 1974: 4)

Since those university days, Freire, mainly because of his education and class, has never been poor or unemployed. He has always been 'invited' to take up his various posts and has never had to look for work. Yet with the security of a job, a wife and family, even with house servants (1970: 10), he felt empowered to create a pedagogy of the oppressed. The contradiction between the radical, subversive nature of this approach to education and the apparent conformity and ordinariness of his early life style and experience is blatant. It seems that the more one knows of the situation and values of his childhood and adolescence the more the choice and motivations of his first steps into radical literacy are unexpected, even out of character. The mismatch is certainly not easy to explain, particularly because a simply chronological or historical bio-text often allows hindsight to impose a logic and orderliness on events which do not reflect the reality of the situation at the time. Often, too, memory sees certain facts with more coherence and certainly with more charity than the lived experience might merit. Therefore, to get at the facts, but before we ask further questions of Freire himself, we need to consider the personal and cultural context in which this radical move into pedagogy was possible.

North-east Brazil

North-east Brazil is 'one enormous region of a country, as large as a continent, one of the most backward areas in the country, marked by truly appalling social conditions – 60,000 square miles of suffering'. Here, in *Death in the North-east*, first published just before the coup in 1964, Josué de Castro is writing passionately about the deprivation of his home region. In his earlier work, *The Geography of Hunger* (1952), he notes that the area was celebrated only for 'the misery of the great majority of its inhabitants, for its periodic, natural catastrophes and for a system of land ownership which was incredibly unjust'. A comparable historical and sociological analysis, which Freire used and which later provided him with one of his key images of oppression – the senhor de enghéno: the mill owner – is equally forcefully written in Freyre's *The Masters and the Slaves*.[3] This was the study which scandalized many at the time of its first publication in 1933 precisely because it attempted to unmask the complex realities which lay behind the eclectic, individual and collective Brazilian national identity. It identifies the fusion of African cults and Indian customs with Roman Catholicism, and exposes a sexually permissive but sexist culture founded on patriarchy, slavery and class oppression. It outlines the sequences of colonial and cultural invasions which help to explain the structures of social and political domination, but it also presents the need for agrarian reform to combat widespread poverty and exploitation.

Freire (1987a: 20) admits that Freyre 'the great sociologist and anthropologist who writes so well was an important, saving influence' but it does not seem that this helped him to see any more clearly the blatant inequalities in society or the privileged position of his own family. On the contrary, although as a teacher of Portuguese Freire used *The Masters and the Slaves* with students, it was only to 'point out syntactical aspects strictly linked to the good taste of their language' (1987b: 34). There is nothing to suggest that he had seen the contradiction between Lucien Febvre's stylish description of Recifé, the Venice of the North, in the preface to Freyre's book, and the poverty and misery which Freyre and de Castro describe in such detail.

There is nothing to suggest either that he had any empathy for the content of one of Brazil's best-selling books ever, *Beyond All Pity* (de Jesus 1970). Written not in the smooth, classical prose of the academics but in the sharp, urgent language of the street, this is the deeply passionate diary of Carolina Maria de Jesus, a woman who lived in the *favelas* (slums) of São Paulo. It has a vital and shocking honesty: there is humour, violence, deep sadness, anger and an insuperable human spirit. It is a book of tears and hunger that clearly explains the expression which Freire later made his own: *los marginados*, those who have been marginalized, those 'who don't have names'. Had his discourse on oppression been her discourse of the oppressed, Carolina Maria could have offered Freire an insight into a world which lay outside his own experience and both a first-hand description of the reality of poverty and oppression and a language to describe that reality which many people in Brazil would have recognized.

What indeed was the reality at that time? As a brief indicator, we are able to compare the North-east in 1960 and in 1970 – the decade which encompasses Freire's first literacy efforts in Latin America.

In their Pastoral Letter, *Eu Ouvi os Clamores do meu Povo* (I have heard the cries of my people), the Catholic Bishops of the North-east (1973) stated that

> Data from the 1970 census revealed that only 3.3 per cent of the economically active population in the North-east earned more than 500 cruzeiros ($83) per month, and only 0.86 per cent earned more than 1,000 cruzeiros ($166). In Piaui and Maranhâo, for an economically active population of 1,470,000 persons, only 955 earned more than 2,000 cruzeiros ($333) per month.

Infant mortality in the North-east as a whole was 180 per 1,000 live births. In the capital, where medical assistance was concentrated, it was still 98 per 1,000. Of all deaths, 47 per cent occurred before 5 years of age.

Drummond (1975), who in 1972 was attempting to develop a nutritional education programme on Freirean lines, noted the evidence of poverty as a major factor in the serious problem of malnutrition:

> Virtually all the children admitted to the Sao Luis hospital are under-nourished, and 3/5 of them have manifest signs of kwashiorkor, including bilateral oedema. (Drummond 1975: 1)

A decade earlier (in 1960) Tad Szulc, writing in the *New York Times*, explicitly criticized the United States for having done so little to help the area around Recifé in peacetime, despite the fact that it was the support base for a string of guided missile tracking stations in the South Atlantic for the United States Air Force.

> There are sections of the North-east where the annual income is about $50. About 75 per cent of the population is illiterate. The average daily intake is 1,664 calories. Life expectancy is 28 years for men and 32 for women. Half the population dies before the age of 30. In two villages in the State of Piaui, taken at random, not a single baby lived beyond one year. (Szulc, quoted in de Castro 1969: 119)

These reports, from very differing sources, cover periods either side of the coup, yet they show very little change in the stark picture of poverty. None the less, many in Brazil, and certainly in Europe, saw this period as the time of Brazil's economic miracle. There was a marked upsurge of economic development which went even further than the already dramatic changes achieved in the earlier Kubitschek period.

His promised 'fifty years' progress in five' was very real. Skidmore (1967), using Celso Furtado's detailed study *Diagnosis of the Brazilian Crisis* (1965), notes that between 1956 and 1961, Brazil had witnessed the most extraordinary industrial expansion. Industrial production grew by 80 per cent, the steel industry by 100 per cent, mechanical industries by 125 per cent, electrical and communications industries by 380 per cent and transportation equipment industries by 600 per cent. The effective real rate of growth was 7 per cent per year, approximately three times that of the rest of Latin America. However, the rate of inflation had increased from 24 to 52 per cent between 1958 and 1959 and had risen to 70 per cent just before the coup in 1964 (Gerhardt 1979).

This darker side of this economic expansion was also seen when the results of the 1970 census were tabulated:

> The share of the total national income of the lower 50% of the population decreased from 14.5% in 1960 to 13.9% in 1970. The lowest 10% of the population saw their share decrease from 1.9% in 1960 to 1.2% in 1970. The exclusion of the majority of wage earners from the windfall of economic growth, together with the high profits of an increasingly de-nationalized industrial sector, brought about the conditions for social movements of dissent and grass roots organisation. (Fernandes 1985: 81)

This was the context in which Freire was working in the mid-1960s: no doubt many saw his Literacy Programme as one of those social movements of discontent. Yet maybe Freire had only ever seen poverty from the exterior, from his 'average house'. The statistics dispute his assessment of what was *average*, and illustrate his position of privilege in those early years. Although he considered himself to have been poor, he was not forced into dissent by his own experience of that poverty and hunger.

> My childhood was partly in Recifé and then in Jaboatao. My family left Recifé in order to survive the economic crisis of the Depression in the 1930s. A great moment of my life was the experience of hunger. I needed to eat more. Because my family lost its economic status, I was not only hungry but I also had very good friends both from the middle class and from the working class. Being friends with kids from the working class, I learned the difference of classes by seeing how their language, their clothing, their whole lives expressed the totality of the class separations in society. By falling into poverty, I learned from experience what social class meant. (1987a: 28)

Freire had fallen into poverty but had climbed out of it: he was never truly 'of the poor'. He encountered the dominated classes through this discovery of his own middle-classness and through the differences of language, clothes and life styles which separated him from the oppressed.

At the time, however, Freire was unaware of the advantages of his own social situation. He later admitted:

> A critical view of my experience in Brazil requires an understanding of its context. My practice, while social, did not belong to me. Hence my

difficulty in understanding my experience . . . without comprehending
the historical climate where it originally took place. (1985: 12)

Only with hindsight did he see himself as following unquestioningly the
normal, educational paths appropriate to his class. This meant going to
university and, in what Gerhardt (1979: 42) describes as the mainstream,
Brazilian intellectual tradition, studying Law and Jurisprudence.

First steps into literacy

This difficulty which Freire has had in identifying and coming to terms with his
past perhaps explains why, at this stage, biographical details remain vague and
unexplored.

Jerez and Hernandez-Pico (1971: 499) suggest that, after university, Freire
worked for several years as a legal assessor in the trade unions – *trabajo durante
varios anos de assessor legal de los sindicatos obreros* – through which, indirectly, he
became involved in education. Drummond (1975), on the contrary, prefers to
see Freire as a pedagogue and less as a lawyer. She says that, having finished
law school but after being presented with his first case and talking with the
young dentist, Freire 'decided he was not meant to be a lawyer. He turned to
the field of education' (Drummond 1975: 4). Both she and Brown (1974) then
take up the story from 1959, the date of Freire's doctoral thesis *Educação e
Actualidade Brasileira* at the University of Recifé.

Both these biographical traditions, which are part of the 'Freirean myth-
ology', gloss over the critical years of 1940–59. Little is known of this period in
Freire's life other than some incidental details about his marriage and some
generalized reflections on his increasing involvement in education. Only in his
latest book, *Education in the City* (1991), has Freire attempted to fill in these lost
years.

As he remembers it now, he had always wanted to be a teacher, but equally
the family budget required him to work. So he started to 'teach' Portuguese
(the emphasis is his, 1991: 52) shortly after he started high school, giving
individual tuition to his fellow students. Later, he was actually employed in the
same private high school: 'When I was a young man, I accepted a position as a
high school teacher of the Portuguese language. Of course, at that time I taught
youths whose families were very well-to-do' (1985a: 175).

At the same time, but for reasons which he recalls with no great clarity,
Freire, still a teenager, was teaching in the slums and shanty towns of Recifé
(1991: 53). He does not explain why or how he came to be there, and he also
chooses to ignore the fact that he was still at university and training to be a
lawyer. What he does not ignore here is his meeting with his first wife, Elza.

If there is a key to understanding or explaining this period of his life, it may
well lie in the importance of Elza Maia Costa Oliveira. Freire (1987a) records,
with a vagueness that is instructive because it is typical of the way he often
records his early life, that

At some point between 19 and 23 years of age, I was discovering teaching
as my love. Also important at this moment, in my affective life, was when I

met Elza, who was my student, and then we got married. I was her private tutor. I prepared her for an exam to qualify for school principal. (1987a: 29)

In fact, Freire was 21 when they met, that is when Elza came to ask him for help to pass the competitive examination which she needed to advance her career. They married a year later (1991: 93).

Elza was a nursery school teacher, but Freire says elsewhere that 'it was Elza who led me to pedagogy' (1985a: 175) and he recognizes that 'she influenced me enormously'. Yet notwithstanding the more than standard acknowledgement of authors – 'Here I would like to express my gratitude to Elza, my wife, and first reader, for the understanding and encouragement which she has shown my work, which belongs to her as well' (1982: 19) there is no misunderstanding the relationship of patriarchy which is revealed in the statement: 'She was my student . . . I was her private tutor. I prepared her for an exam'.

Elza was to bear him three daughters and two sons (Collins 1977: 6), but Freire has spoken remarkably little about his family. One son, Joaquim, who went on to teach classical violin at the Fribourg Conservatoire, was with him in Geneva in 1976 (1989: 19), but little other reference is made to the family, to his own children or to his brothers and sisters. No account is offered, for example, about what happened to the family after his arrest, how the children left Brazil with him in 1964, how they managed the upheaval and stress of moving to Bolivia, then Chile, then to Cambridge, Massachusetts, before settling more permanently in the very non-American setting of Geneva.

Freire conveys this deep uncertainty, in part cultural and in part personal, about his role as father or husband. In a conversation with Macedo (1985a: 198) he admitted that 'As a young man, I thought that living and sleeping with a woman might interrupt my intellectual life. I found that my family did not interfere with my writing and my writing did not interfere with my love for my family.' It is almost as if the personal, family man is quite distinct from the professional persona, even in that public arena which he shared with his wife. Undoubtedly, he 'loved to love Elza' (1985a: 198) and was heartbroken after her death; *Literacy: Reading the Word and the World* is eloquently dedicated to her memory. Yet, although Freire talks of 'later as *we* were teaching', describing 'that praxis which was *ours* in Brazil', there is no evidence that Elza was directly involved in his work in Brazil. On the other hand, he notes (1987b: 63) that 'since 1976, my wife Elza and I have tried to contribute to adult education in São Tomé and Principé', but the ensuing discourse continues emphatically in the first person: '*my* practice renders me a colleague of the national people'.

Without the evidence of a detailed bio-text that would clarify the options and motivations of Freire's choice of career, an objective biographer of those days might be justified in saying simply that Freire was able to turn his initial interest in language and communication to his longer term, professional advantage. His move into education was pragmatic and opportunist: he never was, and has never professed to be, a Messianic figure who was somehow 'born' to save the oppressed masses. None the less, it is this very pragmatism that explains first why he might have wanted, consciously or not, to play down the elitist education which led him from private school to a lawyer's office, and second, why, at the height of his popularity and fame, he preferred to emphasize his pedagogical roots as a teacher and linguist.

It certainly was the case that, after passing his exams, Freire quickly abandoned law as a means of earning his living. However, his path from Portuguese to Literacy was due less to his own sense of vocation than to the guidance and motivation which he received from Elza. Although he may have tutored her, it was she who directed his path from 'teaching privately, in order to get some money, tutoring high school students or young people working in stores who wanted to learn grammar' (1987a: 27). He started teaching in a secondary school, working by intuition rather than by a clearly articulated pedagogy, and gradually he became more and more involved in teaching adults.

This was the seminal period of intense reading and study which justifies the much quoted references to Freire's eclecticism:

> He has reached out to the thought and experience of those in many different situations and of diverse philosophical positions: to Sartre and Mounier, Eric Fromm and Louis Althusser, Ortega y Gasset and Mao, Martin Luther King and Che Guevara, Unamuno and Marcuse. (Shaull 1982: 10)

In his own words

> My interests were in studying the Portuguese language, and Portuguese syntax in particular, along with certain reading I did on my own in areas of linguistics, philology, and the philosophy of language, which led me to general theories of communication. (1985: 175)

At the same time, through Elza, Freire became involved in the Catholic Action Movement, although he never became a full member. In 1944 the Church was still a very conservative force and only gradually was it moved to question the realities of the poverty and oppression which it was supporting and of which it was always aware. Freire himself underwent a similar process of 'conscientization'. He was, and has remained, a practising Catholic: a short period of adolescent doubts ended with his marriage to Elza, but also not without some pressure or support from his mother (Gerhardt 1979). He was, however, able to move from a naive acceptance of the authority of the Church to a more mature, questioning faith that even allowed of criticism, although it was not until as late as 1972 that he was able to write and publish a cogent analysis of the failings of the Church to fulfil its evangelical, prophetic role.

Not surprisingly, Catholic Action was not the answer for Freire. It was rather a very disheartening experience as he discovered the intransigence of the middle classes, forcing him to make a conscious choice: 'We decided not to keep working with the bourgeois and instead to work with the people' (R. Mackie 1980). That 'we', however, sounds to have included the choice which Elza had already made before meeting Freire.

Through his close relationship with Dom Helder Camara, the Bishop of Recifé, Freire became closely involved in the Basic Church Communities (*Comunidades Eclesiales de Base*) which were developing a pastoral ministry through community groups that sought to relate their biblical study to local, social and personal issues. During the 1940s and 1950s this movement had grown to accept the need for a clearer identification with the poor, and for a theology of liberation relevant to ordinary people (Fernandes 1985).[4]

It was through his involvement in the Church that Freire was invited by what he called a 'private industrial institute' (1987a: 29) to be the co-ordinator of a programme concerned with education and culture. This institute was, more accurately, an organization called Social Service for Industry (SESI), a private sector institution set up by the National Confederation of Brazilian Industries (1991: 96), but it was here that Freire was able to rediscover popular culture and the working classes.

This is a point which he makes often. 'Now as a young man, working with labourers, peasants and fishermen, I once more became aware of the differences among social classes' (1985a: 175). He was able to renew the experience which he had as a child when he had been 'associated' with working class children and peasants. This was a 'second chance to reknow what I had learnt about working life' (1987a: 29) when 'at the age of 25, I found myself faced with fishermen, labourers and peasants' (1991: 96). Freire also notes that it was this experience that enabled him to write *Pedagogy of the Oppressed*, a significant comment not least because it tends to confirm that Freire identified the working classes as the oppressed class.

'It was precisely my relationship with workers and peasants then that took me into more radical understandings of education' (1987a: 29). That might be true, but the change did not happen immediately. Although this initial contact with the trade unions and community education was also an introduction to the 'Culture Circles', his primary concern, paradoxically, was less with literacy than with post-literacy: 'I paid little attention to whether the participants in the Culture Circles were literate or not' (1978: 116). He was involved in what was essentially a basic education programme, teaching Portuguese. This did not, however, prevent him from making two important discoveries. First, that this new awareness of illiteracy, the fact that men and women were not able to read or write, provoked in him a profound sense of injustice. 'I remember clearly that these injustices used to touch me, and they took up a lot of my time during my reflections and studies' (1985a: 176).

Second, he found that the method of teaching in 'culture circles' was an effective means of structuring both discussion and collective action. The method, of course, was not new. Although the Culture Circles had their origins in Brazil in the so-called *Peasant League*, a union movement of the 1930s, they represent a long tradition of similar community-based learning groups which were central to the diverse labour movements which were active in the United States, Britain, the former Soviet Union, France and Sweden.[5] This dormant structure of trade union organization and education had been reactivated in the 1950s in the North-east by Francisco Juliåo, a radical, socialist lawyer, creating, according to Sanders (1968), an important catalyst in the opening up of 'new discussions about nationalism, remission of profits, development and illiteracy', just at the time when Freire had been invited to respond to the major problem of illiteracy among the local workforce.

De Castro's (1969: 177) own appraisal of Julião was that he had made a tenacious effort to free the peasants from their silence, by talking to them and by teaching them to talk. His work was uncompromisingly aimed at the destabilization of social structures: for him, to be called a 'social agitator' was an accolade for it meant 'in that patriotic sense, someone who brings a fundamental problem before the people so that it might be frankly debated'.

This 'tap-root' of dialogic learning has more than anecdotal significance. First, it sets the scene for the educational study which Freire presented for his doctoral thesis in 1959, *Educacão e Actualidade Brasileira*, although it scarcely explains his motivation for writing it.[6] Why, at the age of 38, married and with a secure job, did he feel compelled to write up his ideas on adult education? Was it that he was looking to hasten the offer of the teaching post at the university which did, in fact, materialize shortly afterwards? We may never know, but it is clear that that work experience, plus the doctorate, provided the incentive for a confrere of Julião, Miguel Arraes, then the Mayor of Recifé, to invite Freire to construct a literacy programme for the city council in 1961.

Arraes had no doubts about what that programme should yield:

> He surrounded himself with a team of technical advisers, among whom there were Communists, but also Socialists, devout or nominal Catholics, and simple economists and technicians, many of whom had a horror of ideological embroilment. They all worked together to achieve a common goal – the socio-economic transformation of the State of the North-east.
> (de Castro 1969: 170)

Freire probably was to be counted among those with a horror of ideological embroilment, for the direct, political implications of this concerted social development seem to have escaped him at this point. He may refer (1978: 176) to 'those political-pedagogical activities in which I have been engaged since my youth', but his later reflection appears more accurate: 'When I began my educational practice, I was not clear about the potential political consequences' (1985a: 179).

What then becomes clear is that it was not his personal, political association with Arraes and Julião that provided the driving force for what quickly became a very effective literacy programme: the simple motivation was Freire's own delight in teaching. He was not one of Julião's social agitators: he was an educator, loving and needing the adrenalin of the classroom (1989: 12), an intellectual occupying that position of neutrality which later he came to condemn.

As an educator, in 1961, Freire was writing his first book: *A Propósito de Uma Administracão*. This was essentially an appeal for the university to become more relevant to the lives of ordinary people and to create learning that confronted the social realities in Brazil. Universities in developing countries, especially those modelled on European countries, he saw as incapable of combating social alienation precisely because the responses or remedies which they offered

23

were being transplanted from other cultures, disregarding their own particular context and culture.

In this light, it has been suggested (Elias 1972), that Freire did not promote literacy for its own sake, but saw it rather as bringing about the democratiz-ation of culture among the rural and urban illiterates in Brazil. If this is true, then Freire's project did indeed constitute a major effort against the elitism of the university based education system. In the pilot project, some 300 workers became 'literate' within 45 days (Mashayekh 1974).

Freire's position of 'in but against' the university, plus the success of his pilot project, made him the ideal candidate, academically and politically, for the post of director of the newly created Cultural Extension Service at the University of Recifé. Once in post, from early 1961, he had started to confront the enormous problem of illiteracy in the region, bringing thousands of illiterate peasants throughout the North-east into literacy Culture Circles, when he was helped from an unexpected source. From October 1962 to January 1964 the Cultural Extension Service received considerable financial assistance from the United States Agency for International Development (USAID), clearly not without Freire's knowledge and approval (Brown 1974). This shows once again his ability to make the pragmatic choice or compromise: he had the motivation and the need, they had the money. Only later would he view things differently and see as naive his easy acceptance of this archetypal agency of cultural invasion.

Whatever the political or even pedagogic content of this first initiative, its social and media impact at a national level was such that Freire was invited, in 1963, to extend his programme and to become the director of a National Literacy programme.

A National Development Plan was produced which aimed to enrol some 2 million people and to teach them in Culture Circles of twenty-five people, each Circle lasting three months, at the extraordinary, direct cost of some $5–7 per Circle (Freire 1970n). The cost-effectiveness of the programme was achieved in part through the import of Polish projectors which cost $2.50 each, and films costing $1, a fact which, however, brought Freire into disrepute for it aggravated charges against him that he was undermining the national economy and was 'attempting to bolshevize the country'. This was never even remotely true, given his background and personality. He had simply modelled his programme on the very successful Cuban Literacy Project which had been completed a year before. Much of the organizational structure of this Brazilian National Plan, which Freire would use substantially again in Guinea-Bissau, owes much to that Cuban experiment.[7]

This was not just a simple plagiarizing of the Cuban programme but rather that the populist Goulart Government (1961–4), riding on the wave of radical reforms in agriculture, social services and labour relations, was not wanting to be compared unfavourably with Cuba, and was actually seeking a consolidat-ing programme which could be seen as equally 'modernizing' and effective as the Cuban model (Skidmore 1967: 244–56).

The forces for change in the two countries, however, were very different, and Freire found that he had unleashed some unexpected, and not altogether desired, developments. For example, in the State of Sergipé, the number of literate people went from 9,000 to 80,000, and in Pernambuco from 800,000 to 1.3 million (Mashayekh 1974). The implications both for regional and national democracy, and thereby for the ruling classes, were enormous. Under the legacy of Portuguese colonialism, only those who could read and write were eligible to vote (Gerhardt 1989). Brazil in 1960 had a population of some 34.5 million people of whom only 15.5 million were eligible to vote (Collins 1977). Freire's estimates for 1964 were that 4 million school-aged children lacked schools and that there were 16 million illiterates of 14 years and older (1976b: 41).[8]

Almost overnight, therefore, the whole electoral base of the country had been overturned, a fact which suggests that the motivation of the peasants was more than a simple desire for literacy. The central demand for the trade unions and of the Movement for Popular Culture in Recifé, the demand for the vote (and thereby power to demand further economic and industrial reform, the right of free association and security of land tenure), not only had been acquired without bloodshed but also had been given to them by a governmental literacy campaign (Sanders 1968).

Freire was criticized immediately, for example, in the powerful Rio de Janeiro daily, *O Globo*, for bringing the country to the verge of revolution. In fact the country had been on the verge of revolution throughout the Goulart presidency, but it is not surprising that Freire should have been a focus of the right-wing, middle-class backlash that brought about the coup in 1964. Many people saw *Açao Popular* and the Basic Education Movement's (MEB) programme of mass literacy only as a subversive strategy to introduce the agrarian reforms to which they were totally opposed. Skidmore (1967: 254) records how landowners increased their stock of arms, ready to defend their interests by force and how Freire was identified as a target by 'the traditional patrons of the agrarian sector who did not view with indifference the nascent mobilisation of the agrarian masses'.

At this point we need to throw a force-field of political assessment around the simple narrative of dates and events which links the coup with Freire. While it is true that he may have been regarded as a somewhat maverick professor of an otherwise traditional university, and that he was a director of a national literacy programme, he was none the less marginalized geographically by working from Recifé, and the scale of his success was more regional than national. According to de Kadt (1970):

> Freire's work at the time of the coup was still characterized by potential rather than actual achievements. Incitement to revolt was never Freire's objective as an educator, although democratisation was. (de Kadt 1970: 104)

Freire seems to agree with this assessment. As the emotional climate became more intense and sectarian irrationality grew stronger, 'there was increasing resistance to an educational programme *capable of helping* the people move from ingenuity to criticism' (1976b: 20, emphasis added).

In the event, Freire was deemed guilty by association. He was seen to have been part of that socialist/communist *tomada de consciencia* (awakening of consciousness) which had destabilized the country.[9] Gerhardt (1989), who was actually working in Brazil at the time, is pointed in his criticism:

> The first literacy campaigns in the north-east of Brazil (1961–64) which were based on Freire's 'system' show just how far the educators had espoused the political objectives of the programme organizers, that is, of the reformist provincial government. The reality is that the goals of these campaigns were blatantly political. (Gerhardt 1989: 541)

He goes on to argue that only when the programme organizers saw the number of enrolments decreasing was any emphasis put on the merits and advantages of functional literacy.

Does this mean that Freire was more the enthusiastic but naive academic who was used by the socialist coalition for their own political ends? Was he exiled because of their political downfall? Besides the fact that, after his departure, the literacy campaign continued without him in the form of the *Cruzada ABC* with the goal of 'conscientizing the workers' (Duiguid 1970), two other arguments support this demythologized view.

The first is that, although Freire later came to clarify his own commitment to socialism or Christian humanism and was not in disagreement with the aims of the regional government and their objectives for the literacy campaign, he was himself aware of the naivety of his involvements.

> Considering my present and more pronounced experience, I am also becoming aware of this kind of mistake in some of my earlier activities and also from pedagogues who do not see the political dimensions and implications of their pedagogical practice. (Freire 1985a: 169–70)

In effect, Freire is admitting that he was involved as an apolitical actor in a process of education, in which he had not considered the political consequences. He had jested with Elza after his first night working in adult literacy, 'After what I saw today, what I experienced today, possibly I will be jailed'. He had, however, no understanding of *why* he might be jailed. 'I was still not totally clear about the political nature of education. My first book reveals this lack of clarity' (1985a: 180).

Others, however, were clear and had long been observing the consequences. Freire (1976b: 31) saw only with hindsight that 'the country had begun to find itself. The people emerged and began to participate in the historical process'. Yet the *New York Times* had seen that as early as 1960 and was already warning of revolution (O'Neill 1973). Skidmore (1967) documents the fears of the US State Department in his appendix entitled 'The United States' role in Joao Goulart's fall': he clearly felt no need to add a question mark. The White House doubted that a socialist Brazil could reorganize its foreign debts and feared a Peronist-type solution to economic and social problems, a view which explains why, within hours of the coup, the interim government of Ranieri Mazzilli was recognized by Lyndon Johnson who also quickly confirmed a very favourable aid package for Brazil. In return, the United States gained an unequivocally pro-American ally for its foreign policy, particularly in the Dominican Republic.

In this context, it is not surprising that Freire, whose USAID support had been stopped in January 1964, was listed among those who were anti-American. Worse, through his associates, he was listed as being pro-communist. He was among some 10,000 government officials who were immediately dismissed or forcibly retired.

Exile and return

The reactionary nature of the coup allowed the new government to suspend individual and political rights. Along with many others, Freire was imprisoned and interrogated. On his release, he sought refuge in the Bolivian embassy, through whom he was able to arrange an exit visa to Bolivia where he had been granted political asylum.

It is one of the ironies of fortune that Bolivia itself experienced a coup fifteen days after his arrival and he was forced to seek further refuge in Chile (R. Mackie 1980). But forced by what? The popular image is of this 'eminent, influential, and for some, highly dangerous figure' seeking a political haven in whatever country would have him. Obviously there were many problems, politically and professionally, which confronted Freire in this new and unstable country, but it is also the case that other practical factors, much less dramatic, encouraged Freire to leave for Chile. First, he felt that, with the upheaval of the coup, his career prospects were very limited. Second, he was convinced that, after two months in La Paz, he could not cope with the climate and the high altitude (1989: 98). So there were more advantages to be had in moving to Chile.

Interestingly, Freire's bio-text across this period of crisis is again vague. It is only in the kind of conversation with Faundez that Freire mentions this temporary stay in Bolivia; normally, he passes over the events of those months. Although, this time in conversation with Macedo, he recalls the places of his exile, 'Chile, Cambridge, Geneva and la Paz', his preferred recall is that

> After those 75 days, I was taken to Rio de Janeiro for further questioning. And there I was told via the newspapers that I ought to be jailed again. My friends and family convinced me that it would be senseless for me to stay in Brazil. So I went into exile in Chile. (1985a: 181)

Jerez and Hernandez-Pico (1971) suggest that the choice of exile was imagined rather than real. Although he was 'invited' to leave the country – *Setenta dís más tarde le dejaron en libertad, y le 'invitaron' a abandonar el país* – in reality he had no choice but to leave. Yet surprisingly, given the momentous experiences of being let out of prison, being exiled and trying to make a new start in two new countries, Freire has never sought to clarify a certain confusion around all these events. Although, for example, he recalls the detail of his five-by-two foot cell (1985a: 154), there is some uncertainty even about how long he was in prison. He says, 'I was jailed twice before I was exiled, for a total of 75 days' (1985a: 180), but no one else records the two periods of imprisonment, although Mashayekh and Mackie also count 75 days. Other biographers and commentators closer to Freire, like Gleeson, McLaren and Shaull, count only 70 days. Brown (1974), whose work was well known to Freire, is alone in recording that 'Freire was under house arrest until June, imprisoned for 70 days, and finally sought refuge in Chile' (1974: 25). Freire himself recalls (1987a: 63) that he spent only one day and a night in a small closet-cell, but that otherwise he was in a cell with five or six other colleagues, doctors, intellectuals, liberal professionals.

At this point, we need to note a further element which contributed significantly to Freire's exile, but which also, because of his association with Bishop Camara, may also have assured his safe passage from the country. That element, little discussed, was the response of the Catholic Church in initially supporting the coup. With the exception of a few dissenting priests and laypeople, the Church was for the most part wholly positive in its response to the new, right-wing, conservative government. Whatever difficulties that posed for the Church socially or democratically, doctrinally they had found in the leaders of the coup a convergence of interest against the forces of communism. The Church, even according to the differing perspectives of O'Neill (1973) and of Camara (1969), was simply expressing its felt need for an anti-communist government that would protect Brazil's Christian civilization from Marxism, communism and from atheism. It was going to take four long years before the Church in Brazil realigned itself with the poor and the oppressed through its radical defence of human rights and its clear statement of opposition to government policies at the Medellin Conference, held in Columbia, in 1968. In the mean time, it made sense that all Freire's 'communist' learning materials, films and projectors should be not only confiscated but also destroyed, and that the problem posed by his close association with the Church should be resolved, to the short-term advantage of both Church and State, by his exile.

In Chile, where he immediately felt he was 'born again with a new consciousness of politics, education and transformation' (1987a: 32), Freire was able to secure a post at the University of Chile, Santiago. Here he was contacted by Waldemar Cortes and invited to work as a Unesco consultant in a literacy programme which was being proposed by the Department of Special Planning for the Education of Adults. At the time, the government of Eduardo Frei was committed to a dual programme of literacy and agrarian reform. In this way, Freire became involved with the Chilean Agrarian Reform Corporation where he then worked until 1969.

While involved in the training of extension workers, Freire was also writing creatively. In 1967 he published *Education: The Practice of Freedom*, the notes of which he had begun in prison in 1964. The core of the book is his detailed explanation of his method of creating 'generative' words and of reconstructing, syllable by syllable, other words from the learner's own vocabulary. In much less detail is the introduction to his emerging philosophy of education. Learners, as well as teachers, must be seen as subjects who awake to a critical consciousness of reality. They are creators of their own learning, who respond actively through dialogue rather than mechanically and passively to the anti-dialogue of imposed, dehumanizing, massified education.

The tone of the book reflects a style which is now known to be 'typically Freirean'. It combines an appeal to highly charged human values of love, humility, hope, faith and trust with an academic style that seeks to present an objective sociological analysis of alienation.

This was followed, early in 1969, by what was effectively a fusion of his fieldwork in Chile and his longstanding, academic interest in epistemology and communications: *Extension or Communication*. Given his first-hand experience both of the need for land reform and of the need for literacy education, he was able to make a radical examination of extension work or community development. He polarizes the difference between extension and communication as a choice between cultural invasion and propaganda or true, dialogic education. This latter is not now described in terms of Christian virtues but as an approach to knowledge which exists only 'in history', in the praxis of action and reflection. This 'gnosiological state' requires learning to be concrete and practical, and generated by the learner, rather than theoretical and idealistic and imposed by the educator/developer.

The strength of Freire's integration into Chile is perhaps illustrated by the fact that the introduction to this essay was written by Jacques Chonchol, a leading academic and economist who was later to become the Minister of Agriculture in Chile's Allende government. It is worth noting, however, that these two important books or extended essays (the first published in Portuguese in 1967 and the second in Spanish in 1969) were published in English only in 1974, four years after the publication of *Pedagogy of the Oppressed* – a chronology which explains why many English-speaking readers consider this latter work to be Freire's most influential book.

Despite the productivity of his writing and of his involvement in the literacy campaign, Freire was clearly not satisfied to stay in Chile. In 1969, some months before the election of the Marxist Allende government in Chile,[10] he was invited to Harvard to be Visiting Professor at the Center for Studies in Education and Development. Three or four days later he received another invitation, this time from the World Council of Churches at Geneva. Both institutions were offering an initial stay of two to three years, and Freire opted for the 'world-wide chair' at Geneva rather than the limited sphere of work at Harvard; 'however famous or great the university'. He agreed, however, to spend some months at Harvard, because 'I thought that it was very important for me, as a Brazilian intellectual in exile to pass through, albeit rapidly, the centre of capitalist power' (1989: 12).

Important the visit certainly was. This was a time of student and social unrest, especially in Europe, where demands for more freedom within education, for greater personal freedom and independence of thought featured strongly in the 'Student Movement', causing severe anxiety to many academics. The liberalism and openness that characterized or caricatured certain parts of the United States, for example the University of Berkeley, had not been a feature of life at Harvard, and Freire found some very challenging reactions to his views which provided the impetus and encouragement for him to publish two articles in the *Harvard Educational Review* (May and August 1970) which appeared just before the English version of *Pedagogy of the Oppressed* and which later were published together as *Cultural Action for Freedom*.

This marked, at least for Freire, a watershed in his development:

> Let me say in passing that in *Pedagogy of the Oppressed* and in *Cultural Action for Freedom*, I do not take the same position when confronting the problem of conscientisation. My own praxis in the interval between the last two books and the first taught me to see things I had no opportunity to see before. (1975e: 15)

What he had recognized was that conscientization is not simply a personal, psychological process of renewal or change that could be seen apart from other processes of political action and shifts in related power relations. His evaluation of his literacy work in Brazil and in Chile showed him that the motivation for change, however strong that might be and however necessary the change might be, was not of itself sufficient to bring about that change.

It was his attempt to respond to this major criticism of his earlier work, namely that he had created a polarization between the knowledge or awareness of a given reality and the transforming of that same reality, that explains his demand in these two works that we should see critical consciousness as a process of action *and* reflection. It is a dynamic, individual and collective reappraisal of history, that insists that the learner is 'in the world' and able to 'name' his or her world.

The world is the world of the oppressed, where banking education, cultural invasion, domination and silence mark the life of those who are not conscientized, and particularly the lives of those who are non-literate. The pedagogy of the oppressed (the title of the book is in the singular in the original Portuguese but is usually read in the plural sense in English) requires that they should be able to read and to write, to enter into an equality of dialogue and so name their world, in order to transform it and thus be makers of their own history. The means and the ends of such a pedagogy are a critical awareness of reality (knowledge) and the eradication of the inequalities which exist between the oppressed and their oppressors (power).

Within a wide range of movements of questioning, reform and confrontation, particularly within education, the publication of *Pedagogy of the Oppressed*, plus the impact of the two Harvard articles, quickly established Freire's international reputation as a radical, even revolutionary, pedagogue. He became a symbol of the time, fashioned by the rhetoric, the liberalism and the romanticism of the post-1968 era. It was this reputation and the potential of his pedagogy rather than any published, quantifiable results from particular literacy programmes, that Freire took to the World Council of Churches when he was appointed consultant in their Office of Education at Geneva. There he set up the Institute of Cultural Action through which he had the opportunity of more direct involvement in the struggles of other Third World countries, mostly in Africa. His consultancies, as well as a host of seminars and international conferences, took him to Mozambique, Peru, Angola, Tanzania, São Tomé and Príncipe, and Guinea-Bissau.

Among all these activities, it was perhaps his work in Guinea-Bissau which was the most crucial in the development of his ideas and practice. *Pedagogy in Process: Letters to Guinea-Bissau*, a collection of letters written to educators and politicians between 1975 and 1976, shows Freire moving towards a much clearer position about the power relationships between learning, conscientization and freedom (Youngman 1986). He locates his pedagogy and his praxis within the context of overt political and economic activity, and he manages to be comfortable with the neo-Marxist but very African ideology of Amilcar Cabral in a way that could not have been imagined ten years earlier.

Ironically, at the very point at which he had moved towards a clearer political statement about literacy and conscientization, he found himself included, contrary to the expectations of many, in a general amnesty granted by the Figueredo government in Brazil in September 1979. Freire, ever Brazilian, returned to Recifé in June 1980 to work initially at the Centre for Educational Studies (Centro de Estudos em Educacåo) and then to take up a post as Professor of Philosophy of Education at the Pontifícia Universidade Católica de São Paulo and the public Universidade de Campinas in São Paulo.[11]

So commenced a period of reintegration, marked by no major publications in English until *The Politics of Education: Culture, Power and Liberation* in 1985. This is essentially a reprint of selected articles and interviews, first published between 1965 and 1975, including the two Harvard essays of *Cultural Action for Freedom* and the article which first appeared in *Study Encounter* and which gives crucial evidence of the politicizing of Freire's thought: 'Education, Liberation and the Church'. Although the book aims 'to stimulate more discussion on current major issues in education' (p. xxvii), the only new material is an interview/dialogue with Macedo recorded in 1984.

The same themes re-emerge in his next publication in 1987, *A Pedagogy for Liberation: Dialogues on Transforming Education*.[12] This is a series of dialogues with Ira Shor which have been transcribed, the 'talking book' being itself a device to create a 'dialogue' with the reader who can then both see and hear Freire's explanation of the development of his pedagogy. The constant anchorage in Freire's theory of communication and his view of what constitutes knowledge is still there. What is added to the discussion which prevents it from being merely as restatement of *The Pedagogy of the Oppressed* is Freire's reflection on his wider experience and Shor's more incisive logic and disciplined analysis.

Freire has clearly a great enthusiasm for such 'talked books'. The same device, this time again with Macedo, forms the base of *Literacy: Reading the Word and the World* (1987b). The edited dialogues focus less on the techniques of literacy teaching (which so marked his early works) and more on restating the goals of literacy as the acquiring of the *language of possibility*. This 'pedagogy of liberating remembrance', to borrow Giroux's sumptuous phrase from the introduction, is embedded in history. It is a literacy which is an act of knowledge but in which 'it is no longer possible to have the text without the context' (1987b: 43).

31

This elision of text and context takes Freire beyond Berthoff's 'pedagogy of knowing' to a pedagogy of questioning. *Learning to Question: A Pedagogy of Liberation* is his latest book published in English, co-authored or conversed with Antonio Faundez.[13] The dialogues centre on selected biographical details and the different experiences of exile which the two men had endured. There is a detailed examination of the relationship between learning and power but the book serves primarily as a means for Freire to answer criticism of his work in Guinea-Bissau and for him to repeat his view that literacy acquisition should be in the natural language of the people and not in the dominant language of the educator or of the cultural invader.

None of the work which Freire has published in English since his return to Brazil in 1980 shows a radical change in his thought or in his practice. Little approaches the passion of *Extension and Communication* (1969e) or the clarity of Education, Liberation and the Church (1973a). Yet, before the discourse of pleasant conversations and of comfortable nostalgia come to be all pervasive, there will be an English translation of Freire's latest work, *Education in the City* (1991).

This reveals a renewed Freire, in a series of ten reprinted interviews or dialogues which took place between 1989 and 1990. The text, unusually, gives considerable biographical detail and because of that reveals much more of Freire as a person. It is almost as though he feels himself liberated from certain elements of his own past and therefore able to talk with a new energy and vigour. Three points are of particular note, bringing this bio-text up to date.

First, Freire is able to speak about his second wife, Ana Maria Araujo. She is the daughter of the high school director who had given him a free place to continue his schooling so many years before. She is twelve years younger than Freire and had also been a student of his when he taught Portuguese at her father's school. Nita, as she is familiarly called, is an educator and literacy tutor and an author in her own right.[14]

Freire's new-found love and joy allows him to reveal just how devastated he had been at the death of Elza. She had been a far greater influence on him than he had as yet been able to admit and her absence brought to a close a unique relationship and a long period of working and teaching together.

Second, and perhaps because of that, Freire launched himself in 1989 into a new political career. He had been invited by the mayor of São Paulo, Luiza Erundina, to create an adult literacy programme. He was appointed Secretary for Education in January 1989, and set about organizing, together with the Church and the university, a literacy movement (MOVA) which aimed to reach 60,000 people in some 2,000 culture circles. Additionally, he had the task of building or rebuilding 546 schools to meet the needs of the vast number of children in the area who were not attending school. The first results of this programme, which Freire calls a restatement of the *Pedagogy of the Oppressed* in action, appear to be very positive.

Behind the decision to co-ordinate this project lay an overt political decision on Freire's part. The logic of his position within the local government was that he was, even in Geneva before his return to Brazil, one of the founder members of the Workers' Party that convincingly won the local elections in November

1988. This is the first time that Freire has committed himself to a political party and he has done so because it is a people's party, rejecting elitism and authoritarianism. In this case, he sees his role as administrator and decision-maker as wholly coherent with the principles and goals of *Pedagogy of the Oppressed*.

Finally, after two and a half years of intense work, having achieved some success but having also suffered sharp criticism from the press and opposition parties, Freire resigned from his post as Secretary for Education in May 1991. He has returned to his books and his writing. His time in the Town Hall had served to convince him that his real skills and ambitions lie in being a political educator rather than an educated politician. He has taken up his post again in the university, and is now occupying himself with 'three or four projects' which he has laid aside in these recent years.

There is no doubt that this experience will serve, in the strict sense of the word, as a pretext (pre-text) for Freire to write a consolidated version of his philosophy and practice of education. He will continue, as he has always done, to pose the simple, provocative question: What is the relation between literacy, liberation and learning?

The contemporary Freire, teaching in a modernized Brazil, will have cause to reflect upon the changes in texture and context through which his pedagogy has lived. The bio-text of his experiences and the grapho-text of his work have given us not just a writing of his life (a biography) but a reading of his world. Both assert the possibility of a liberating pedagogy which is commonly known now as the 'método Paulo Freire'. What they do not assert as clearly is that, if we rewrite this text by reading it in more detail, we shall find that, despite its apparent novelty, such a pedagogy is not new and that behind Freire lies the weight of other traditional pedagogies and a large library of other philosophers of education and of liberation.

TWO

Backgrounds and borrowings

A review of selected sources
and influences

Introduction

To say summarily, as many commentators do, that Freire's thinking is eclectic is to underestimate the degree to which he borrowed directly from other sources, and the affinity which he found in other authors on whom he was confidently able to rely for support. An avid reader, there is no doubt that he was also an erudite poacher who sought out and repossessed other ideas in order to enlarge and restock his own intellectual domain. Consequently the text which Freire offers is actually a complex tissue of his own work and the threads of other pedagogies and philosophies which he has woven all together across the loom of his experience and his genius.

The unravelling of these trace elements within the filigree of his ideas and his practice is made all the more difficult because Freire's library is actually more syncretic than it is eclectic. His analysis of history and culture leans heavily on Althusser, Fanon, Lukacs, Mao, Marcuse and Marx, as much as on Aristotle, Descartes, Hegel and Rousseau. His theology is compiled from Bonhoeffer, Gutierrez, Niebuhr and Rahner as well as from Buber, Fromm and the traditions and practices of the 'Church Triumphant'.

> Freire's work and study on many continents enable him to quote at will from scores of philosophers, psychologists, sociologists, political scientists, educators, revolutionaries, and theologians. It is possible, however, to identify some of the major accents in his writings and the personalities whose thought to a greater or lesser degree contributed to his philosophy. (Collins 1977: 27)

This means that the reader will find references to Aristotle side by side with arguments from modern French sociology, traditional Catholic theology

34

explained by radical Protestantism, and descriptions of cultural poverty or oppression enlightened by international Marxism or Jewish mysticism.

The efficacy of such syncretism or, in other words, the coherence of Freire's personal philosophy, means that it is not possible to unravel neatly the diverse skeins of influence in the multi-layered appliqué of his thought. What is possible is to paint in the background, identify the ingredients which Freire has used to make his own particular work of art (to borrow his own provocative image of the educator as an artist) and, within that, to concentrate on those key elements which have been the most formative in the creation of his pedagogy.

A European heritage?

The French connection

We have already referred to the major influence of French academics on Freire's early reading and have noted the presence of the much underrated figure of Lucien Febvre. He was one of the first contingent of émigré professors at São Paulo University and co-founder, with Marc Bloch, of the French journal, *Annales d'histoire économique et sociale*, which introduced into a traditional approach to the teaching of history the important innovation of the sub-disciplines of economic and social history. Their 'social contextualizing' of history led to the investigation of culture and ideology as the construct of historical events. History is not the chronicling of dates and epochs but rather the intersecting of 'cultural moments' which according to the mentality of the time (or according to the mentality of the historian) were deemed to be significant.

These later cultural studies focused on the centrality of language and a 'history of mentalities'. This was the subject of a series of lectures which Febvre gave in São Paulo University. Through his analysis of a history of conscious and unconscious forms of thought, he provided Freire with the notion that consciousness was stratified but capable of accelerated or retarded evolution. He also provided an introduction to *discourse analysis* as a method of studying language, illustrating its usefulness in the identification and construction of the various historical 'stages of consciousness'. Freire's explanation of the development from naive to critical consciousness in *Pedagogy of the Oppressed* is a development of Febvre's categorization of consciousness, and the technique of *decoding* in the Culture Circles is effectively a specific application of discourse analysis.

For Freire and for Febvre, words are social 'witnesses' of their time and history (*mots-témoins*). Freire played much with this idea of historicizing, where history is the means of revealing reality. He then reversed the current of Febvre's logic, arguing that history was brought into being, revealed only by the word: critical consciousness is where individuals are able to insert themselves in their own history by 'naming the word/world'. The word is their reality (*mots-choses*).

It is worth noticing the ripple effect of Febvre's influence which touched

Freire indirectly but significantly. It was he who, in the second year of the *Annales*, initiated a separate section in the journal which was entitled *Les Mots et les choses* (words and things) the purpose of which was to explore the etymological archaeology of key words and phrases, creating a history of words and ideas which was specifically an analysis of the social and cultural contexts of those ideas. This is exactly what Michel Foucault proposed in his book of the same title, *Les Mots et les choses* (1966), which was translated into English as *The Order of Things* (1970). It is a study which 'traces language as it has been spoken', but 'Quite obviously, such an analysis does not belong to the history of ideas or of science: it is rather an enquiry whose aim is to *discover on what basis knowledge and theory became possible*' (1970: xxi, my emphasis added).

This critical definition of the central relationship of Power and Knowledge is also clear in Foucault's *Archaeology of Knowledge* (1969), where he makes the direct link between his approach and the *nouvelle histoire* of Febvre by insisting that the core focus of the power-knowledge dilemma is the fundamental questioning of the world as it has been written (*la mise en question du document*). Historical documents should not be treated as cold monuments to the past, inert monoliths of culture, but as living evidence of what people have done and said, of relationships, of people 'in the world'. The problem (and interestingly, Foucault resorts to the neologism in French *problématiser*, just as Freire did in Portuguese *problematizaçâo*: problem-posing) is to 'protect the sovereignty of the Subject' by insisting that the individual in history is not an object (Foucault 1969: 22, 54). In a contrapuntal echo of Febvre, which is testimony to his influence, we can hear Foucault's 'textualizing of the world and history' essentially as the obverse of Freire's 'writing the world'. Both assert the mutual valencies of the history of writing and the writing of history.

Beyond the importance of this historist attempt to structure mentalities or consciousness, Febvre's other major contribution was that it was he who initiated, both through the *Annales* and through the university in São Paulo, the co-operation and involvement of many French intellectuals who came, some for periods of two years, others (like Roger Bastide) for many years, to teach at the university. Many of them wrote for the *Annales*, and for Mounier's *Esprit* which, from the early 1960s, was available in Brazil in Portuguese translations. Among those who, collectively and individually informed Freire's thinking were Lévi-Strauss, Goldman, Barthes and Althusser.

The structuralist ethnology pioneered by Lévi-Buhl which found further expression in Lévi-Strauss's *Anthropologie structurale* (1958) also emphasized the contribution of linguistics in the social sciences. It underpins Freire's explanation of culture and art in Picture 7 of his literacy method (see Chapter 5). Freire knew *La pensée sauvage* (Levi-Strauss 1962) and he made full use of the important distinction between 'the savage and the scientific mind' (naive and critical consciousness), as well as Lévi-Strauss's construction of history (1962: 307). 'History is never history, but history-for . . . History-for-me can make way for the objectivity of history-for-us'.

Freire cites Goldman both in 'Cultural Action and Conscientization', in explaining the state of perceptive clarity which Goldman calls 'the maximum of potential consciousness' beyond 'real consciousness' (Freire 1970i: 471,

474), and in *Pedagogy of the Oppressed*, to express the difference between 'real consciousness' and 'potential consciousness' (1982: 85, 100) and the impossibility that reality can be transformed 'mechanistically'.[1]

Barthes's 'Histoire et littérature: à propos de Racine', which appeared in the *Annales* in 1960, reflects Febvre's social history of literature in criticizing the view that one can read social structures homologously as one can read texts, and highlights the Freirean question of how one can write text and so 'write' society.

Although Althusser is named as one of the major influences on Freire (1982: 10), precise references to him are scarce within Freire's work. In fact the only references quoted all refer to his *For Marx* (of which Freire had a copy in French) and to his ideas of 'superstructure' and 'overdetermination'. Freire was able to accept Althusser's *structure* as a means of distinguishing economic, political and ideological practices, but he clearly could not follow the argument that theory and practice cannot be considered in some kind of conceptual isolation through to the creating of that ruptural unity which would have made the revolution which Freire proposed forcefully self-determining and realizable.

L'éducation nouvelle: *reformed education*

In that context of French teaching and reading, Freire was introduced to a wide range of more formal statements of that pedagogy which came to be known as *l'éducation nouvelle*. A number of key elements of this approach can be found in Freire's works. Although he so completely assimilated them and made them his own that acknowledgement is rare, it is none the less possible to distinguish the interpenetrating influences of Freinet, Claparède and Petersen.

Freire (1970l) refers to Freinet as 'one of the great contemporaries in education for freedom'. In Africa he had seen a training seminar based on the teaching principles of Freinet and he regarded him as a 'practical political pedagogue', placing him in the company of 'Amilcar Cabral, Samora Machel, Fidel, Nakarenko and Nyerere' (1978: 33, 157). What perhaps had caught his attention was that Freinet centred his pedagogy on literacy, on enabling the child or adult to write their own text for themselves (Freinet 1968) but the philosophy which lay behind that and which had created the context of the 'live-in' school which Freire visited in Guinea-Bissau represented a wider contextualizing of education. The central tenet of *l'éducation nouvelle* was that education is nothing less than life itself.

Freire arrives at the same point in his book with Frei Betto (1985b): *Essa escola chamada vida* (This School Called Life), but the initial assertion lies embedded in both French and German education of the late 1920s.

'If education is supposed to be a preparation for life, but is not actually a way of life itself, then it can never be the preparation which it claims to be'. So ends Claparède's *L'éducation fonctionnelle* (first published in 1930). Here, while it is interesting to note in passing the wider focus on 'functional education' some fifteen years before the expression 'functional literacy' became popular, the important idea is that the lived-in-school is also the school-in-life. Freire obviously found close affinity with this. Claparède (1973), in *L'éducation fonctionnelle*, insists that education is a way of living in which the educator is an agent of social change but where the function of the teacher has to be transformed to allow the school to become a place of experimentation for work, play and social relations. The teacher has to be able to learn from the pupil in a context where success is not guaranteed and where the process of 'trial and error' (*tâtonnement*), like dialogic education, may well result in failure.

Claparède follows Vygotsky and Dewey (both of whom Freire knew well) in his proposition that learning is created by breaking into what is accepted and unquestioned: 'to the degree that an action is automatic, it is unconscious'. Learning becomes possible only when we become conscious of our actions and when, through a process of decoding the obvious, the learner and educator can arrive at an understanding of their underlying needs. Learning is thus predicated on this identifying of needs, the process of which parallels Althusser's ruptural principles: 'destabilization (*la rupture d'équilibre*) is the driving force of all activity' (Claparède 1973: 59, 51).

By strange coincidence, Freinet and Petersen had met at Locarno in August 1927 at the Fourth International Conference of the New Education Fellowship. The theme of the conference was 'The Meaning of Freedom in Education' and among the participants, mostly from Europe and the United States, were representatives from South America, particularly from Chile. It was here that Petersen presented in detail what later became known as the *Jena Plan*.[2] He proposed a *Lebensgemeinschaftsschule*, a school-which-is-the-living-community. The similarities in language alone provoke the question: Did Petersen foreshadow Freire, or did Freire apply and develop Petersen?

According to Petersen, 'Education is a function of existence as original and as powerful as life itself. As such, it makes the spiritualization and the liberation of humankind possible' (Spies-Bong 1989: 91). Unmistakably here, the concept and practice of spirituality and freedom would reinforce for Freire what he would read in Maritain:

> I know myself as subject by consciousness and reflexivity. Subjectivity is known or rather felt in virtue of a formless and diffuse knowledge which, in relation to reflective consciousness, we may call unconscious or pre-conscious knowledge. (Maritain 1957: 76)

Petersen, and with him Freinet, aligns education with a 'change of consciousness', an idea that provided Freire with a further rationalization of the quest for liberation and 'hominization' which he would find as one of the core themes in Teilhard de Chardin. That, plus the insistence by both pedagogues on the need for a change in the basic relationship between student and teacher, would lead Freire equally to redefine that relationship and to express the process of such change within the spirituality of an 'Easter experience' (Freire 1982: 103).

In this *nouvelle pédagogie* the first responsibility of the teacher is to create the possibility of questioning (Freire's problematizing), in a pedagogical situation where each person is active and empowered to take decisions. Spies-Bong (1989: 101) calls this 'a pedagogy of learning' (*une pédagogie de l'enseignement*), an expression which is but the parallax image of Berthoff's description of Freire's 'pedagogy of knowing' (1987b: xv).

The teacher is the animator of the conversation which takes place in 'core groups' (*Stammgruppe*) or *Learning Circles*. According to Spies-Bong (1989):

> The Circle allows for the raising of general questions or topical issues proposed by the children, or of facts relating to their experiences or observations. The fact of being in a Circle should be beneficial: each communicates with the other as an individual. (Spies-Bong 1989: 104)

This prioritizing of the individual as subject within an authentic, personal conversation does not diminish the centrality of the co-ordinator/teacher in the Circles. Whatever the equality of the relationship in dialogue, there is still the need for authority and control. Petersen (1965: 31) talks of the fundamental *Gesetz der Gruppe*, a self-imposed discipline but still insists that 'the teacher is the animator . . . who still remains the expert'.

Freire, like Petersen and Claparède, has never fully resolved this ambiguity of roles, as we shall see more clearly when we look in detail at his Method. Despite his dialogic rhetoric, and his warning about the dominance of the educators in the Culture Circles, his practice reflects wholly the principles of Petersen and Claparède. While that may be a criticism when viewed against other pedagogies, here it simply serves to impress how far Freire was imbued with the spirit and the practice of *l'éducation nouvelle*. It provided him with a linguistic structure and pedagogical outlook with which to articulate his own specifically Brazilian learning programme. It does also explain to a great degree why his work is based on a psycho-pedagogy rather than on functional competencies and applied apprenticeship.

What is clear, however, is that, when seen schematically, Freire, Claparède, Freinet and Petersen are all hanging their work on the same pedagogical skeleton. For example the three essential principles of Freinet (Pomes: 1989), namely free expression, experimenting and rehearsing, and action (*expression libre, tâtonnement expérimental et coopération*) represent a parallel formula to Freire's basic method of *See–Judge–Act*, a difference of style but not of philosophy. Freire's frequent assertion that 'knowledge emerges only through invention and reinvention, through restless, impatient, continuing and hopeful enquiry which people pursue in the world, with the world and with each other' is perhaps only a culturally South American translation or transposition of Petersen's equally culturally Germanic *Pädagogische Tatsachenforschung*, that intense and continual researching of knowledge and learning.

The triptych of personalism, existentialism and hominization

Much has been made elsewhere of the influence on Freire of Maritain's *existentialism* and Mounier's *personalism* (Collins 1977; R. Mackie 1980). What has been overlooked, however, is that these philosophers and writers together gave Freire not only the text, but also the intellectual context in which to forge a pedagogy of liberation. Paradoxically, their main influence on him was to be felt not directly through the university classroom but indirectly through the Catholic Church.

Freire came to find himself cast on the horns of the Marcusian dilemma: 'One of the decisive social tasks of affirmative culture is based on the contradiction between the insufferable mutability of the bad experience and the need for happiness to make such existence bearable' (Marcuse 1968: 118). As an educator, Freire found himself committed to a process of cultural affirmation: as a Catholic, he found himself neutralized by the Church's palliative theology that explained undeserved injustice today by the promise of an earned happiness later. The Church has never believed, or never acted in the belief that 'The meek shall inherit the earth'.

In the early days of Freire's literacy programme, the Church was still emotionally and theologically a long way from the declaration of Cieneguila in Peru 1969, and from the statement in the same year made by Dom Helder Camara (Bishop of Recifé) and Dom Antonio Fragrosa (Bishop of Ceara) which was also signed by some 350 diocesan priests. They concluded that, faced with the obscenity of social injustice, 'the revolutionary option, which has scandalized so many, can well be the result of the purest act of conscience' (Gerassi 1971: 48).

All had been influenced by Mounier, who had campaigned, particularly through *Esprit*, in support of the worker-priest movement, arguing that the Church should identify 'authentically' with the people and that revolution was potentially the clearest expression of love.[3]

Authenticity was one of the key themes of the age. Mounier had come to reject the Augustinian view that *freedom to be* was ultimately discrete from the *freedom to do*. Freedom could mean only 'freedom in action'. Hence the title of Freire's books are deeply significant: *Cultural Action for Freedom* and *Education: The Practice of Freedom*. 'Every educational practice implies a concept of humankind and the world' (1970h), but that concept has value only in the case where being human means being authentically free.

For Freire (1976b: 34), this contrasts with the massified society which makes people 'passive, fearful and naive'. What is required is the humanization of mankind[4] which, both for Freire and for Mounier, was to be achieved through a Christian view of history, melding together 'the unity of God, the unity of history and the unity of the human race' (Mounier 1951: xv).[5]

This was to be nothing less than a spiritual revolution, the first steps of which were political and economic revolution (p. 117), made possible by the here-and-nowness of each person in their own history: 'I am a me-now-here, perhaps even more heavily, a me-now-here-like this-with these people-with this past' (p. 127).

It is in engagement with others that we are completely free: 'There is no liberty for humankind except in creating engagement: there is no engagement without creating a liberty' (p. 141). Engagement refuses the consciousness of solitude because it is in relationship 'towards the other, in the other, towards the world and in the world before being in itself' (p. 150).

'To be human is to be a being-in-the-world' (p. 159) full of 'wonder and interrogation' (p. 164), whose liberty comes 'not from following history' (p. 166) but from making history.

This admittedly selective presentation of Mounier[6] is all that is required to reconstitute the main historical and social themes of *Pedagogy of the Oppressed*. Add that to Maritain's Christian existentialism and the foundation of Freire's pedagogy is almost complete.

Maritain (1957: 83) restates the importance of authenticity: 'To be known as object, to see oneself in the eyes of one's neighbour, is to be severed from oneself and from one's identity'. For Freire, this severance from identity, resembling the *non-being* of Heidegger and Sartre (*das nichts, les néants*) is a central problem: 'The struggle begins with people's recognition that they have been *destroyed*. . . . Teacher and students, co-intent on reality are both *Subjects*' (1982: 44).

As subject, each person IS: they do not simply EXIST. So Maritain's statement 'To exist is not and cannot be cut off from the primary concept of being, that-which-is' (1957: 33) is echoed with the same import in Freire (1988: 89) 'Unlike animals, human beings not only live but exist' (*Os homens, ao contrário do animal, não somente vivem, mas existem*).[7]

As such, each person is a 'being in action', an expression which, for Maritain, is an existential tautology. Potential existence is revealed only through action – *potentia dicitur ad actum* (Maritain 1957: 45). Following a very Thomist view which Freire also accepted, Maritain states (1957: 70, 76): 'Only subjects exist, with the action which emanates from them, and the relations which they bear to one another . . . I know myself as Subject by consciousness and reflexivity.'

Freire (1976b: 146) restates that as 'The *prise de conscience*, which is a human characteristic, results in a person's coming face to face with the world and with concrete reality, which is presented as a process of objectification'. This is none other than Teilhard's *Noogenesis*, each person discovering themselves in their own mirror (Teilhard 1965: 201). It is a permanent process of conscientization, of personalization (Teilhard 1965: 192), 'what Teilhard calls *Humanisation*, when human beings made themselves capable of revealing their active reality' (Freire 1975e).

Consciousness is not a reflection of, but a reflection upon reality which transforms that reality, humanizing it (Freire 1970i: 454; Teilhard 1965: 183). 'Consciousness takes possession of itself, not just knowing, but knowing that it knows'.[8]

Freire here quotes directly from Teilhard, but mostly he absorbs and applies his ideas: that intelligence must overcome the encircling illusion of proximity (Teilhard 1965: 239); that '*thinking the world* gives it a form of unity it would otherwise lack' (Teilhard 1965: 274); that the evolution of a progressively more conscious mind is a process of *complexification* (Teilhard 1965: 16).[9]

A Marxist infrastructure?

One of the themes raised by many of Freire's critics and commentators is his uneasy relationship with communism in general and with Marxism in particular. His experiences during the Brazilian coup of 1964, his life in Chile under the pre-Allende government, his stay at Harvard and his longer involvement with the World Council of Churches all attest to the complex and sometimes ambivalent *aggiornamento* between Catholicism and Marxism which so marked both the preparations for the Second Vatican Council and the new dialogues of liberation theology, particularly in South America. Yet while many of these commentators focus on Freire's reading of the 'early Marx' and on his selective application of Gramsci, no one has yet paid attention to the highly significant figure of the militant Czech communist and Marxist philosopher, Karel Kosik, who so influenced Freire's humanistic Marxism.

Even Youngman's (1986) careful study of Freire's pedagogy in the light of the nine principles which he proposes as a coherent guide for action for socialist adult educators makes only a passing reference to Kosik and so ignores the fundamental contribution which he made to Freire's work.

Born in 1926, Kosik was an active member of the Labour Movement and played an important role in the political and social debate during the 1960s that led to the liberalization of the country. After the 'Prague Spring' of 1968, he was dismissed from his post and from the party.[10]

Personally, Freire would have identified with Kosik: both were educators, both were arrested because of that, and both were exiled, Freire to another country and Kosik to internal anonymity where he was not allowed to teach. Beyond that, what seems to have struck Freire initially was Kosik's idea of a 'concrete reality': that institutions, ideas and concepts – what he would later come to collectivize as *Culture* – are also a part of the reality of daily life which human beings are able to change (Freire 1982: 73). Earlier, he had argued that the adult literacy process, as an act of knowing 'implies the existence of two interrelated contexts. One is the context of authentic dialogue . . . the second is the *real, concrete context of facts*, the social reality in which people exist' (Freire 1970h: 214).

In both these instances, Freire quotes from a 1967 Spanish edition of Kosik, *Dialéctica de lo Concreto*. The French version of *Pedagogy of the Oppressed* notes that 'On this subject, Karel Kosik's *La dialectique du concret* (Maspero, Paris 1970) must be read', and the latest Portuguese text of *Pedagogy* (eighteenth edition) now quotes Kosik in a Portuguese third edition.

Freire is therefore acknowledging Kosik in a way that he does not do with other authors (Fromm or Unamuno, for example), yet it is still very difficult to evaluate the importance of his contribution. In *Politische Alphabetisierung: Einführung ins Konzept einer humanisierenden Bildung* which first appeared in the *Lutherische Monatshefte* in 1970, Freire asserts that human beings have a presence in the world which reflects the constant 'unity of action-reflection'[11] and he adds the footnote: 'On this, see the extraordinary book *Dialéctica de lo Concreto* by Karel Kosik, Grijalbo, Mexico, 1967. N.B. There is a German edition of this book'. This note, which is retained in the original typescript translation of the article into English at the World Council of Churches, Geneva, is suppressed in the most recent translation in *The Politics of Education* (1985a: ch. 8).

Kosik, however, appears elsewhere, reinforcing for Freire the insight of *l'éducation nouvelle* that the essential context of literacy learning and teaching is everyday life. 'We have no right so to submerge ourselves in the drama of our own life that we lose ourselves in daily triviality' (Freire 1985a: 129); human beings cannot escape the tension between past and future, death and life, hope and despair, being and non-being. Here, in *Education, Liberation and the Church*, with a direct reference to Kosik, Freire is not merely asserting the key idea that reality is 'concrete' but also insisting that such reality is historical, that time is three-dimensional. Human beings have a present because they have a past and a future, but they must discover that for themselves through discovering their history. They find their true selves, not in some utopia or other world, but in their daily lives which they must seek to understand.

In this early works, Freire never refers to Kosik by name in the text as he does with Althusser, Gramsci, Marx, Niebuhr, and Teilhard, among others. However, in *Pedagogy in Process* – which interestingly Youngman (1986: 154) suggests is much closer to a Marxist approach to adult education than Freire's previous books – Kosik, is quoted directly. 'From this base they form a kind of practical intuition of reality in the midst of which they carry out their own lives of practical activity and feeling' (1978: 135).

Freire comments that simply existing, in some naive consciousness, does not give a sufficiently critical comprehension of life to be able to 'live', a point which he makes again explicitly in *Learning to Question*.

> One of the basic features of our experiences in everyday life is precisely that we pass through it, taking account of the facts, yes, but not necessarily gaining real insight into them. As I say this, I am reminded of that outstanding book by Karel Kosik, *A Dialética do Concreto* in which he engages in critical discussion of the significance of everyday life. (1989: 20)

The precise context of this statement, a discussion with Faundez, is important. In describing Kosik as one of the intellectuals who have attempted to enter in the history of the society in which they lived 'of which daily life is a vital part', Faundez recalls that 'they [Lukacs and Kosik] were the thinkers who bound us to the reality we were experiencing at that time when changes were taking place in Chile. They were the ones who made us reflect on everyday life' (Freire 1989: 20, 24). All of which leads us to question what perspective Kosik had on everyday life that made his book so extraordinary or outstanding and how important an influence that was for Freire.

Freire first read Kosik in 1967 when he was working in Chile in a political context where the pro-Marxist Allende government was seeking radical social reforms which included his national literacy campaign. The popular discourse of the day was openly and militantly Marxist in a way that had never been achieved in Brazil, even in the early 1960s. Freire, from his still deeply Catholic background, then met this powerful statement of neo-Marxism which was argued as a critique, not only of Marx (although that also gave Freire a much wider bibliography of Marx and Lenin than he had previously known), but also of a wide spectrum of classical and Marxist pedagogy and philosophy which included Aristotle, Descartes, Rousseau, Husserl, Hegel, Gramsci, Lukacs and

Wright Mills,[12] to name but a few of those subjected to the analysis of Kosik's enormous erudition.

Freire found in Kosik key points of convergence which allowed him to use the structure of Kosik's argument throughout his work. The core theme of the book is that human beings exist in nature, in history and in economics. Nature is that reality which is living, which is not fixed or given but which is in a state of becoming. It can be understood by human beings only to the degree that they fashion it themselves, recreating it in three-dimensional time. This awareness of history as past and future is what distinguishes human beings from animals. Their insertion in history is achieved through dialogue, through praxis and through work. These are the three processes of humanization which provoke social revolution, that is economic revolution, for it is economic categories which form the scaffolding of society and which define a human being not as an individual but as a function of the system. This renders the individual anonymous, depersonalized, hence the need for a *prise de conscience* which enables individuals to set themselves in opposition to what is given and to reinvent for themselves a liberating praxis in which they know themselves as Subjects.

That in fact is a summary of *Dialectic of the Concrete*, but it could easily serve as a summary of the argument which connects *Cultural Action for Freedom, Pedagogy of the Oppressed* to the more self-consciously Marxist analysis of *Pedagogy in Process*.

The essential influence of Kosik, however, predates Freire's work in Africa. We have just considered the content of Kosik's philosophy which Freire found so extraordinary, but when we look at the structure of his argument we can see just how deeply Freire had absorbed it.

The argument of *Dialectic of the Concrete* can be presented schematically:

Chapter 1 Intellectual and social reproduction; the total, concrete reality.

Chapter 2 Homo oeconomicus vs social banking structures; the growth of rationality, conscious or unconscious views of reality; art as history and culture.

Chapter 3 The reading of text and the reading of the world; human beings as Subjects/Objects, in the context of work and self-fulfilment.

Chapter 4 Praxis, history and freedom, the nature of humankind, consciousness and the reality of the world in history.

Now, when we look at the structure of *Pedagogy of the Oppressed*, we find a parallel argument:

Chapter 1 Justification for a pedagogy of the oppressed and explanation of the reality of oppression.

Chapter 2 Banking education vs problem posing education; man as a consciously incomplete being in the process of becoming more humanized.

Chapter 3 Dialogue between people as Subjects, the social practice of freedom, and the stages of consciousness.

Chapter 4   Dialogics and antidialogics: the matrices of praxis; Being in the
world and the nature of oppression, conquest and liberation.

The correspondence between the two books is too close to be mere coincidence,
and the essential point is not furthered by detailed quotation. The common
themes are clear: social reproduction and the reality of oppression; social
banking structures and educational banking systems; reading the world and
dialogic conscientization; the praxis of freedom and the practice of education.

That is not to say, and perhaps the point should be made unequivocally, that
Freire 'copied' or plagiarized Kosik. Not only would that be a gratuitous insult
but also it would completely devalue the exciting and creative processes which
take place within an eclectic mind. Freire absorbed Kosik, as he had discovered
and absorbed other pedagogies, and he repossessed this 'concrete reality' as his
own. Kosik simply brought out the crypto-Marxism in Freire which was to
become more evident in his later work. He also provided Freire with a refreshing
critique of 'classical' philosophy which enabled him to rework and restate
particularly his own understanding of Aristotle and Hegel. Through Kosik,
admiration, annunciation, theory-practice-praxis, being-in-the world became not the
hallmarks of traditional pedagogy but the prerequisites of a new, revolutionary
futurity (Freire 1982: 57).

A classical lecture sequence?

In constructing his pedagogy, Freire was seeking something definitely other
than what he saw negatively as Socratic intellectualism and the other-
worldliness of Platonic dialogue. He wanted a pedagogy that existed in Kosik's
world of the concrete, in that 'relationship between the *theoretical context*, in
which representations of objective facts are analysed, and the *concrete context*,
where these facts occur' (1970h: 217–18).

If we can now hear a double echo, first from Kosik, but behind that, from
Aristotle, we should not be surprised, given that Freire was in fact, initially, only
secondarily involved in literacy. Within the University of Recifé in the early
1960s, his primary role was as Professor of the History and Philosophy of
Education. It was in this role that he presented a 'classical' lecture sequence on
the development of pedagogy which modelled many such courses in other
European universities which, in one form or another, treated the history of
education 'From Aristotle, via Hegel to Rousseau'.

It is worth looking at this in some detail because it reveals some of the
structures of Freire's thinking, as well as the degree to which he first absorbed,
then creatively retranslated, Aristotelian and Hegelian philosophy to express his
own pedagogy.

Aristotle

Freire, even in writing and then translating *Pedagogy of the Oppressed*, preferred to
use the classical Greek terms of *doxa* and *logos* rather than find a suitable
expression in the vernacular (Freire 1976b: 110). In doing this, he was not

intending to mystify: rather he was so imbued with Aristotelian thought that he is able to restate his own pedagogy not as a simple translation of Aristotle but as a recreation of Aristotelian principles. Several key examples will illustrate this remarkable reinvention of classical pedagogy.

The first point of contact for Freire was the debate about theory and practice. Pythagoras had described the *theoros*, the spectator, as the only truly free person because he or she could stand back and see things as they actually were. However, for Aristotle, this was not an absolute freedom. Such a person did not live in a vacuum any more than freedom itself could exist without a context: it could exist only *in* the world, with its own purposes, its specific intentionality. In other words, *theoria* (theory – which today we might call 'scientific inquiry', or which Freire might call 'critical consciousness') is *a reading of the world* (*Metaphysics*, Epsilon, 1, 1,026).

This idea conjoins the notion of rigour and 'seeing reality' which is evident in Freire's understanding of conscientization. He argues continually that, in order to perceive this reality critically, one has to be *in* the world, and not just *with* the world (1982: 49). It is also an understanding of reality which is not engendered by mere intellectual curiosity any more than it is created by practical necessity; rather it arises from a *sense of wonder* and an awareness of one's own ignorance (*Metaphysics*, Alpha, 2).

This awareness or *theory* is the prerequisite of true knowledge. In talking about *doxa* – the alienating knowledge, and *logos* – true knowledge, Freire says 'Knowledge begins with the awareness of knowing little . . . and knowing that they know little, people are prepared to know more'. Earlier, he had argued for 'an education that would lead people to take a new stance to their problems, one oriented towards research. An education of "I wonder" instead of merely "I do"' (1976: 36, 117). The image certainly is that of the spectator who sees more of what is happening precisely because he or she sees things from a distance: that is the very essence of the process of conscientization (1991: 103).

'Merely doing' (Freire's *activism*, 1982: 60), the phrase used to contrast with 'admiring', is also Aristotelian. He frequently contrasts *doing* (*poiésis*) with *action* (*praxis*). Essentially, *doing* only fulfils itself, is an end unto itself, acting upon objects: once it has stopped, it has no value. *Praxis*, on the other hand, is realized through the effect it has on others: it may not even exist without others for it is fundamentally exoteric, other-seeking, dialogic. It is that 'productive quality exercised in combination with true reason – *logos*' (*Ethics*, 6.4. 1,140). It is interesting that, in the light of Freire's argument about oppression, banking education and the people who have been marginalized, Aristotle is heard to say that 'life is *praxis* not *doing*'. Mere doing is the function of a slave (*Politics*, 7.2. 1,325, 1.2. 1,254).

What distinguishes human beings from slaves (the oppressed) and animals, is that human beings can 'create, can act for a purpose'. This is because humankind has a *logos*, a reason characterized by intentionality and a capacity to deliberate (*Ethics*, 6.1. 1,139). This intentionality, which is the essence of consciousness (Freire 1982: 52), is how Freire explains that knowing is the task of subjects, that is those who are free, not slaves, not oppressed. He quotes the person from São Paulo who said 'I want to learn to read and to write so I can change the world', adding his own observation that that person was someone 'for whom *to know* quite correctly means *to intervene in his reality*' (1976b: 99, 50). For Freire, as for Aristotle, this purposeful action in the world, *praxis*, cannot exist without *theory*, because it is only together that they constitute knowledge. They are not polarities but rather are two dimensions of human existence that can be distinguished but not separated.

Freire (1982: ch. 2) speaks powerfully of reflective action and active reflection. It is in the context of this dialectic that he explains the equally 'classical' concept of *admiring*. This is the ability to gain distance from an object, to objectify the 'not-I' which is, for Freire, a 'dialectic operation which characterizes human beings, differentiating them from animals' (1970h: 215). For Aristotle, it is the essential requirement of knowledge, and a product of that role taken by the *spectator* which creates an 'engagement with reality' (*Ethics*, Book 6). Freire agrees but nuances or reinterprets the idea by translating it as 'a commitment to', or 'conversion to' reality (1982: ch. 1).

Later Freire (1970h) presents a condensed summary of the *Ethics*, Book 6, perhaps echoing the use of this passage in a lecture:

> For dialogue to be a method of true knowledge, the knowing subjects must approach reality scientifically in order to seek the dialectical connections which explain the form of reality. Thus to know is not to remember something previously known and now forgotten. Nor can *doxa* be overcome by *logos*, apart from the dialectical relationship of people with their world, apart from people's reflective action upon the world. (Freire 1970h: 218)

What Freire (1982: 71) calls the 'dialectic operation which most characterizes human beings, differentiating them from animals' is almost a direct translation of Aristotle's statement (*Politics*, 1.1) that 'human beings alone of the animals have *logos*'. What is meant here by *logos*, however, was not primarily the distinguishing factor of rationality or cognitive abilities. For Aristotle, *logos*, above all, means the ability to express oneself in speech: it is to speak, to name one's world. To have *logos*, and the rights to speak the word/the world that go with that, is to be truly human.

For Aristotle, to be human also means to be a political being, a *politikon zoon*. It is against this background that we must hear Freire insisting that dialogue (the creating and using of authentic *logos*) is a human (political) encounter, mediated by the world, in order to name the world (1982: 61). Dialogue is no less than an existential necessity, providing the means for achieving critical awareness (Freire's and Aristotle's *logos*). That is why the process of conscientization is also a process of humanization: 'as human beings, as beings of *praxis*, to transform the world is to humanize it' (1970i: 455).

That is also why the literacy process has 'to relate *speaking the word* to transforming reality, and to each person's role in this transformation'. At its most basic, 'learning to read and write ought to be an opportunity for us to discover what *speaking the word* really means: a human act implying reflection and action' (1970h: 213).

Finally, Freire insists (as does Kosik) that the process of conscientization is never complete. For him, the uncovering of social reality and the discovery of the person in that reality 'is not something to be grasped as something *which is*, but as something which is *becoming, in the making*' (1975e: 14).

This takes us to the essence of the challenge of Aristotle. In talking of the freedom of the individual and of what it means to be rationally human, he describes humankind as 'capable of being other', having a capacity to see and make things, including themselves, other than what they are now (*Metaphysics*, Theta 5). However, he recognizes that real life can also be 'potency limiting': 'the question of what it is to be human is one thing; actually being human is another' (Analyt. Posterior 2.6). On the one hand, this is a way of recognizing that we can only be human in this world. On the other, it is a way of emphasizing that we need to look at the concrete history of being human, that is we must consider ourselves as historical beings in what Freire would call our 'limit situations' (1982: 71). *Pedagogy of the Oppressed* itself could almost be retitled 'A Pedagogy in Limit Situations'.

Stated in that way, Freire's pedagogy is self-evidently and fundamentally Aristotelian. None the less, the similarities do not end there: two final points are worth noting. First, Aristotle also considered that words themselves might be a guide to help us understand the nature of things. In the *Metaphysics*, Book Delta, he collected instances of usages of common, key words, effectively compiling a lexicon of generative words. Second, he was aware of the pedagogic potential of alphabetizing the language. In talking of causality and the four most evident types of causes, he refers to matter, fire and earth, the parts of the whole and *the elements in the case of syllables* (*Metaphysics*, Delta, 12).

That reality can be dissected in a way wholly comparable with the dissecting of a word into syllables is an insight that lies at the root of Freirean pedagogy. It is almost as if Freire read into, or read out of, Aristotle's alchemy of learning his own psycho-pedagogy. Thus he is able to assert, with Aristotle, that to think correctly, to have *logos*, is to be able to construct and reconstruct one's world.

Hegel

If one can construct the world, by definition one can then construct history, and vice versa. This is one of the fundamental hypotheses of Freire's pedagogy for which he found evidence in preparing his own university course on Hegel, analysing particularly the series of lectures on the *Philosophy of History* which Hegel delivered in 1822–3.

This hypothesis, which so marks *Education: The Practice of Freedom* and *Pedagogy of the Oppressed* is based on a view that history offers both an epistemological and metaphysical perspective. It concerns itself with that body of knowledge of past human actions (the nature and possibility of historical truth) and with that part of the theory of reality which is concerned with meaning and the purpose of history as it was and is being made.

For Hegel, history was not to be ascertained simply as so much fact, but as the reasons *why* the facts happened as they did. It is primarily the unfolding of the story of the development of freedom which seeks to explain the parallel development of the functions and authority of the State alongside the safeguarding of the rights and interests of the individual within the State. History does not seek to parade the past, any more than it can try to predict the future: it aims instead to present the Now of this moment. In this Now, as Freire says (1976b: 3), 'through reaching back to Yesterday, coming upon Tomorrow through recognizing Today', human freedom for any individual is the same as their consciousness of their freedom. One cannot be free unless one is conscious of being free. To study the development of freedom is, therefore, to study the development of consciousness.

Freire would have found this sequence of ideas congenial. Hegel had taken the focus on the present moment from Schiller (as he took the idea of the world realizing itself in self-consciousness from Schelling, and the stages of consciousness from Fichte) and from the idea of *history-which-explains-contemporaneity* which Vico had proposed in his *Scienza Nuova*. Here Freire was encouraged by Kosik's (1988: 93) distinction between History and false history and his acknowledgement that it was from this same root (Vico's 'Verum et factum convertentur') that Marx developed the theme that human beings make their own history.

This is a restating of the Aristotelian *logos*, for Hegel insists that what is important in human activity is not the actions of people seen simply as events, but the thought or consciousness of which the actions are outward expressions. It is *logos*, critical awareness, which is the mainspring of history. Thus, in summarizing his view of history in the Preface to his *Philosophy of History* as 'What is rational is real and what is real is rational', Hegel exposes Freire's conditional hypothesis of history and of pedagogy. If what is rational is *logos* (correct thinking or reason), then *logos* itself is the means of making rational for the attainment of *logos* represents a process which is intrinsically humanizing. For Freire, this means that only what accords with critical awareness can be accepted as authentically human. What is dehumanizing and what is the product of naive consciousness (*doxa*) cannot be tolerated.

For Hegel (1892: 103) the thought processes which underpin this actualization or conscientization are logical and, because they evolve dialectically, history itself is inherently dialectical. Thesis provokes antithesis, and the ensuing conflict or contradiction between them is resolved in synthesis, leading to a new thesis. This gave Freire a disciplined mode of thinking which protected him to some limited degree from the otherwise circular Manicheism to which he was prone. 'People, because they are aware of themselves and thus of the world – because they are conscious beings – exist in a dialectical relationship between the determination of limits and their own freedom' (Freire 1982: 71).

In other words, people become aware of their freedom through the stages of consciousness by which they recognize 'their not being free' (the limit situations), but they also recognize that these are not 'given', they are not immutable. Accordingly they are able to intervene in those self-same limit situations and create the possibility of them being otherwise:

Neither does the discovery by the oppressed that they exist in dialectical relationship as antithesis to the oppressor who could not exist without them (see Hegel's *Phenomenology of Mind*) in itself constitute liberation. The oppressed can overcome the contradiction in which they are caught only when this perception enlists them in the struggle to free themselves. (Freire 1982: 26)

It is interesting here, in passing, that in *Pedagogy of the Oppressed*, Freire quotes in English, even in the Portuguese text, from an English version of Hegel's *The Phenomenology of Mind* (1967). As there is no reference to the *Phenomenology* in any of Freire's work prior to the *Pedagogy*, the strong influence is that Freire read this work of Hegel via Kosik, who equally makes the interesting link between Rousseau, Hegel and Marx (Kosik 1988: 118).

The importance of Hegel's *Phenomenology* is that he describes here three phases or stages of consciousness. There is an historical or historicized progression from consciousness of the 'object' (*Bewußtsein*) to that of consciousness of the 'self' (*Selbstbewußtsein*) and finally to that of consciousness of reason (*Vernunft*) which is the actualization of *logos*. Only this final stage, which Hegel identifies as the synthesis of objectivity and subjectivity, surpasses the stoic or unhappy consciousness (*das unglücklicke Bewußtsein*) or what Freire (1976b: 18) calls the passive, intransitive consciousness.

The celebrated image by which Hegel explains this transition is that of the differing perspectives of the master and slave, an image used extensively by Freire.[13] For Hegel, while the consciousness of self demands the recognition of the self-hood of others, the master of the slave 'by not recognising the slave as a real person, deprives himself of that recognition of his own freedom which he originally demanded' (Hegel 1967: Part 3; Freire 1982: 25). It is in this sense, that Freire with Hegel came to see the relationship of master and slave, oppressor and oppressed, and even teacher and learner, as *dehumanizing*, because it is a denial of self-hood.

Conclusion

The disciplines which make possible a history of ideas are primarily those of the archaeologist and the genealogist. However, the fertile terrain of such an analysis is not, in the first instance, verbal or conceptual, but rather textual. As illustrated in the above arguments, the first decoding of Freire requires not so much a history of thought (*Begriffsgeschichte*) as an historical appraisal of written sources (*Redaktionsgeschichte*) in order to disentangle the multi-layered threads of argument and description from a whole library of texts which Freire has used and refashioned into his own writings and lectures.

This does not diminish Freire nor deny the originality of the fusion of ideas which are particularly his. However, it does expose those complex stratifications of philosophy and pedagogy which lie beneath the surface of his work. This enlarged textuality provides the reader with a lens that is both convex and concave. The latter brings into focus Freire's specifically South American profile, educated and educating as he was in a provincial University in North-east Brazil. The former provides a much wider perspective which situates Freire firmly within the mainstream of European intellectualism, denying by such a pedigree, that the pedagogy which he engendered is in any way novel, quaint or transient.

THREE

Education and liberation

The means and ends of Dialogue and Conscientization

Dialogue and Conscientization

The notions of Dialogue and Conscientization are so closely associated with Freire, and with the *Pedagogy of the Oppressed*, that, as the hallmarks of his philosophy, they explain in large measure both his frequent marginalization and his cultic status. The development of this association, however, is difficult to date mark. Freire (1979: 11) claims not to have used the word 'Conscientization' since the early 1970s: 'I stopped using this word because the word was so corrupted in Latin America and in the States. It does not mean that I reject the process which the word means'. None the less, he has never yielded to the pressure (1985a: 185) to find an appropriate English translation that represents his first understanding of *Conscientização*.

Freire has never claimed to be the author of the idea. It is now clear that the word *Conscientização* emerged from a discussion group within the Higher Institute of Brazilian Studies where it was popularized particularly by Dom Helder Camara, the Bishop of Recifé, at a time in the mid-1960s when the Catholic Church was increasingly involved in the Moviemento de Educação de Base (MEB), successfully using radio learning and the national media for its literacy campaign. Freire does claim, however, to have been consistent in his use of the word. Conscientization is a process of developing consciousness, but consciousness that is understood to have the power to transform reality. He denies (1979: 3) that 'objectivity is *created* by consciousness, as if, somehow, we could transform reality through speech alone, through convictions. I cannot transform the world inside my consciousness'. Merely thinking that one is free, or even asserting that one is free, does not achieve 'freedom'. Freire frequently had to combat that allegation, and he was adamant that he had never said that speech, literacy or education could bring about social transformation.

However, he does claim the obverse, namely that radical social transform-ation, revolution in itself, is an educational process.

It is naive to continue to insist that by education we can transform reality. (1975d: 3)

Education rather *reproduces* the dynamism which characterizes the historical-social process. It is an act of knowing and a *means* of action for transforming the reality which is to be known. (1972b: 180–1)

The question remains: How does Freire break into this cycle of causality? On the one hand, he is asserting that education is a means of transforming reality, by which he means 'the social reality'. On the other hand, he also insists that the education system, or at least 'radical change in the educational system', is contingent upon the radical transformation of society. This begs the question of how that radical, societal change is created, particularly as he seeks to prevent us from considering the educational option: 'I have insisted on the impossi-bility of considering the educational system as an instrument of social transformation' (1976a: 70).

How then are we to consider the educational system: is it not therefore an instrument of social control? Freire will certainly want to argue that it is, that 'banking education' lies at the heart of oppression, yet it seems that he fails to undertake any serious analysis of the questions which underpin the debate about power and knowledge, teaching and learning, schooling and society. It may almost be that we have to confront the possibility, as does Berger's (1975) sharp critique, that 'liberating education', that is that Dialogue which leads to or results in Conscientization is a contradiction in terms.[1] To do that, we shall need to examine carefully Freire's intentions and his claims for Dialogue and Conscientization.

Freire's initial goal, as stated in *Education: The Practice of Freedom* (1976b: 43), was 'a literacy programme which could be an introduction to the democratiz-ation of culture'. It is in this light that the dialogic theme of *Pedagogy of the Oppressed* should be interpreted, namely that the naming and transforming of the world through the democratization of culture is possible precisely because Dialogue is both a 'human phenomenon' and 'the encounter in which the united reflection and action of the dialoguers are addressed to the world which is to be transformed and humanized' (1982: 61).

The need for a dialogic form of education arises directly from the unequivo-cal statement that education is not neutral, and indeed can never be neutral 'because it is always an action either for the domestication of people or for their liberation' (1985a: 99). This is the essential dichotomy – the distinction between education as an instrument of domination and education as an instrument of liberation – which provides the starting point of the *how of conscientização*, that process in which 'we take the role of agents, makers and remakers of our world' in 'a permanent, critical approach to reality in order to discover it and discover the myths that deceive us and help us maintain the oppressing, dehumanizing structures' (1971a: 24).

The next questions leap off the page: what are those myths? What are those dehumanizing structures? There we are thrown on to the horns of a dilemma that recurs throughout any analysis of Freire and which reflects the deep Manicheism which underpins his thinking. Constantly we are forced back on to the schism of reality, into a world of polarities which comprises teachers and the taught, the oppressed and the oppressors, the necrophilic and the biophilic, light and dark, subjects and the objects, liberators and liberated.

This polarizing is a useful heuristic device that can induce clarity, as is shown in Kelly's (1955) extremely useful dichotomous construct theory. The problem arises, however, where the device is allowed to *create* the reality, where this world of bi-polarity becomes the only known reality. It induces an overall simplicity that actually impedes the way in which we give meaning to experience. Freire relies heavily on this device, but the clarity of his argument allows us to see accurately only at the poles of the inter-arching continua which he has constructed: it allows little light into the central canopy of everyday life where most people live.

Is it possible that Freire has rationalized a world of false dichotomies? Is it the case that education, to take but one of the constructs, is not simply *either* about liberation *or* about domination but rather about *both*? Berthoff, in her introduction to *Literacy: Reading the Word and the World* (p. xix), actually avoids this question by finding a triadic rather than a dual construction in Freire's thought. For example she suggests that he juxtaposes the traditional, liberal and prophetic church, or a consciousness that is naive, astute or critical. While this is not untrue, it represents only a surface reading of Freire. First, it does not take into account the degree to which his catholic discourse, culturally and spiritually, cannot escape the bind of Manicheism. Second, the detailed text suggests that Freire is concerned only with the transiting from one polarity to the other and that his 'middle terms', in the few cases where he gives them, serve primarily as rhetorical pointers to the preferred direction.

This is certainly true in the instance where Freire, having stated that 'every educational practice involves a concept of the world and of what it is to be human', starkly contrasts two forms of such practice: Banking – Digestive Education and Dialogic – Liberating Education (1982: chs 4 and 2).

Freire's description of the former is well known and highlights the emphasis on transferring knowledge, on the passivity of the learner, on the distance of the teacher from the learner, on the selective rather than the global perception of reality and on the alienation created personally and culturally for the learner who is regarded as a 'deposit' or 'object'. The temptation is that, if we simply accept Freire's Manicheism, we attempt to combat banking education by creating a new model from those elements which lie on the opposing poles. In so doing, we arrive logically at the concept of 'education for freedom', but without questioning whether, ontologically, this new, proposed polarity can actually exist.

However, for Freire this is more than a step of logic. He claims that the ingredients of a counter-education can be identified, if they are posited on an act of knowing which is fused from two interrelated experiences. First, there is the creation of an authentic Dialogue between the learners and the educators as equally knowing subjects, and second, there is the awareness of the real, concrete context of facts, that is of the social reality in which we are living (1970j: 214).

This again begs the question: whose reality constitutes the real, concrete context of our experience? Freire does not explain his own understanding of epistemology or ontology, yet those perspectives are fundamental to his argument. In an interesting lapse in *The People Speak Their Word*, he asks rhetorically: 'What do we mean by challenging you to think correctly?', but he then answers his own question by explaining only the word *challenge*. The definition of *correctly* is stated but is not for question: 'To think correctly means to try to discover and understand what is found to be hidden away in things and in facts that we observe and analyse' (1987b: 87). This act of knowing then becomes 'a truly gnosiological situation' which enables the learner to 'truly enter into the problem' and thus to 'make his or her own History' (1976b: 145ff).

It is clear in this passage that Freire draws little distinction between epistemology and ontology, knowing and being. For him, the Cartesian *cogito ergo sum*, 'I think therefore I am', becomes 'I know therefore I am', and he aligns himself with a classical Piagetian psychology which views cognitive development as personal development. (Freire 1979 is entitled 'To Know and To Be'.) The confusion of these two different perspectives is highlighted here when, in order to combat banking education, we ask: What kind of reality must a teacher or learner be able to see? What is it that they need to know correctly, so that they can engage in a relationship which is not oppressive?

The obviousness of this question makes it all the more significant that it is here that Freire is at his most mystical and abstruse. Authentic Dialogue, he says, requires the resolution of the teacher/learner dichotomy. In part this will come about as the learners achieve their own consciousness, but primarily it will be brought about by the 'Easter Experience' or 'Class Suicide' on the part of the teacher.

> The educator for liberation has to *die* as the unilateral educator of the educatees, in order to be born again as the educator-educatee of the educatees-educators. An educator is a person who has to live in the deep significance of Easter. (1970l: 9)

This experience, Freire argues, brings about a different kind of learning, or at least the potential for a different kind of learning, because it can become 'an act of knowing and a means of action for transforming the reality which is to be known' (1972b: 180). The essential factor of this form of learning is that it is *problem posing*, not concerned with simplistic questions to be found only within the given. It is about the 'problematizing of human beings and the world, not the problematization of human beings isolated from the world, nor the world isolated from human beings' (1976b: 152).

Freire thus makes the relationship of an individual with the world the pivotal link in the process of Conscientization, but misses the other cardinal point which is the articulating (in both senses of the word) of the act of knowing *and* the means of action for transforming the reality of what is known.

Praxis

The result is that, for Freire, it is the locating or annunciating of knowledge-education within history, rather than the articulation or denunciation of knowledge-power, which creates the possibility of *praxis*. Perhaps 'historical praxis' is itself a tautology, yet it is not immediately evident how Freire wishes the idea to be understood.

At one level, given that he is both a product of, and a mirror of, the ambivalent response of the Catholic Church in Latin America to Marxism, Freire might deny any underlying tension between the Christian and Marxist elements which converge in his use of the word 'praxis'.[2] Although he was able to say (R. Mackie 1980: 126), 'God led me to the people and the people led me to Marx', he had to reaffirm his orthodoxy by adding 'When I met Marx, I continued to meet Christ on the corners of the street – by meeting the people'. This apparent compromise, none the less, allowed him, encouraged by his reading of Kosik, to resort to the political and economic descriptors of Marxism to explain the need for Dialogue, liberating education and a counter-oppressive society. It gave him the advantage of a linguistic and phenomenological currency that had a known value and immediacy for many people of the 'oppressed world'.

Freire, however, was never converted to Marxist, revolutionary politics. When he makes his appeal for the creation of those conditions which will combat oppression, his core argument is couched not in the language of Marxism but in the biblical terms of love, faith, hope and humility (1982: 62). As with his idealizing of revolutionary leadership, or his view that Conscientization is primarily a process of 'humanization' and that Dialogue itself is the fulfilment of one's 'ontological vocation', the language of the Christian faith is more than the mere clothes for dressing and presentation: it is actually the skeleton or underpinning of his philosophy and social analysis.

At this stage, we have to note that the accommodation of Marxism and Catholicism does not necessarily create a marriage of ideas out of which praxis is born. On the contrary, Freire's redefinition of the term creates a further tension or polarity for it is based on an assumed, non-Marxist, dichotomy between theory and practice, reflection and action.

Freire is clear in stating that praxis can be defined as the action and reflection of people upon their world in order to transform it. He pillories those who are merely activists, who are busy expending their energies for the cause, unthinking followers, doers, just as he attacks the theorists who hide in the ivoried towers of policy-making, educational administration or political rhetoric. What is actually required, according to Freire, is *active reflection* and *reflective action*. 'The role of reflection is to react to the action and to reveal its objectives, its mean and its efficacy' (1976b: 110). Reflection in that sense is coterminous with 'correct thinking':

> Finally true, Dialogue cannot exist unless it involves critical thinking – thinking which discerns an indivisible solidarity between the world and people admitting of no dichotomy between them – thinking which

perceives reality as process and transformation, rather than as a static entity – thinking which does not separate itself from action, but constantly immerses itself in temporality without fear of risks involved. (1982: 64)

As such, praxis may be easier to proclaim than to achieve. Clearly, it comprises three elements which have common valencies: *thought, reality* and *perception*. These adhere together to form that web of ideas spun by Freire around the deceptively simple, but much used concept of *process*. If *reality* is a process, *Conscientization* is a process, *humanization* is a process, *Dialogue* itself is a process, then we need to pause to question the nature of this process or these processes. What are they a *PROCESS* of?

With praxis providing the linkage between ontology and epistemology, one immediate answer is that they are all processes of the *Practice of Education*. We could even complete the circle and add to that the idea which Freire used as the title of one of his key, early books *Education: The Practice of Freedom*. It is almost as if the core ideas of process, praxis and practice might be mutually interchangeable, a view supported by the fact that, within Freire's writing and lectures over the past twenty years, there has been this constant scoring of the three ideas to construct subtle variations on the theme.

How then is the 'practice of education' or the 'practice of freedom' to be construed? What is it a practice of?

Carr (1987) raises this very point in an interesting and pertinent analysis of the confusion that arises when practice is defined or understood on a continuum opposed to *theory*:

On this view, practice is everything that theory is not. Theory is concerned with universal, context-free generalisations; practice with particular, context-dependent instance. Theory deals with abstract ideas; practice with concrete realities. Theorising is largely immune from the pressures of time; practice is responsive to the contingent demands of everyday life. (Carr 1987: 164)

This is a dichotomy which, on these terms, Carr and Freire reject. One cannot simply dissect out the principles of education from the practice of teaching/ learning. What is required is not the separation of theory and practice but the ability to distinguish between them.

This is the specific task of philosophical reflection. When this is done, what perhaps did not previously appear as the theory of action, is now revealed as such. If there is no dichotomy between theory and practice, reflection on our actions reveals the theory – without which the action or practice is not a true one. (Freire 1976b: 110)

Essentially, Freire is wanting to assert the distinction between theory and practice because, as in the argument above, he wishes to contrast the nature of the dialogic person who is *Subject* (who sees the theory behind the reality) and the person who, without Dialogue, is oppressed as *Object* (who has only a naive consciousness of reality).

It is this further, all-embracing bi-polarity, however, which serves to protect Freire from the critical debate which concerns the nature of this *person*. Whether I am conscientized or not, who is the 'ME' who is learner or teacher? If I name my world, to use only one of the generative statements of his philosophy, who is the 'I'? Following Carr's (1987: 166) useful definition of an educational practice as 'an ethical activity undertaken in pursuit of education-ally worthwhile ends', we can look again at both the process of Dialogue and locate the 'I' and the 'We' of those who construct the Dialogue.

Dialogue and transformation

Freire argues that the truly revolutionary project, enabled by the process of Dialogue and mediated by the outcomes of Conscientization, creates a *'process in which the people assume the role of subject in the precarious adventure of transforming and recreating the world'* (1970i: 486). By 'people', he means those who address themselves as 'I' or 'We', not in some nominative sense of the grammarian, but as *Subjects*. The word has a flavour of independence, status and integrity, reflecting the preferred value system by which he consistently asserts that Conscientization, engendered by Dialogue, is the means of transforming Objects into Subjects, the Oppressed into the Liberated.

The rhetoric is clear, but how it is to be realized is not. The fact is that 'transforming' and 'recreating' are primarily value judgements. How is transformation achieved? We have the elements of a possible reply on Freire's part, even though he remains, as before, rather mystical and enigmatic. Obviously he would say that the purpose of problem-posing education, by which he means that dialogic education which he also describes as 'revolution-ary futurity', is to create a critical awareness of the present reality where 'I am' and 'We are' (1982: 57). We have to re-educate ourselves to an understanding that rejects the assumption 'that we are merely *in* the world, not *with* the world and with others:[3] that we are spectators and not recreators' (1982: 47). It is this possession of a social consciousness, of being-in-relationship, that identifies us as social and political beings.

Freire describes the new consciousness which is brought about by Dialogue in various ways, but most notably he speaks of the 'unmasking of reality' as the identifying of 'limit situations'.

> Conscientization implies the critical insertion of the person into the demythologized reality. It is first of all the effort to enlighten people about the obstacles preventing them from a clear perception of reality. (1970i: 30)

This demythologized reality presupposes a regard that is 'biophilic', a further bi-polarity which Freire took from Fromm. 'Authentic thinking, thinking that is concerned about *reality*, does not take place in ivory-towered isolation, but only in communication' (1982: 50). Because of the very processes through which it has evolved, new learning, which is now also correct and authentic thinking, does not leave the learner isolated:

The thinking subject cannot think alone. There is no longer an *I think* but *we think*. This co-participation of the subjects in the act of thinking is communication. (1976b: 135)

The logic here is seductive, suggesting that five premises accumulatively provide the infrastructure of a pedagogy of the oppressed:

1 The individual deprived of Dialogue is oppressed.
2 Dialogue is the Process and Practice of liberation.
3 The individual engaged in Dialogue is liberated.
4 Dialogue, by definition, requires more than one person.
5 More than one person can be called a Society.

Given these premises, it must therefore be the case that *the Process and Practice of Dialogue liberates Society*.

There is an interplay here of ideas and structures some of which relate to the individual and some to the society in which such individuals might find themselves. It is, as it were, a deliberate fusing of micro and macro perspectives. The difficulty lies in trying to make sense of what this fusion produces. At one level, Freire is construing society in an almost scholastic sense, as something which is an entity in itself, an *ens a se*. Starting from the premise that 'People, among the uncompleted beings, are the only ones which develop. As historical, autobiographical *beings for themselves*, their transformation (development) occurs in their own existential time, never outside it', Freire then creates the new hypothesis: 'If we consider society as a being . . .'. He then goes on to state:

It is obvious that only a society which is a 'being for itself' can develop. It is essential not to confuse modernisation with development. In order to determine whether or not a society is developing, one must go beyond criteria based on indices of *per capita* income. The basic, elementary criterion is whether or not the society is a 'being for itself'. (1982: 130)

By now we can anticipate the dualism embedded in Freire's thought. In contrast to the developing society which is a being for itself, there is the metropolitan society which cannot develop because it is alienated. The political, economic and cultural decision-making power is located outside the society, in the invader society. By extension, it follows that the metropolitan society is an oppressed society: it is 'massified', dehumanized and alienated (1976b: 112).

So how is such a society, 'being for itself' to be recognized? What are its economic structures, how is it administered, who within the society has power and responsibility? What is the relationship between the *individual* (that micro perspective which exposes questions of personal independence and liberty, self-development, and personal individuality) and the *society* itself (the macro perspective which questions 'the common good', the role of the state, those duties and responsibilities which make demands on the individual)? Nowhere does Freire confront these questions, a failing which considerably encourages his critics to question the relevance of his theorizing.

All that we really know of Freire's utopian society is that it bears the hallmark of Dialogue. In *Cultural Action for Freedom*, he refines further the content of Dialogue: it is about the processes of annunciation and denunciation.

> A utopian pedagogy of denunciation and annunciation such as ours will have to be an act of knowing the denounced reality at the level of alphabetisation and post-alphabetisation, which are in each case cultural action. (1970h: 221)

It is thus tempting to see cultural action as social action, as one way of bridging the gap between the micro/personal and the macro/societal. What we do see, however, is that the process of Dialogue, manifested as the literacy/post-literacy process, is essentially an *act of knowing*:

> Conscientization occurs simultaneously with the literacy or post-literacy process. It must be so. In our educational method, the word is not something static or disconnected from people's existential experience, but a dimension of their thought-language about the world. (1970h: 222)

Freire is here using the means of Dialogue, the WORD, and the process of 'thought-language' in a very specific way in order to 'reflect critically on the process of reading and writing itself, and on the profound significance of language' (1970h: 212).

> Insofar as language is impossible without thought, and language and thought are impossible without the world to which they refer, the human word is more than mere vocabulary, it is *word-and-action*. Learning to read and write ought to be an opportunity for people to know what *speaking the word* really means: a human act implying reflection and action. As such it is a primordial right and not just the privilege of the few. Speaking the word is not a true act if it is not at the same time associated with the right of self expression and world expression, of creating and recreating, of deciding and choosing and ultimately of participating in society's historical process. (1970h: 212)

The fact or the claim that learning to read and write ought to be an opportunity to speak the word clearly allows for the possibility that this is not necessarily the case. Indeed, Freire admits that for some 'even if they can occasionally read and write because they were "taught" in humanitarian – but not humanist – literacy campaigns, they are nevertheless alienated from the power responsible for their silence' (1970h: 212).

We are left with a caricature of what it may mean to be both oppressed *and* literate. Like the illiterate, the oppressed literate does not know that 'human actions as such are transforming, creative and recreative'. It is not their actions which are different but the fact that *they do not know* that their actions are different. Within the culture of silence they suffer the double jeopardy of the exterior silence of oppression and the interior silence imposed by the absence of critical perception.

The conclusion therefore is that there seems to be no ontological imperative that necessarily correlates literacy with transforming knowledge. At best, the wish can be expressed that, through 'calling forth the critical reflection of both the learners and educators, the literacy process might relate *speaking the word* to *transforming reality*, and to each person's role in this transformation' (Freire 1970h: 213). What is significant is not the actual learning to read and write but rather that relationship between the word, reality and the ways in which the latter is transformed by the former.

Critical consciousness

This is the tension that underlies authentic Dialogue. As the word is not static, neither is the outcome of that Conscientization which uncovers social reality. It must be 'grasped not as something which is, but as something which is becoming, as something which is in the making'. This is authentic when the 'practice of revealing reality constitutes a dynamic and dialogical unity with the practice of transforming reality' (1975e: 15).

What then is the causal connection between 'revealing reality' and actually 'transforming that reality'. What is the content of 'our ontological vocation' which Freire recognizes as Teilhard's 'humanization'? (1982: 20)

Freire (1970m: 4) does not help his cause by his mystic explanation that this process of humanization is 'the individual and instantaneous leap from instinct to thought'. However, elsewhere, he does identify a sequence through which the individual consciousness could or must develop. It is a process which he called the 'archaeology of consciousness', in contrast to the 'archaeology of irrationality' – the myth pursuing, falsification of consciousness which is the hallmark of domesticating education (1970n: 16).

In outline, Freire sees the excavating or evolution of critical consciousness as a move away from a state of either naive consciousness or even magical consciousness. The former perceives causality as a static, given fact, and is thus deceived in its view of the changing world. The latter apprehends change but attributes to it powers beyond human control, and is thus released from responsibility for it. In rejecting both these perspectives of the world and of change as less than human, Freire argues that only 'critical consciousness' perceives the true causality of the world *and* the human potential to direct and influence that change (1976b: 44).

Later, in the *Cultural Action for Freedom* Freire speaks of the stages of 'intransitive awareness', 'naive-transitive awareness' and, finally, of 'critical-transitive awareness'. In his view, these three stages correlate to those development stages experienced within a society which is *closed*, which then undergoes *splitting* and which then has to choose between becoming *massified* or actually achieving *critical consciousness* (1970i: 457–67).

Again, we are faced with the tension or confusion of what happens to the individual and what happens to society. A closed society has, 'as one of its structural components, the silence of the masses. When this closed society then begins to crack, silence is no longer seen as an unalterable given' (1970i: 462).

61

What is not clear is whether this breaking of the silence, or splitting of the society, is the cause of Conscientization and critical awareness, or whether it is the product of it. Freire is content to talk of the 'awakening consciousness on the part of the masses', but he does not explain how this process is experienced by the individual. Unless some causative connection or correlation can be found between the mind changes which occur at the level of the individual and the social changes which occur at the level of the masses, then there must be the likelihood that the fundamental premises of Freire's argument are flawed.

His rebuttal of this charge lies in his claim that the connection is actually made through the process and function of education, that is Dialogic Education, for he is absolutely clear that the *sine qua non* of that process is that education presupposes, by its very nature a political intention (1980: 1).

> The pedagogy of the oppressed [is] a pedagogy which must be forged *with*, not *for*, the oppressed (be they individuals or whole peoples) in the incessant struggle to regain their humanity. This pedagogy makes oppression and its causes objects of reflection by the oppressed, and from that reflection will come liberation. (1982: 25)

Yet notwithstanding that this is the explicit intention of the educator, Freire is also clear that 'a radical transformation of the educational system is contingent upon the radical transformation of society' (1976a: 68).

It is important, therefore, to consider how society itself contributes to Dialogue and Conscientization and how the dualism inherent in the role of education is resolved. If the role of oppressive, banking education is functional, serving the interests of the elite, then Freire (1976a: 70) seems to be in a very weak position in insisting 'on the impossibility – which is evident to me – of considering the educational system as an instrument of social transformation', while offering the consolation that 'I do not, however, deny the use of making serious efforts within this system'.

If there is a coherence to Freire's view at this point, it would be found in the understanding that education is not a system or element outwith society. On the contrary, it is one of the primary elements without which we cannot have an understanding of society.

Freire follows Jaspers in asserting that Dialogue constitutes the essence of societal structure and societal change:

> Dialogue is the only way, not only in the vital questions of political order, but in all the expressions of our being. Only by virtue of faith, however, does Dialogue have power and meaning: by faith in humankind and in their possibilities, by faith that I can only become truly myself when other people also become themselves. (1976b: 45)

So the core construct of Freirean Dialogue is revealed: against the matrix that Dialogue is 'loving, humble, hopeful, trusting and critical', it expresses his ontological view of humankind. More simply put, Freire is arguing that, without Dialogue, one cannot be human. In a very real sense, Dialogue precedes Monologue.

Dialogic Conscientization, which we can now understand in Tomas Atencio's phrase 'awareness and respondability' (Marrero 1971), cannot be authentic unless it elicits a creative and liberating response. Since his experience in Africa, Freire has been consistent in saying that this, ultimately, implies the 'political organization of the oppressed to take and achieve power' (1975c: 16). This effort will be realized through 'communication and cooperation, unity and organization that give witness to the fact that the struggle is a common task, and cultural action' (1982: 135–48).

It is interesting that Freire has long since preferred to talk of 'cultural action' rather than of 'education'. His first main text was *Education: The Practice of Freedom*, but his Harvard papers were entitled *Cultural Action for Freedom*. More recently (1991: 82), he has indicated his own preference that that should be properly understood as 'Cultural Action for Liberating'. In which case, what then is the relationship between cultural action, dialogic education and liberation?

The choice of words here is important: education is preferred to action, and liberation to revolution, because Freire has openly denied that his pedagogical methods had as their goal or objective the bringing about of revolution.[4] However, he has always insisted that the processes which he advocated, especially that of Dialogue, would be, in some sense, liberating.

This (dis)connection of literacy, literacy education and development, and revolution is highly significant not least because it exposes a development of Freire's thought. In comparison with his early work, his later writing, influenced particularly by his reading of Fanon and then Cabral, indicate a reinterpretation of his ideas of Dialogue and Conscientization from what might be seen as his initial, 'naive' position.

Frantz Fanon appears *passim* in the *Pedagogy of the Oppressed* where his presence is acknowledged, although he was far more instrumental in the formulating of the argument in *Cultural Action for Freedom* where he is not acknowledged. His shocking, violent book, *The Wretched of the Earth*, Freire knew well, yet he never seems to have been tempted to use either Fanon's illustrative case-study approach or the passion of his expression. It was, however, from Fanon that Freire took the ideas of the metropolitan and dependent society, the colonial mission land, the closed society that had no authentic voice, and the personality schism whereby the 'alienated' find themselves both oppressed and oppressors.

The main significance of Fanon, in this context, is that he proposed an overtly revolutionary model which Freire did *not* use, despite the obvious parallels between the experiences of colonialism in Brazil and Algeria. Of course, Freire never intended writing a primer of cultural revolution, but why could he not have used Fanon to apply his theory of Dialogue to concrete situations? Was it the case that, despite insistence on the historicizing of theory, Freire could not challenge the icon created by his own rhetoric? To have placed his theory under the lens of anti-colonial, anti-oppressive practice would have possibly created a situation where Althusser's (1969: 99) *ruptural principle* would have taken pedagogy beyond Freire's control and would have forced him into a directly revolutionary and political statement.

At that time, Freire was unable to resolve that contradiction, perhaps because, in the final analysis, he was being forced to a level of critical awareness about himself and his own role as one of Fanon's *assimilados*. What his treatment of Fanon suggests is that, in this 'literacy phase', he wrote *Cultural Action for Freedom* as the intellectual outsider.

Conscientization and action

From a period of the mid-1970s, however, symbolized most clearly by the publication of *Pedagogy in Process* in 1978, there is a change in the definition and interpretation of these terms which is quite evident. The book was proposed as the first instalment of a record and review of Freire's work in Guinea-Bissau in 1975–6. He had gone there from the World Council of Churches following an invitation to assist the new government in the reconstruction of their education programme.

This was a seminal experience for Freire as is evidenced by the change in his mood and language. 'For me, education for liberation implies the political organisation of the oppressed to achieve power' (1975c: 16). 'Revolution in itself is an educational task. Educators are also politicians' (1979: 4). 'The question is not only to replace a certain social class by another one as regards the power over the means of production, but above all it is also a question of changing the whole approach towards production' (1974c: 3).

Dialogue and Conscientization are now being explained in terms that are clearly more radical and more Marxian. Across this watershed lies the influence of Amilcar Cabral. In preparing his visit, Freire notes how they had begun 'to read everything we could find, especially the works of Amilcar Cabral' (1978: 9). Cabral was undoubtedly the pivotal figure in the liberation movement in Guinea. He was assassinated by the Portuguese early in 1973, but his extensive writings (Freire quotes mostly from a French edition of *Unité et Lutte*, published in 1975) have formed a primer both for African development and for the anti-colonial struggle world-wide.

According to de Andrade (1980), Cabral was both a theoretician and a man of action, a revolutionary leader of outstanding ability who was 'indefatigably in pursuit of reality, by revealing the deep roots, the fundamental causes, so often blurred in the tumult of revolutionary action'. His was a radical practice and pedagogy which seems to have provoked in Freire a change of focus, a new mind-shift, a different awareness of the process of conscientization.

It was from Cabral (from a widely reported speech in Havana, January 1966) that Freire took the notion of 'class suicide' where 'the revolutionary petty bourgeoisie must be capable of committing suicide as a class, to be restored to life in the condition of the revolutionary worker completely identified with the deepest aspirations of the people to which they belong'. It was also he who identified the 'vegetable silence' to which the oppressed were subjected and to which they subject themselves. He insisted on the need of the oppressed to 'acquire consciousness of reality' through which they would achieve the potential to transform that reality (Cabral 1980: 83, 136).

This consciousness reveals, without a sense of shock but as an obvious response to imperialism, that 'the normal road to national liberation . . . is armed struggle'. The very nature of *national liberation* demands not only the Conscientization of the people (it is the oppressor who calls them the 'masses') but also the violent eradication of that principal characteristic common to every kind of imperialist domination, 'the violent usurpation of the freedom of the process of development of the productive forces' (Cabral 1980: 134, 141).

What then was Freire's response to this kind of argument which was able to consider control of the means of production through violence as the key means of collective liberation? The evidence from the text is that it altered his rationale for literacy training, enabled him to be more explicitly political, and engaged him in issues that previously he had circumvented. In confirmation of this view, it is also interesting to note Kozol's reaction to the *Pedagogy in Process*. He emphasizes the point that Freire's *revolutionary posture* is 'unevasive'. There is a 'revolutionary passion' in which Freire has extended his vision and his consciousness of pedagogic struggle (Freire 1978: 2).

Kozol did not indicate how this vision has been extended, but there are three important points to be noted that impinge on our new understanding of Dialogue and Conscientization: the changed status of Conscientization, the role of dialogic learning, and the relation of both of these to issues of the class struggle and control of the means of production.

Conscientization is no longer a process of becoming aware of the oppressor and of understanding the means by which oppression is sustained. Nor is it just the eradicating of the exterior, physical oppression which makes a person free. Freire has moved beyond that formula (which *Cultural Action for Freedom* may well represent) to insist that 'being conscious is not a slogan but a *radical* form of being, of being human' (1978: 24). It is more creative than recuperative. Reflecting Camara's view (1969: 33) that 'the days of colonialism or oppression may be over, but internal colonialism still remains', Freire sees the need for a more directive form of Conscientization, one which concerns itself with re-conversion, re-Africanization.

Paradoxically, this shift into radicalism implies less political action and more cultural invasion than Freire's naive stance. Conscientization has become more a psychotherapy, a 'detoxifying' (to borrow Brookfield's power-aware phrase, 1986: 151) that places the radix of the problem within the person of the oppressed. It re-echoes loudly the overt, political education-for-action of Moses Coady and his 'mobilization and attitudinization' (Armstrong 1977).

The force-field of Conscientization, or in Bakhtin's term 'the speech zone' of Dialogue, clearly centres over the learner/oppressed person. The process of Conscientization has become a process of changing the conceptual horizon of the victim. Dialogue has become the polyphony, or cacophony, of the authoritative discourse of the educator which is competing with the internally persuasive discourse of the learner (Bakhtin 1981: 342).

This does not align with Freire's initial insight into oppression. If, in this analysis, each person is to be responsible for their own liberation, then they are equally responsible for their own continued domination. That is the logic, but it contradicts the lived experience of gnosiological, historical and cultural oppression where Freire wants to insist that matrix of power-knowledge has to be constructed around the society and not around the individual.

Consequently, although the initial logic of his language brings us to this micro-level, psychotherapeutic focus of Conscientization, Freire turns steadfastly towards a macro-restatement, towards Conscientization as it effects the system of education and society. In so doing, Freire is deliberately redefining the terrain of Conscientization. In this new zone of development, the educator is now a militant whose actions have to be coherent with an overt, political and revolutionary stance (1978: 12) of which Literacy is only one element in a range of social developments.

> If literacy efforts are to achieve their primary objective, that of contributing to national reconstruction effectively, then it would be necessary to establish a dynamic relationship between them and all other forms of social intervention in any way related to or dependent upon literacy. (1978: 25)

Literacy is not about personal development but about national development: the concomitant process of dialogic learning has 'to be seen within the context of literacy, post literacy and production *and* the total plan for society' (1978: 10).

It is this total plan for society that is important, and this for three reasons. First, Freire, while talking about Dialogue and Conscientization, has moved away from a 'revolutionary pedagogy and its role in society' (e.g. *Pedagogy of the Oppressed*) to talk about 'a revolutionary society and its use of creative literacy' (1978: 11). The *raison d'être* of his literacy programme is not now the primary need to read and write but the demands of national reconstruction. Second, what was once a literacy campaign has now become a *Basic Education Programme* that encompasses health education, agricultural development, and management training needed to support the growth of co-operatives (1978: 31). Finally, *Pedagogy in Process*, posited on the contribution of Conscientization to the national liberating process and on the extended content of dialogic learning, is now able to address the previously unconsidered issues of class and the control of the means of production.

At this point, we have arrived at the broadest possible statement of Education as *Cultural Action* which redefines the means of that action (Dialogue) and its goals (Conscientization). Dialogue is now a process within which 'the unity of theory and practice establishes the unity between education and productive activity as a dimension of the concrete order' (1978: 21). In the emerging society, the role of education is to 'create the fundamental background necessary for the full participation of every citizen in the development of the new society' (1978: 42), but the formulation of this programme of Basic Instruction must be considered in its relationship to the means of production (1978: 56). By 1979 Freire could even say 'We have to forget the concept of adult literacy itself. I think the only way is to increase our political clarity and also our commitment to the oppressed class' (1979: 4).

Class consciousness

There seems to be little difference between this education in the *national interest* and the *investment* in education described by Bowles and Gintis (1976). At best, Freire seems to have rendered Banking Education more benign and to have created a new form of education which is concerned not only with cultural autonomy but also now with economic and political liberation. Does this mean that Conscientization through Dialogue is now seen as a strategy of the class struggle? Is Freire suggesting, for example, that Marx's working class is the same as his oppressed class?

Regrettably, among the most conspicuous failures in Freire is the absence of a clear definition of the 'oppressed' and the 'oppressors' (Stanley 1972) and the lack of clarity about what constitutes 'class' (Youngman 1986). This omission is important, first because the analysis of 'class' would allow us to look at both the causes and the consequences of oppression or liberation, thus exposing the way in which *inequality* is conceptualized. Second, it would help us distinguish the dialogue which takes place between individuals from the dialogue which takes place between oppressors and oppressed, and the different dynamics that take place inter- and intra-groups.

Freire (1982: 31–3) assumes as incontestable the generalization that 'any situation in which A objectively exploits B or hinders their pursuit of self-affirmation as a responsible person is one of oppression'. As oppression is essentially about preventing a person from being more fully human, by definition, therefore, the peasants, the illiterates, the colonized and the poor are all oppressed.

This description of the oppressed class or classes does not clarify the notion of *class* itself. When Freire says of *Pedagogy of the Oppressed*, for example, that it was 'rooted in concrete situations and describes the reactions of workers (peasant or urban) and of members of the middle class whom I have observed directly or indirectly during the course of my educative work' (1982: 16), it is not clear whether the distinction between the workers and the middle class is meant as an illustration of the oppressed and the oppressors.

In his later writing, there is no greater clarity. He says that 'in the contradiction of the dominant and the dominated, there is a cultural and class conflict' (1985a: 192). Here he does attempt to clarify what he means by culture, but he does not expound on the meaning of class. If he is intending to interpret *class* as *culture*, then there are important implications for the processes of Dialogue and Conscientization.

Bourdieu (1971: 190) defines culture as that common code which 'enables all those possessing that code to attach the same meaning to the same words, the same type of behaviour and the same works and, conversely, to express the same meaningful intention through the same words, behaviour patterns and works'. In this light, there is a real danger that, in breaking into the Culture of Silence which is the culture of the oppressed, with the intention of conscien- tizing, the educator actually becomes engaged in a process of de-culturation through the creation of radical change. The process, nominally created through the objectives of literacy for the individual, actually calls for changes of behaviour, interaction and language at a social level. Conscientization then becomes a *means* of radical change because it is led by those who have power or who, at least, have the power to teach. But what is it a means of? What are its objectives? In whose interests does the process work?

Freire clearly wishes it to be in the interests of the oppressed, but for that to be anything other than wishful thinking there must be some convincing evidence. It will not suffice to say that the dangers implicit in this perception of the power of Conscientization are, or ought to be, counterbalanced by the creativity of the Dialogue which engages not just individuals but the whole 'cultural community'. Before we can accept that *cultural action for freedom* is the same as *class action for freedom*, we need to know what are the characteristics of this class, what are its interests and its struggles, what is its class strategy for survival, and who are its class opponents.

In reviewing the grapho-texts of Freire, one cannot find as yet any substantial answer to these questions. He uses the language of class, class solidarity, even class suicide, but the word *class* is almost wholly denoted as a cultural phenomenon. The force of the criticism is that it creates a major dislocation between Freire's writing and his practice. It denies his own emphasis on *praxis* and this despite the evidence that he knew and understood the 'early Marx'. He shares with Marx an epistemology that focuses on the issues of being human, on consciousness and alienation, on culture and nature. It is interesting that this Marx (of the *Theses on Feuerbach, The Paris Manuscripts*, and *On the Holy Family*) which Freire quotes most, was also the Marx with whom the Catholic Church was most comfortable. Apparently neither Freire, despite the influence of Kosik, nor the Church felt able to follow the development of Marx's thinking to encompass the issue of class and its economic base.

Added to that, from Freire's bio-text, from his practice, especially in Guinea-Bissau, it is immediately obvious that his development of schools and co-operatives was an educational initiative overtly intended to restructure the means of production. Effectively, each literacy unit became a new, economic unit, creating its own local economy and independence while contributing to the overall structure-plan of national development. Thus we find a Freire who is a long way from the writer of the *Pedagogy of the Oppressed*:

> Freire is convinced that literacy work has more relevance when related to the introduction of new production techniques and the need to increase the community's ability to take charge of its own development by providing its own basic services. (Bee 1980: 48)

Nothing here distinguishes Freire from an educator in the Banking System which, equally, is centred on social development. One cannot disguise the fact that Banking Education has successfully taught sufficient numbers of people to read and write in order to maintain a viable base of both production and services. Is it possible that Dialogic Education, as much as Banking Education which it opposes, is itself actually the means within society by which people learn to oppress and to be oppressed? If the oppressed are to be seen as a class, and clearly that is Freire's view, then more thought must be given to that analysis and to how education is the prime creator of *class consciousness*. Freire cannot simply assert that 'every approach to the oppressed by the elites, as a class' forces the oppressed 'to see themselves in contradiction with the oppressors' (1982: 103, 122). The construction and definition of 'oppression' is critical, because that will in turn define the action which results from someone becoming critically conscious of their oppression.

Conscientization and change

The question of what kind of action ensues through the processes of Dialogue and Conscientization is as critical for the educator as it is for the oppressed. What is the *product* which is offered as the goal of the processes of education-liberation?

The first goal is psycho-social, for Conscientization requires that the individual changes his or her attitudes, perception or beliefs. The essential virtue here is that of non-acceptance: there is nothing given, nothing that cannot be questioned. Conscientization is a form of 'paradigm shifting' (Dunn 1971) in which an individual experiences the redefining of their total boundary systems and a recreating of their own self-image. Inevitably, that must lead on to the validating or rejection of the individual's cultural base, which includes the common codes of accepted behaviour and those 'master patterns' which Bourdieu argues have been previously assimilated.

Herein lies the most subversive element of Freire's pedagogy for, while focusing on the individual and enabling them to name the forces which shape and control their lives, he is able to conceal the secondary agenda which lies in motivating them to strive collectively towards a second goal. This is no less than the moving beyond the new perception or reflection into action, into understanding experimentally how to act upon the causes and processes that generate those forces.

Paradoxically, it is at this point, when Dialogue and Conscientization are seen functionally as psycho-social processes that contain within them a potential extension into socio-political processes, that many critics charge Freire with being utopian. The charge is not easy to rebut, first because Freire himself relies a great deal on the idea yet plays on the very ambiguity of the word. Second, and particularly in translation into English, the concept itself is much misunderstood. Rebuttal is possible only if the word 'utopian' (French *utopique* and Portuguese *utopico*) is taken in its strict sense, that is 'the refusal to accept the *status quo*, contestation, re-appraisal, a demand for the potential and the better rather than the given and the mediocre' (Furter 1974).

By definition, therefore, utopian education implies both individual and social shifting, micro and macro change.

> People stop believing in what once may have been true and has now become false. They withdraw support from institutions which may once have served them but no longer do. They refuse to submit to terms which may once have been fair but no longer are. Such changes are a product of true education. (Reimer 1971: 96)

69

The problem is how to explain or rationalize such 'true education' without being seduced by two widespread fictions. The first is that there is something called Truth, and that there is a Reality which those properly conscientized can perceive. Freire has always been too Catholic to consider this as anything other than the *a priori* of the created world. Consequently, he is frequently in danger of presenting his pedagogy as a form of Social Gnosticism which can be understood only by those who accept the first premise of his act of faith.

The second fiction is that utopian education, even with its related educational practices, cements the gap between such practice, praxis and revolutionary action. However effective a mind-shift it may create at the level of the individual, however wide the impact of its social repercussions, it is not, as an idea, sufficiently self-explanatory as a *causal element* of revolutionary action.

Literacy education, of which Conscientization is the process and Dialogue the means, does not have of itself sufficient effect to control or define the kind of change implicit in any understanding of revolutionary action. This is because, from its conception, it does not have the potential to fuse theory and practice into that Althusserian *ruptural unity* of contexts, currents and circumstances which give revolutionary action its force and potential.

Freire would probably concur with this point: 'In that it constitutes a superstructure, education functions as an instrument to maintain the infrastructure in which it is generated' (1972b: 175). None the less, the difficulty lies in judging the nature of that 'maintenance' and the processes by which it is expressed. Conscientization, given that it is based on Dialogue, has to be a process that is at best *consensus*, and at least *convergence* seeking. It is fulfilled in the reflective action necessary between people who *create together*. It is therefore at the obverse of those strategies which are based on a conflict mode of change through confrontation. The disparity between the two modes is revealed in the expectation that one can enter into an authentic, human dialogue with one's oppressors and, at the same time, engage in revolutionary action against them.

Conclusion

The resolution of this dilemma, without which the concepts of Dialogue and Conscientization cannot be realized in praxis, requires the constructing of some theoretical framework against which to plot the position of education (which must be anti-Antidialogic and at least convergent) and that of revolutionary action (which, for it to remain authentic, must be divergent but also anti-Antidialogic). Such a framework suggests a continuum of attitudes from revolution to reform, maintenance to conservation, where the first value or mode is conflict oriented and where the second, alternative value or mode is consensus oriented.

We need to find a route through the maze which Freire has created by his descriptions of the *product* of literacy education in the first mode, while claiming that the *processes* by which that is achieved should be in the second mode. In order to do this, but without distorting the problem, we can revert to the Freirean technique of exposing elements of contradiction.

We find that there are two interrelated but distinct continua:

a: that which represents the forces in society which define the content and the scope of education, the contrast between the learning agenda as set by the educational institution (that *system* of education which, for Freire, is the Banking System) and the agenda required by the learner in a non-banking system (that *process and product* of learning which arises from Dialogue);

thus:

institutional [IA] —————————————————————— learner's [LA]
   agenda   agenda

b: that which represents the tension or conflicting positions inherent between an educator who is a banker/teacher and an educator who is committed to dialogic learning;

thus, using Freire's language:

the teacher/[TB] —————————————————————— the teacher/[TL]
   banker   the learner

The potential of any form of education to be capable of revolutionary action at the macro level or even of conscientizing at the micro level has to be seen within the context, not only of attitudinal or philosophical variables, but also of the contradictions implicit within the interplay of these two continua. What these continua expose is a previously covert dynamic of those causal elements which both describe and define the *locus* of possible change and revolutionary action. In each quadrant of the intersecting continua lies very differing understanding of *change*, and thereby differing processes and outcomes of Dialogue and Conscientization.

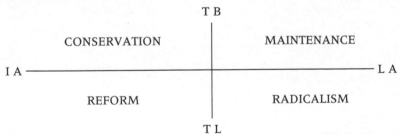

This simply restates the fundamental contradiction implicit in Freire's work. The *language* of his philosophy, hinged around a Dialogue that creates liberation for the learner, clearly reflects a *radical* pedagogy. It focuses on the engagement of the learner and prioritizes his or her agenda, dialogically animated by an educator who is both teacher/learner and learner/teacher.

However, the *practice* of his method, while it would aspire to praxis (reflection and action), is so severely constrained by the social realities within which education takes place that it almost wholly occurs near to the **I A** pole of the contextual continuum. But that is also the *terminus ad quem* of Conscientization, the target which an anti-oppression (liberating) pedagogy has to confront, not least because the **I A** pole, the system of education, also protects the sources of domination. The degree to which action can follow upon reflection will depend on what kind of educator is involved in the process. Given either a dialogic **T L** or an anti-dialogic **T B** teacher, the outcomes will veer either towards conservatism or reformism.

Prior to that, however, the outcomes of Dialogue are also directed by the educator. The *terminus a quo* of Dialogue is firmly at **LA** (in the jargon, one 'starts where the learners are at'), but equally the goals of Dialogue will be fulfilled or denied, at least heavily influenced, by the other person involved in the dialogue, the educator. In the end, the learner will either be liberated and able to 'name their world', or he or she will be domesticated, sentenced (even by the sentence of Banking Literacy) to remain in silence.

In reviewing the diverse possibilities which expose the contradictions inherent in the ideas of pedagogy and literacy, it seems clear that Freirean dialogue is not, and could never be, revolutionary, although there is a sense in which it could be 'revolutionable', in the sense of 'actionable'. In summary, *Dialogue may provide the grounds for revolutionary action, should the need and the circumstances arise.*

Conscientization is then, in its turn, the process which creates the possibility that such need and circumstances could arise and could be met. In summary, it is a process which achieves its goal (its product) to the degree that it creates *that level of awareness and respondability which can authentically sustain a revolutionable conscience.*

Perhaps the great genius of Freire was to conceal the enormous complexity of such a pedagogy within the apparently simple technique of an alphabetic learning method. It is that which we must now consider in detail.

FOUR

The 'Método Paulo Freire'

Generative words and generating literacy

Principles and methodology

The genius of Freire was to bring together a range of pedagogies and learning/ teaching techniques to create a method of teaching which is now known throughout the world as the 'Método Paulo Freire', a method which is both a process of literacy acquisition and a process of conscientization. It is based on the simple but fundamental technique of *problematizing* or 'problem posing', and is therefore the antithesis of Banking Education which seeks solutions or gives answers. It consists of daring to interrogate what is given, bringing into question known structures, and examining conventional or taken-for-granted 'explanations' of reality. It discovers and then reacts to possibility of 'contradiction', identifying ways in which things can be said, done, or exist differently.

In *Education: The Practice of Freedom*, Freire explains the details of his method which has changed very little over the years. It is a three-stage investigation, which poses three fundamentally different questions. First, there is a NAMING stage where one asks the question: what is the problem, what is the question under discussion? Second, there is a REFLECTION stage: why is this the case? How do we explain this situation? Finally, there is the ACTION stage: what can be done to change this situation? What options do we have?

It is a pedagogy which describes certain processes of learning rather than prescribing certain required outcomes, acceptable results or attainments. In the jargon of educationalists, it is process-centred, not product-centred.

It is a permanent, critical approach to reality in order to discover it and discover the myths that deceive us and help us to maintain the oppressing, dehumanizing structures. It leaves nobody inactive. It implies that people take the role of agents, makers and remakers of the world. (1971a: 24)

The three-stage structure of the method, however, was not Freire's creation. It parallels a process popular in the 1960s within the Basic Ecclesiastic Communities (*Comunidades Eclesiales de Base*: CEB) in Brazil. As the basis of their social education programme, especially in the literacy campaign broadcast nationwide by the Church's Basic Education Movement (MEB), they used a method known widely as *See–Judge–Act*: what is the case, why is it so, and what can be done about it? The method found favour, particularly within the Catholic Church, partly because it was simple and practical, and partly because it represented the secular application of the three stages of prayerful meditation as taught within the Jesuit tradition since Ignatius of Loyola. Brookfield (1984: 5) finds the same rural-radio link in the Canadian Association of Adult Education and their *Farm Forum* broadcasts in the 1940s. The scheme, which he describes as an early implementation of Freirean praxis, had as its motto 'Read, Listen, Discuss, Act'.

Freire was thus using a tried and tested method, as Cartesian as it was Catholic, within a learning context which was equally well known to many people both through the CEB and through the trade unions, that is in the *Culture Circles*. These groups became very much associated with his method, although the idea behind the Culture Circle is again, as we have seen, neither new nor particularly South American. What Freire saw was the potential of such a group for the Portuguese lessons which he gave to workers and peasants. Later, it seemed a natural context for his literacy programme. Only very much later did he see the political possibilities which the CEB had been deliberately exploiting for some time.[1]

Two linguistic theories, which Freire constructed through his creative reflection on his own teaching experiences, underpin his method:

1 Adults can learn to read with ease words with which they are already orally familiar and which are, therefore, immediately meaningful. In Freire's expression, 'No one is orally illiterate'.
2 It is possible to identify, within a phonetic and syllabic language like Portuguese, a small number of words (sixteen or seventeen) which contain all the phonemes of the language.

He then describes (1976b: 49–53) the five stages or phases of the design of a literacy programme in which the educators and the participants of the Culture Circle work together in

1 researching the needs, interests and activities of the group and understanding its ordinary, everyday language;
2 identifying a short list of 'generative' words, selected on the basis of the phonemic value of the word, its phonetic difficulty and its immediate relevance;
3 creating the 'codifications', that is the typical situations which the group would recognize as reflecting their daily lives and interests;

4 elaborating an agenda or structure for the discussion in order to analyse and 'decode' the given situations;
5 preparing flash cards or slides to be used in the process of word recognition and word creation.

Freire (1987b: 136) has always been aware of the importance of training the educators, co-ordinators, in this sensitive role of leading such a group. The problem is not so much the techniques or technicalities of the scheme but the creating of the required attitude on the part of the educators, namely a willingness to enter into a dialogue. The period of instruction, he insists (and the point is emphasized by Ewert)[2] must be followed by dialogic supervision, to avoid the temptation or danger that the educators behave in a way which is anti-dialogic.

Regional word lists

In *Education: The Practice of Freedom* Freire includes, after the sequence of ten pictures or codifications, the list of seventeen Generative Words which he used in the State of Rio.

1 favela	=	slum
2 chuva	=	rain
3 arada	=	plough
4 terreno	=	land
5 comida	=	food
6 batuque	=	Afro-Brazilian dancing
7 poço	=	well
8 bicicleta	=	bicycle
9 trabalho	=	work
10 salàrio	=	salary
11 profissåo	=	profession
12 govêrno	=	government
13 mangue	=	swampland
14 engenho	=	sugar mill
15 enxada	=	hoe
16 tijolo	=	brick
17 riqueza	=	wealth

These words are intended to reflect Freire's practice of negotiating the key words and the generative themes of the community which will be implicit in the codified situations presented to the Culture Circle. Each word can be parsed syllabically (TI JO LO; TA TE TI TO TU; JA JE JI JO JU, etc.) and new words can be made from the 'discovery card': for example, luta = struggle, loja = store, leite = milk, tela = screen (1976b: 54).

A comparison with other word lists used in the programme is interesting. Brown (1974) includes four such lists in her 'Literacy in 30 hours' from different areas: from a rural area in Rio (the list given by Freire); from a slum in

Recifé, Cajueiro Sêco; from Tirini, an agricultural colony near the city of Cabo; and from Maceio, a city on the sea coast.

The four lists have fifteen, sixteen, sixteen and seventeen words respectively. Of the sixty-four words, eight are used more than once:

tijolo	=	brick	voto	=	vote
máquina	=	sewing machine	engenho	=	sugar mill
mangue	=	swamp	enrada	=	hoe
comida	=	food	trabalho	=	work.

A further three ideas are expressed in two groups through the use of different words:

$$\left.\begin{array}{l}\text{milho}\\\text{farinha}\end{array}\right\} = \text{flour} \qquad \left.\begin{array}{l}\text{terra}\\\text{terreno}\end{array}\right\} = \text{land} \qquad \left.\begin{array}{l}\text{cacimba}\\\text{poco}\end{array}\right\} = \text{well}$$

Only one word, tijolo/brick, appears in all four lists, while two other words, voto/vote and engenho/sugar mill appear in three of the lists.[3]

The fact that three of the lists, that is all except Freire's, begin with the same two words, *tijolo* and *voto* (brick, vote), immediately raises the question of how far the content of each list was actually constructed *with* the individual groups rather than suggested or imposed by the educators. It is highly significant that *tijolo* is the guide word which Freire uses in his explanation of his Method in *Education: The Practice of Freedom,* and it seems evident that the educators were relying heavily on the model which they had received. There is no other, immediate answer why three groups, one in a city slum, another in a coastal town, another in an agricultural colony, should all select *a brick* as their key, generative word.

Again, the use of *voto*/vote seems to have been imposed. The one list (again, Freire's) that does contain key words of *government, profession* and *salary*, does not, perhaps surprisingly, include *voto*. However, the other three lists (which do have the word) do not have other words which might suggest the context or the content of the discussion around *voto*. One possible conclusion, therefore, is that rather than reflecting the principles of negotiated learning and the stated processes of creating the generative words, the use of *voto* reflects more the interests and personalities of some of Freire's co-workers.

Although Freire was strongly against the use of primers or prepared texts, mainly on the grounds that they were mechanical, redolent of Banking Education and destructive of the flexibility required on the part of the educators in the Culture Circles, two of his colleagues in the Popular Culture Movement had written a short Primer *Viver é Lutar*. Using Freire's method of syllabic parsing, they introduced initially just five words:

povo	=	people	voto	=	vote
vida	=	life	saúde	=	health
pão	=	bread			

Their first sentence reads *O vote é do povo* (The vote belongs to the people) and the Primer ends with 'The North-east will only have peace when the roots of its ills have been eradicated' and 'Peace grows out of justice'.

In the context of that Primer and of the large-scale literacy programme which MEB undertook through the trade unions in 1963–4, the content of the three lists which Freire did not use takes on a new focus. *Tijolo* was used to give an example of syllabic parsing, and *voto* was used to create the climate of the discussion which was overtly about oppression and liberation. The themes of the groups were about hunger, employment, food and exploitation, the *senghor de engenho*, and the role of the unions and the controls of the market.

It is these lists and codifications which leads Gerhardt (1989: 541) to suggest that Freire's early programme was overtly political, having espoused the politics of the reformist, regional government. Clearly the bass line provided to support the melody of the discussion within the Culture Circle is that of a radical Marxist analysis. The hint that Freire was not wholly in sympathy with this view is that, at the time of writing *Education: The Practice of Freedom*, he would have had these lists to hand, but he makes no reference to them, preferring instead his list from Rio even though that was not his own home area.

This only emphasizes the point that, despite the claims of dialogic learning, the hidden or personal agenda of the educators has had a controlling influence on the formulation of all four lists of generative words. There is a directiveness required for the presentation of this programme – a view which is supported by the analysis of the ten 'codified situations' offered by Freire – which contradicts the principles of negotiated learning. The educators, including Freire, have influenced the choice of words in a way which reveals them to be (benign) banking educators. The groups have not been completely free to choose their generative words, because the educators themselves had a message (or a mission?) to bring to the discussion groups, that was the twin process of conscientizing through literacy and achieving literacy through conscientization.

An analysis of these word lists suggests that the methodological principles enunciated by Freire were more a post-hoc rationalization of a practice which had proved itself to be effective. Although, in reality, the practice was more a form of enlightened Banking Education, he preferred to regard it through the lens of his idealism and ambitions, and, precisely because it was effective as a method, preferred to see it as a product of dialogic teaching and negotiated learning.

The word lists may confirm the trend of previous analyses, but they also open up new questions which underpin the pedagogy of teaching/learning literacy.

Nouns, nominalism and naming

It is worthy of note that, in a pedagogy constructed around the idea of liberation and the fact that 'no one can liberate themselves', and which is based on the social nature of learning, not one of the lists includes words relating to personal or family relationships: there is no mention of wife, husband, children, parents or friends, no mention of family or community.

Additionally, it is significant that all the words in the four lists are all *nouns*: there are no verbs, prepositions or adjectives. That is to say that, not only are there no words to describe relationships, but also that there are no words with which one can relate one word to another. It is as if, in learning to read a foreign language, one were to learn only selected nouns (for example the cat, a pen, the table, the hat, a beer, etc.). No matter how well one might know the words, one could not converse, nor could one read with any security what other people have written.

In proposing the idea of a generative word list, Freire nowhere explains the process of language acquisition through which one learns to connect the given nouns in such a way that one can construct sentences. For example a generative word list may have *voto*/vote and *povo*/people, but how does one learn to read or write: *O voto é do* povo: *The* vote *is of (belongs to) the* people?

The lack of explanation is all the more surprising, given Freire's work in São Tomé in 1976 which develops his basic methodology. The word lists are still there, but evidently not negotiated as before with the community. The texts are 'designed to meet the objectives of the literacy campaign, namely, for the people to participate effectively as subjects in the reconstruction of the nation' (Freire 1987b: 65). The word lists include 'school, plantation, land, product, people, health, radio', as well as 'unity, discipline, work, vigilance', and are more socially mature and more overtly political than previous lists. But still, although the two *Popular Culture Notebooks* also include points of grammar, no attention is given to how pronouns and verbs are to be learnt, and no explanation is given as to how, phonologically or semiotically, pronouns and prepositions can be used as generative words.

This is not simply an academic question as to whether one can learn a language or learn to read and write without some understanding of the grammar of the language. It is rather a question of whether it is possible to identify a list of words which are absolutely essential, if one is to read or write a language. Specifically, in terms of this analysis of Freire's method, if the use of generative sight-words indeed provides a base for an animated and relevant discussion among non-literate people, how does such discussion aid their transition to actual literacy? Is there a difference between 'seeing' a word and 'reading' that word?[4]

The kind of in-depth study made by Otto and Stallard (1976) of the use of sight words as an aid in the teaching of reading is very relevant here. It shows that Freire's method of selecting common, key words as a basis for reading has indeed a long pedigree, given that there is evidence of regular use of word lists even from 20BC. In more recent times, the development of *Look and Say* teaching methods have led to the revival of such aids.

Word lists can be created through the methodologically simple technique of counting the frequency of words that occur in oral and written samples of children's and/or adults' communication. Otto and Stallard (1976) concluded that, by comparing a wide range of such sight words, 'it is possible to identify a list of one hundred words that could be accepted as *essential* sight words with some confidence'.

Two of their subsequent observations are also pertinent here: first, that the words which occur frequently in children's speech also tend to be frequent in adults' speech, and second, that the core words from adult writing are also the core words in children's writing. It therefore seems reasonable to transpose this research to the question of Freire's literacy teaching method, in supposing that the same essential words would be needed within any such literacy programme.

In contrast to Freire's method, Otto and Stallard include no nouns in their list. The largest number of words (32 per cent) are basic verb forms (be, have, see, come, go, be able, do, know, like, look, make, put, say, take, think, and want); 16 per cent of the words are personal or possessive pronouns, and a further 16 per cent are prepositions. Essential adjectives (6 per cent) include big/little, new/old, good and right.

The advantage of such a list is that it creates the immediate possibility of what Freire would call the dialogue of literacy, the language of possibility. A person who has the ability to read and write these words can be the subject of his or her own learning. Unlike Freire's lists, this essential word list leads the learner towards the making of a statement which is, potentially, immensely personal. I can write 'I am', 'I think', 'I have' and 'I know'. I can also write in relationship: 'you can', 'you said' or 'we want', 'we are'.

Phonetically, this list of 100 words, syllabically parsed according to the Freirean method (hat, het, hit, hot, hut; an, en, in, on, un, etc.), covers most of the essential phonemes even of the English language and provides a framework for the constructing of sentences. It may, initially, be more laborious in the teaching/learning of how *to read*, but the fact that it demonstrably reflects essential word units would greatly facilitate the teaching and learning of how *to write*.

There is an almost shocking simplicity in the sight word list that is lost in the complexity of Freire's generative word list. It is also more sympathetic, as a process of literacy and conscientization, to Freire's pedagogy of annunciation (I announce, I name, I act, I am) which is contradicted by the limitations imposed on the discourse of literacy through the use of only nominal, rather than prepositional and pronominal, language.

The divergence between the two lists represents not just a difference in linguistics but a polarizing of two traditional pedagogies. In Cartesian terms, the processes of learning through the creation of a *synthesis* and a logical progression from the simple to the complex are to be distinguished from those processes which propose an *analysis* of what is accepted as complex so as to perceive an underlying simplicity. Freire is clearly following Descartes in seeking to *name* only that reality which he can assert without doubt: I know it, therefore it is. His literacy method reflects therefore a direct application of two of Descartes's fundamental rules:

The second rule was to divide each difficulty into as many parts as possible. . . . The third was to conduct my thoughts in an orderly fashion, starting with what was simplest and easiest to know, and rising little by little to the knowledge of the most complex, even supposing an order where there is no natural precedence among the objects of knowledge. (Descartes 1960: 50)

The confusion arises in that most *Look and Say* literacy methods are based on analysis rather than synthesis. Words are not constructed or made up of syllables: they communicate directly to the reader as 'words'. We do not say 'What do these syllables mean?' but 'what does this word mean?'[5]

Traditionally, within those frameworks which Freire would identify with Banking Education, the teaching of reading has been incremental and synthetic, building upon the learner's gradual development of conceptual and linguistic capacities. Freire's own method, while ostensibly synthetic and syllabic, is primarily analytic, asking the learner to confront the complexities of the whole word, the whole world of reality, through 'naming their world'. In order to do that, the learners need the names, in the strict sense of the word – the nouns.

Using Chomsky's distinction, Freire argues (1970h) that all codification has both a superficial and a deep structure. Decoding or conscientizing is the process of searching beneath the obvious, the given, in order to uncover a new, previously hidden, reality.

But that reality is itself given, for through the use of *nouns*, the learner can only *read*. 'Naming the wor(l)d' does not and cannot mean inventing, creating the world. This is the singular and most important outcome of this analysis for it reveals that Freire's method is fundamentally contradictory. It proposes naming the world as a means of conscientization, yet it can never realize its objective of *praxis*, that process of active reflection *and* reflective *action*. The nominalist discerning of the world cannot turn to action because, by definition, it can never go beyond the passivity of a 'reading' of a word. As such, the use of nominative word lists is fundamentally anti-dialogic, for it never allows the learner to *personalize* the processes of reading and writing.

The evidence is twofold. First, there is the lack of evident action to change the world within the many and varied Culture Circles organized on Freirean lines. As MacEoin (1972) notes:

> For years I have been searching for an instance in which peasants have broken out of their oppression, even at a local level, but I have found none. When I asked Freire, he admitted that neither has he. (MacEoin 1972: 1)

Second, there is Bernstein's (1970) linguistic analysis that explains the view that the nominal forms lead to universalist perspectives, whilst the pronominal forms particularize. He reads this distinction, particularly with a class variable, in a story-telling study (which is just another form of coding and decoding) where middle-class children used thirteen nouns and six pronouns, but where working-class children used only two nouns and fourteen pronouns. Besides this factor of class, which must surely be significant when one is considering a literacy programme for working-class or sub-working-class peasants and labourers, the instructive point is that nominal forms led to universalist statements, while pronominal forms were particular, personal and situation specific.

It is, therefore, this latter form of expression which supports a process which is intended to be deeply personalizing. The nominalist learner may be able to recognize the word for a brick, or a mill, or discuss the importance of the words for employment, wages and the price of bread. But, unless he or she can read and write 'I can read' and 'I can write', there will always be a sense in which they are condemned to remain sub-literate. Only the person who can write 'I can' is in a position to begin to change the world, for it is the *I can* which is the catalyst to the process of conscientizing. This, in turn, breaks the bonds of the culture of silence and enables the learner, as Subject, to say *I am*. The resulting new statement of liberating literacy, '*I can, therefore I am*', becomes nominative, in a way that the nouns on Freire's word list could never be.

FIVE

Generating literacy

Decoding Freire's ten learning situations

Introduction

The one-time thriving business of Freireology has produced, over the years, critiques, reports, theses, literacy programmes, development plans and educational initiatives. It has spawned related projects in health, nutrition, race-relations, community development, theatre, art, music and prison reform. All the more striking, therefore, that little attention has actually been given to the Culture Circles and the content of Freire's method. Most analysis has been content either with a linguistic appraisal in terms of language acquisition or communication theory, or with a philosophical assessment of the ideas of dialogue and conscientization.

If Freire's method actually works, why does it work? What actually happens in the Culture Circles to create or sustain the achievement of literacy and conscientization?

The only way to consider these queries is to subject Freire's method to the rigour of his own system, problematizing what apparently looks uncomplicated by posing three questions: what is the content of the teaching in the Culture Circles? What purpose does Freire intend it to serve? What are the implications for an educator who works in/with such a learning group?

The main evidence remains, even after all these years, Freire's presentation and explanation of the situations discussed in the Culture Circles in the Appendix to *Education: The Practice of Freedom* (1976). To illustrate these discussions, Freire uses a later version of the codified situations which were drawn by Vincente de Abreu. The original pictures, commissioned from Freire's friend, the well-known Brazilian artist Francisco Brennand, had been confiscated by the authorities in 1964.

The other source of this material is in Brown's (1974) study 'Literacy in 30 hours'. She had copied and printed, with Freire's permission, eight of the first series of pictures from slides still in his possession and had added two (pictures 5 and 8) from the published series. Brown's explanation of the method is extremely important here because she was clearly writing with the support and acknowledgement of Freire himself.

Given that degree of co-operation and involvement on the part of Freire, it can therefore safely be assumed that Brown's presentation of the literacy process reflects Freire's own thinking and is an accurate record of his manner and approach as well as a summary of the content of the actual teaching sessions. This makes it possible to combine the two sources and to create an in-depth analysis of the potential for teaching and learning in a Culture Circle.

Within the structure of the pictures, Figure 10 is intended as a summary of the overall debate, a recapitulation, while Figure 1 serves the purpose of agenda setting. The whole sequence is intended as an accumulative process of conscientization, a fixed menu – not to be taken à la carte.

There are three points of note: first, in order to get closer to the original reading of the text/situations, the author has suspended for the moment his practice of modifying texts which indicate an overt level of sexism. The use of language here, textually and visually, which relates to the processes of literacy is itself informative; both Freire and Brown exhibit a use of language (e.g. *man's* culture-making, *his* house, *his* clothes, *his* tools) which has a significance beyond the obvious explanation that, in its time and culture, such language was considered not only acceptable but also normative.

Second, to avoid the constant repetition of references to the same text, all references in this chapter, unless otherwise indicated, will be taken from either Freire (1976b:62–4) or Brown (1974:25–32).

Third, both sets of pictures have been used in this analysis in order to make a composite argument of the various elements of which they are illustrations and to compare them where that is appropriate. Figures 1–10 are the scenes from Brown's article and mostly depict Freire's original pictures. Reference to these will be as Version 1 (or V1), or the reader will be referred back to a particular numbered figure: Figure 1, Figure 2, etc. The single, enlarged pictures in the text (Figure 1a, Figure 2a, etc.) are from Vincente de Abreu's version in *Education: The Practice of Freedom*: reference to these will be as Version 2 (or V2).

The Sequence of Ten Codified Situations

1 Man in the world and with the world, nature and culture
2 Dialogue mediated by nature
3 Unlettered hunter
4 Lettered hunter (lettered culture)
5 The hunter and the cat
6 Man transforms the material of nature by his work
7 A vase, the product of man's work upon the material of nature
8 Poetry
9 Patterns of behaviour
10 A Culture Circle in action – synthesis of the previous discussions

Figure 1

Figure 2

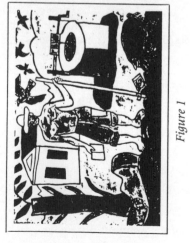

Figure 3

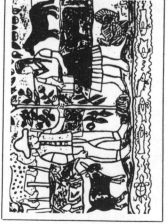

Figure 4

Figure 5

Figure 9

Figure 10

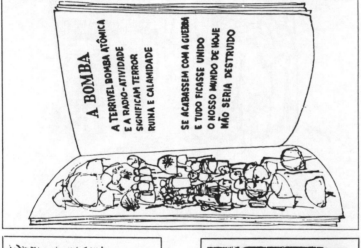

Figure 8

Figure 6

Figure 7

Figure 1a

First situation: Man in the world and with the world, nature and culture

The situation (Figure 1)

Brown (1974: 26) describes this as 'a familiar image from which a non-literate from North-eastern Brazil can use his knowledge to distinguish between nature and culture'. In Version 1, in the foreground, there is a picture of an obviously healthy farmer/peasant. At one side, there is a basket in which he has perhaps been collecting the fruit of his labours: on the other side, a plump pig is truffling. The farmer/peasant, bare-chested and bare-footed, poses with a mattock in one hand and an open book in the other. In the wider frame, there is a very stylized tree and four birds on the wing. In the background, there is a small house and a structured, cemented well from which water can be drawn by means of the handle and spindle.

Version 2 (Figure 1a) has some important variations, most critically in the background. There is a picture of a woman leading a child by the hand back to the house. She is walking perhaps from the well towards the house which now has a more solid construction and a tiled roof. The well itself is evidently both wider and deeper than that in Version 1, with a bricked head and a longer rope. This abundance of water may account for the overall, more prosperous feel of Version 2: while the farmer/peasant is still barefoot, he is no longer bare-chested. Although the pig has disappeared, the mattock remains, perhaps to suggest that the property is still too small, or the people too poor, to have a plough.

Application

Freire argues that, through the discussion of this situation, the participants arrive at the distinction between two worlds: that of *nature* and that of *culture*. They are meant to perceive 'the normal situation of man as a being in the world and with the world, as a creative and re-creative being who, through work, constantly alters reality'.

The co-ordinator leads the discussion by asking 'Who made the well?' 'Why did he do it?' 'With what materials?' The intention is to contrast the answers to those questions with the response to the apparently less ambiguous enquiry: 'Who made the tree?' This leads to an extended discussion, with an almost Thomist simplicity, in reply to the question 'Who made the pig, the birds, the hoe, the book?'

Brown suggests that the discussion moves to the conclusion that people use natural materials to change their situation, to create culture. Freire explains that this insight emerges through the clarifying of two basic concepts: that of *necessity* and that of *work*. Clearly these are not offered as new concepts to the group of non-literates: Brown says the discussion gives them the words to name and clarify what they already know. Even if what they describe is a subsistence way of living, 'at the end of the discussion, participants are conscious of being cultured'.

There is, however, an additional overlay which is suggested by Freire. He describes this initial situation as 'man as a being of relationships', and he returns to this point at the end of his brief summary.

> From this point, one discusses with the group, in obviously simple but critically objective terms, the relations among men, which unlike those discussed previously cannot be either for domination or transformation, because they are relations among Subjects. (Freire 1976b: 63)

Commentary

On the surface, this is indeed an image familiar to a non-literate person in North-east Brazil. The singular and intended novelty in the picture is the presence of *the book*. The picture has to be viewed in the context of the fact that, in 1960, in the capital of the North-east region, Recifé, there were some 80,000 children aged from 7 to 11 who did not attend school: adult illiteracy was estimated at 60–70 per cent. It was, therefore, 'abnormal' to be literate.

The stark impact of the picture, and why Freire could use it to such good effect, is that it not only describes the daily reality of the peasant/farmer in Recifé, but also prescribes the importance of the book, giving it an almost totemic significance. It symbolizes something that is different, and not just that a non-literate peasant can now read. It is clearly intended to suggest that the book is as central and as useful to the life of the peasant and his family as is the mattock, or the well or the house. *The individual who is Subject cannot live without the book.* This is the agenda that is set for the literacy programme. Freire obviously intended that the book should be a symbol of a new relationship between men and men and between men and the world, a relationship which, he says, is not marked by domination or transformation.

We shall have to consider that formal agenda later. What is interesting here, however, is the hidden agenda of this picture in the means by which Freire achieves the discussion he requires. He says that the participants 'arrive' at the distinction between nature and culture. More honestly, Brown (1974) says 'The co-ordinator leads the discussion into the distinction between nature and culture'. Whatever the professed distinctions between the learner/teacher and the teacher/learner, the reality of the situation here requires a deft use of manipulation to achieve the objectives of the session.

In the first place, some key questions have to be avoided. The answers to the simple questions about who made the well, the pig, the hoe, the house, the book, etc., are flavoured with the piety of two illusions or acts of faith. The first is that there is some deity, some God who is Lord and Father of all mankind who 'made' the natural world, 'all things bright and beautiful, all creatures great and small'. So, in the pictures, the birds and the trees, the pig and the earth, the water in the well are all part of *Nature*. When Nature is altered by Work, through the use of natural materials to change their situation, men create *Culture*. This leads to the second illusion: that men, or rather, that this particular man has created his own culture.

There is, of course, an alternative sequence of responses to Freire's questions:

Who made the well?	The Landlord paid men to brick and cement it;
Who made the length of rope?	I traded a pig for it;
Who made the hoe?	I bought it in the market;
Who made the clothes?	A cotton manufacturer in the South;
Who made the book?	The Missionary.

Those fairly obvious responses are in fact removed from the discussion by means of the second illusion, namely the illusion of the enlightened peasant (enlightened except that he cannot read) who has the skills and resources to make everything for himself. He bears the imprint of thrift, practicality and ingenuity. His culture, even at this primary level of subsistence, is self-made. It is the culture of a man who is Subject, who 'relating to the world, made the latter the object of his knowledge. By work, he submitted the world to a process of transformation'.

Illusion though it may be, the image of the enlightened peasant is important precisely because he or she is the model of the ideal student. By definition, their enlightenment means that they already know what it is that they are supposed to know, except only that they do not know it in the way that the teacher knows it. In what is really an example of pedagogic bad faith, the peasant is enlightened because he or she has been judged to be 'in the image and likeness of' the teacher.

Such an image is meant to motivate and encourage the learner. It also serves, however, to preclude an equally important discussion about work itself, about whether the peasant/farmer is working for himself or for someone else, about whether he and his family actually eat what they grow or whether he has to sell it in the market-place. It therefore avoids the need to reflect on how the peasant is controlled or even dominated by the market place where he might have to buy all his tools, the grain he needs and the clothes he wears, and where he will not always get a just price for his pig.

Freire will want to get to a discussion of domination and oppression in due course, but it is clearly his intention not to do so through this route. It is not that he cannot or will not challenge the illusion of the self-sufficient, autonomous farmer/peasant. It is rather that, in the cultural and social context in which he was working, and even for himself personally, there was a taboo surrounding any discussion of the first illusion which assumes the presence of a caring God.

To achieve their stated aims, educators using this first picture have to direct the discussion: in this they are strongly aided by the degree of 'mind-guarding' that is created by the first illusion. Even in the pursuit of objective, critical consciousness, the existence of the deity cannot be questioned. This is not on the grounds of some theological *a priori*, but rather because a tactful silence on this matter is needed to preclude other more revolutionable questions. Why did God make some people poor and some people rich? If God is looking after the birds of the air and the flowers of the field, why is he not looking after me? One might even reflect on whether or not it is part of that natural order of things that there are rich and poor, hunters and hunted, oppressors and oppressed?

However valuable or enlightening, such a discussion would misdirect the potential learning of the group members. The picture was not intended for that and the educators would have to ensure that the discussion did not end in that impasse.

It was clearly Freire's intention that this picture should rather set the agenda for a discussion on social relationships. None the less, he begins to explore that theme not by stressing the social nature of relationships but by stressing that human beings are 'Subjects'. This is surprising for, whatever way they might have articulated their own understanding of being in the world, it is unlikely that oppressed, illiterate peasants in the Culture Circles would choose to describe themselves as Subjects who transform their world by their work. Their lived experience within what Freire describes as the 'Culture of Silence' denies

Figure 1b

that kind of self-expression. The educators might wish that, by the end of the discussion, participants are conscious of being cultured, but that seems to miss the whole *raison d'être* of the exercise, that is that the people who participate in the Culture Circles have had their culture imposed on them. They are, almost by definition, not Subjects: they could even be surprised or shocked at Freire's insistence to the contrary.

How can this dilemma be resolved? How did Freire intend that this contradiction should be resolved? The answer for him, and therefore for all other parties, teacher and student, co-ordinator and peasant, lies in the *totemic status of the book*. It is the book and all that it symbolizes that makes the difference. A comparison between Figures 1a and 1b loudly proclaims Freire's real intent.

The picture actually has no value unless it leads directly to a discussion that is centred not on the presence of God but on the presence of the book. The

Figure 2a

discussion has got to explain *the book*: not just 'Who made it?', but 'What is it for?' and 'What does it say?'

The argument, directed by Freire or his co-ordinator, is that the person who can answer those questions is someone who can *read the book*. That in itself is significant, but not significant enough. The discussion will have failed unless it moves beyond even that notable discovery and raises the possibility that that same person could also *write the book* and, maybe, could even *make the book*. Freire will want to reject the notion that reading is a passive activity. He will insist that being literate goes beyond being a quiescent reader: it requires the person to become an active writer, and thereby to become a maker of their own world, their own history.

In this way, the Book reveals its totemic significance: it stands as an analogy for the reading and the writing and the making of history, that self-determined engagement of the person in and with their world. It represents a person's relationship with the world as a Subject, a 'being-in-the world' in the fullest Heideggerian sense of the term.

This is the agenda set for the analysis of the subsequent pictures, creating a process which engenders certain words which can be not only spoken but also now read. If such words can be read, then they can be written. This is the simple logic of the literacy campaign: what we have to see is the degree to which these learning/teaching objectives can be sustained and achieved through the use of the other pictures.

Second situation: Dialogue mediated by nature

The situation (Figure 2)

In Version 1, Figure 2 shows a man and a woman in the centre of the picture, and around them are a number of animals. The man seems to be planting a tree, while the woman is gesturing to something which she may have found in the book which she is holding.

The pictures of the animals, drawn in a very stylized form, show a horse, an ox and a turkey on one side, while on the other side there is a leopard, a lamb and a goat. Underneath the people and the animals, there is a line indicating water in which there are fish and a turtle.

Version 2 (Figure 2a) is more direct. This time the couple are standing under the tree: the man has nothing in his hands and he is gesturing, as if in discussion. The woman is holding the book and either pointing to a particular passage or reading from the book. They are still poor: although they are both dressed, neither is wearing shoes. Beside the woman is an empty household basket, and behind the man there are no other animals except one cow.

Application

Freire's use of this picture is best presented through the short paragraph which he himself wrote:

> In the first situation, we reached the analysis of relationships among men, which, because they are relationships among Subjects, cannot be those of domination. Now, confronted by this second situation, the group is motivated to analyse dialogue, interpersonal communication, the encounter of the consciousnesses; motivated to analyse the mediation of the world – as transformed and humanized by men – in this communication; motivated to analyse the loving, humble, hopeful, critical, and creative foundations of dialogue. (Freire 1976b: 65)

Brown takes the overall sense of Freire's objectives, but clarifies two particular points. First, that the picture can be used to show that culture is something created by people: animals cannot create their own culture. Human beings can do that because they can communicate with each other, both orally and graphically. Second, and especially using Version 2, the proper relationship among people is that of subjects communicating with each other, not as

Objects, but as Equals. Communication takes place as a dialogue between equals, with the perception of each person having equal validity. Where this is distorted or denied, the communication is not a true dialogue: rather it is an exchange by communiqué.

Commentary

The Christian values of dialogue are clearly evident even on the surface of Freire's comment: love, hope, humility. Of more significance, however, is the subliminal faith which is portrayed in the pictures.

Version 1 presents an 'Adam and Eve' scene of man and woman in the garden, surrounded by the animals. It is the scene on which Freire's use of the expression 'naming the world' makes most immediate sense and clearly can be used to create a very powerful reinforcement of the view that the literate person can somehow control their world, can name their world, and can live in a world of their own making. He uses this strong undertow of biblical imagery. The tree is the Tree of Life: the book is the Book of Life. The Adam and Eve figures are faced with a choice. However, in contrast to Eve, who came bearing the apple, the temptation which resulted in sin, labour, and misery, the new woman comes bearing the book, the invitation to literacy, a new life and a new history.

The idea of the 'new woman' is not unimportant. Yes, she is a new woman in that she is different from Eve. But she is also the new woman, the *mujer nueva*, who with the *hombre nuevo*, formed the cadre of the revolutionary movements throughout South America (Gerassi 1971: 294). She is the life-force of change, even of change as fundamental as that occasioned by revolution.

It is all the more interesting, therefore, that Freire should have chosen this picture to raise the theme of dialogue. Given the gender stereotyping of Latin American culture, and indeed the role given to men throughout the other pictures, it is significant that the conversation between a man and a woman should be seen as the strongest example of a dialogue between equals. The dialogue which Freire is seeking, therefore, receives its validation from two divergent sources of authority: on the one hand, it receives its strength from the transferred strength of the traditional view of the family, of marriage and of gender roles. On the other hand, in contrast to the macho values of society (of which the family, marriage and gender roles are a part) the values of the new, *authentic* dialogue are reinforced by the Book, in the hands of the woman.

This dramatically announces a new dialogue which differs from the 'communication by communiqué' which preceded it because it is an 'encounter of consciousnesses'. But what kind of encounter is that? What kind of dialogue does it engender? Once the rhetoric and the mysticism has been removed from Freire's speech, what is the actual content of this dialogue?

In Wilkinson's (1985) analysis of dialogic communication, although from a very different disciplinary base from Freire, there are a number of insights which are very relevant here. In support of the hypothesis 'I communicate, therefore I am', Wilkinson posits three basic models of communication

(Transmission, Reciprocity and Internal Dialogue) which can be illustrated schematically:

Transmission	A $\rightarrow$ B	
Reciprocity	A $\rightarrow$ B	then B $\rightarrow$ A
Internal Dialogue	A $\rightarrow$ A	

The fact that I communicate at all is because 'I am as I am'. I exist as a personality, as a social being with a self-image and with an identity in the social world, albeit that I communicate with that social world in different ways at different times.

Transmissive communication is, at its most simple and banal, a transmission to somebody or something else which is outside of me. It is usually exhibited in a declaratory mode, the classic mode of the giver of information. It is essentially within this mode that we can recognize the teacher/taught relationship which Freire calls banking education. It is not a communication that accepts the equality of the person to whom one is communicating. Sometimes it does not even require that anyone else is there at all. It has no need of hope, humility or love. It needs only a means by which it can know that the transmission has been effected: a noise has been made, a statement issued, a communiqué published.

The communication model of reciprocity is quite different. It is based on a practice of social exchange theory (Secord 1974) and on a real perception that the communication from A in some way 'creates' or 'validates' B, who in turn is able to create and validate A through his or her response. In essence, such communication, both in its content and in its form, is about intersubjectivity, what Freire refers to as the 'encounter of consciousnesses'. It creates not transmission, but *conferment*, in that it confers on the communicator and on the receiver the status of active and mutual creators of the communication.

In the event, however, where one of the partners in this potentially reciprocal communication is 'disabled' (Freire would say oppressed, en-cultured into silence), then the conferment, to the degree that it is real at all – if that is not a contradiction in terms – reinforces a low, non-adult status, or even a non-person status. This is the anti-dialogic mode of communiqué and banking education.

The processes of reciprocal communication, authentic dialogue, are the principal means of conferring or creating both the identity of the people engaged in the communication *and* their understanding of the reality within which that communication is taking place and which cannot be separated from the communication.

That reality cannot just exist in the mind. Things do not become real simply because I choose to think that they are. Like the communication through which reality is unmasked, reality itself is my engaging with the actual world, which is the world external to me. In a very real sense, we construct social and natural realities through our human communication.

That is why the internal dialogic mode, auto-dialogue is not authentic as a means of identifying reality for, in this case, the very self-hood which is engaged in the monologue lacks external validation. Like the nominalist,

Freirean word lists, the nominative of the monologue is not in relationship. There is only the *I*, for in the monologue there is no need of the *You*.

This is a very complex perspective on the use and nature of language that leads us to ask whether one could expect such a level of discussion within a Culture Circle. Freire would claim that the main argument is certainly possible. He has often argued that people are not 'orally illiterate', that while they might not be able to read or to write, they can nevertheless communicate their ideas and feelings verbally. It is because they can articulate their responses and reaction that the individuals in the Culture Circles are able to create the *generative words* which form the first stage of the writing process.

Freire has an optimistic view of the adult learner for the use of this Codification requires not just an ability to enter into dialogue, into reciprocal communication. It also demands, as a prerequisite, a certain level of *meta-linguistic skill* on the part of the participants and of the co-ordinators. The elements of this picture illustrate perfectly the kind of 'communicative competence' analysed by Habermas (1970). The fact that the (re)construction of a competence is a necessary preliminary to the study of its acquisition is as important here as is the distinction between the *communicative performance*, 'the actual use of language in concrete situations' and *communicative competence*, 'the ideal speaker-hearer's knowledge of the language' (McCarthy 1978). It is in this context that it would be important to assess whether Freire was aiming to achieve literacy performance or literacy competence, the former being constructed by the person-becoming-literate, while the latter is taught or constructed by the teacher.

Whose then is the correct interpretation of these pictures? The question is thrown into relief by Fuglesang's exciting study where he argues that the meta-linguistic skills on which this approach is based cannot be presumed. He does so by challenging the assumption that pictures are some kind of 'intercultural language'. Contrary to Freire who accepts without question that people can always interpret pictures accurately, he says that 'it is probably right to say that pictorial illiteracy is almost as widespread as illiteracy itself. People have to learn to read pictures' (Fuglesang 1973: 62). We are then faced with a sudden, unanticipated question that learning to 'read a picture' might be just as difficult as learning to read a text. Nor does it follow that someone who can read a text, for example the literate teacher/co-ordinator, is any more capable of reading the picture than the non-literate peasants.

This in part underlies Brown's note of caution: the co-ordinator begins the discussion with the question 'What do you see in the picture?' because 'this naming of objects is important because people not accustomed to graphic representations may not easily identify what is meant to be shown' (Brown 1974: 26). There is even a hint of subliminal Banking Education in the implicit judgement about people's pre-literate awareness of themselves, that is to say that the non-literates, the oppressed, are ready, willing and able to become literate. Non-literates are seen almost as a ready market, potential consumers (the words themselves are redolent of Banking Education) for the educator's dialogic skills. It is taken as given that they have the prerequisite attitude and skills that will enable them to participate (invest) in (our) liberating education just as effectively as they might in some other, so-called domesticating education.

That may seem a harsh condemnation, but there is certainly a hint either of contradiction or of condescension in the assumption that non-literate people can correctly 'read' a picture, and thereby express their understanding of oppression, of relationships, of independence, when, unconscientized as they are, they are obviously not able to view critically and accurately the world in which they are living.

The level of pictorial literacy required by Freire's use of this Codification is certainly high, if he wishes to draw from it the kind of discussion which he has indicated. We shall have to return later to the debate that, while attention seems to have been given more and more to the relationship between literacy and post-literacy, less attention has been paid to the requirements of pre-literacy, and in particular to the assumptions about language and communication which are implicit in these early stages of Freire's literacy programme.

For the moment, there is a further important distinction to be made here, if the co-ordinator/educator is truly to attempt a genuine dialogue through the use of this picture. It is a distinction based on Fuglesang's usefully provocative insight into that communciation which he calls *exclamation* and that which he calls *articulation*. He gives numerous examples, pointedly to argue that exclamations are always genuine, while articulations may be both humanly inadequate and concealing. The former creates a foundation on which genuine dialogue can be built, while the latter has a strong, in-built tendency to be anti-dialogic. Yet it is this latter form of communication which Freire is attempting to elicit through the use of Figure 2.

What Fuglesang instances as articulation – thoughts, ideas, conceptions, intentions, facts – is primarily the substance of a systematized thinking, a schooled assessment. It is often the mode of expression which we use to discuss an idea or a theory without committing ourselves personally. Sometimes it is unashamedly calculated, for example where educators talk of being unbiased, of having a 'professional approach' that does not allow personal feelings or views to intrude into the exchange of ideas. It is almost as if the more critical, insightful, reasoned or well argued any communication might be, the more objective and impersonal it must become. 'The facts speak for themselves'.

On the other hand, Fuglesang argues, exclamation is about sensations, feelings, experiences, hopes as much as fears. It is the communication of authenticity, not least because it is immediate, honest, incautious. An exclamation is an expression that has not been filtered through the control mechanisms of 'second thoughts'.

The difficulty is that the lettered educators (because of their experience of systematized education) and the unlettered learners (because of their culture of silence) have both developed defence mechanisms which preclude communication through exclamation. They have been encultured, either through schooling or through fear of reprisal, into articulating (or not-articulating) their thoughts and ideas in a particular way. They have learnt that their responses ought to be considered, thought through (expressed in an appropriate manner); balanced (cautious); and well articulated (with carefully chosen words). In short, the sanctions which govern the way in which we express ourselves lead us to resist *exclamation* and to devalue it as uncontrolled outburst. By contrast, *articulation* is seen as a product of mature and considered thought: the more such expression bears the hallmarks of political and social acceptability the more it is valued and appreciated.

Faced with this picture, the educator or co-ordinator has a difficult choice. He or she has already made an analysis of the picture/situation and is able to communicate that at the level of an articulated statement. They must provoke a response from the learner/peasant. If this response is itself an articulated response, then it has already been manufactured, tuned to the needs and interests of the learner and their view of what the educator most needs to hear. Even if, therefore, the educator can provoke a response at the level of exclamation, a genuine response conveying feeling and immediate reaction, there is still a danger that, no matter how valuable that exclamation on the part of the learner may be, the ultimate outcome is still only a reproduction of Banking Education under the guise of a false dialogue. Critical consciousness or critical awareness is, after all, the outcome of a measured and objectified analysis of the world – the roots of which lie in an articulated expression which reflects a person's true position in society, in the world. Exclamation has the immediacy of the language of the Culture of Silence but this is primarily the language of transmission or of internal dialogue which creates not Dialogue but Anti-dialogue.

Freire himself would argue strongly that the measure of equality required of authentic dialogue cannot be achieved in the situation which has the hallmark of patronage. Yet this is what the use of these Codified Situations can provide. The educator or co-ordinator on the one hand encourages the learner to entrust to them their 'exclamations', their genuine, immediate views and feeling, yet they (the educators) are only able to reciprocate at the level of their own articulations, their carefully contrived and balanced opinions. Is it unavoidable, even required, that the educator becomes 'objective', depersonalized, as de-authored as the texts shown in the slides? Is the process of literacy acquisition itself a process not of humanization but of depersonalization?

This is a critical question for the dialogic educator who is trying to avoid the constant danger of Banking Education. Despite, or in spite of, the directiveness needed to achieve the objectives of Figure 2, is it actually possible to respond in a way which is authentically dialogic? On a wider front but with a related question, is it possible to subscribe to the use of this picture, with its hidden agenda, in a way which is not fundamentally dishonest?

One view would be to admit simply that the objectives set by Freire require a high level of manipulation on the part of the co-ordinator/educator but that, none the less, the ends justify the means. Notwithstanding the rhetoric, we may have to accept that the role of the educator *is* pivotal in this process, precisely because the oppressed or the non-literates do not have the awareness to channel their understandings or perceptions relating to the picture into what Freire would call 'cultural action'. The educator is necessarily an activator who is engaged in a form of cultural invasion, notwithstanding that it is an invasion for liberation and therefore acceptable to those who find themselves in the 'occupied territories'. Lloyd (1972) suggests that educators, 'by their broader perspectives', have the primary function of 'posing problems', but this does not conceal the fact that it is the educator who is setting the agenda.

Freire was not unaware of the problem of motivation. 'The leaders do bear the responsibility for co-ordination and, at times, direction, but leaders who deny praxis to the oppressed thereby invalidate their own praxis' (1982:77). The educator, while being a partner of the students, none the less has to be interventionist, albeit that they must always 'strive for an even greater clarity as to what, at times without their conscious knowledge, illumines the path of their actions' (1970h: 212).

This creates in practice the dilemma which disables so many educators and which, classically, is articulated by Rousseau: how is it possible to educate for freedom, given the need to direct the learner along a path which otherwise he or she would not know? How does one liberate the mind of someone indoctrinated by the values of that very society which one wants to change, yet avoid reindoctrinating that person with a new set of values?

The dilemma hinges on this issue: if education, that is dialogic education, is always about annunciation and denunciation, how can the educator lead the learner to announce or denounce what evidently they do not yet know? There is a fundamental tension between the *theoretical* position that conscientization is about being able to see one's own reality sufficiently clearly to be able to denounce that which dehumanizes and announce that which humanizes, and the *practical* demands that the educator works only from spontaneous themes generated by the participants/learners themselves, without being coercive and directive. This is the very idealistic model of the teacher/learner which Freire has so emphasized, yet it is clear that the use of the content and the agenda set for Figure 2 poses some severe questions for such an educator. We therefore need to examine whether the use of the other pictures makes it easier to achieve a truly dialogic communication which can provide a pedagogically sound base for furthering the development of literacy learning.

Third to fifth situations: Unlettered hunter
                                                 Lettered hunter (lettered culture)
                                                 The hunter and the cat

The third, fourth and fifth situations within the Literacy Process need to be taken together: they project the development of one major theme, namely the difference between *Nature* and *Culture*.

Nature and Culture are presented each as the converse of the other, the two sides of the same coin which should be distinguished rather than separated. The vividness of the pictures and the argument of the accompanying script reinforce the apparent logic of the situations and the learning objectives which they support. Despite that, however, these three situations also reveal Freire at his most vague or inconsistent. The strength of his argument may lie, not in the evident authenticity of the analysis which he makes of these day-to-day

Figure 3a

scenes, but rather in the selectivity of his perception. It is almost as though Freire has come to these events, wittingly or not, with a kind of tunnel vision for, in order to direct the learners to the required themes, again a high degree of mind-guarding is required. The end result is an argument that amounts almost to special pleading. If this is the case, then these three situations may indeed represent the Achilles' heel for Freire of both his method and his philosophy.

The situations (Figures 3, 4, and 5)

The three situations reflect different hunting scenes. In the first, Version 1, there is a very stylized, even stereotypical drawing of an Indian, complete in feathered headdress, perhaps naked except for a decorated loincloth. He is

Figure 4a

hunting in a forest or in a clearing at the edge of a forest and he obviously has had some success: a bird lies dead at his feet and other birds look in imminent danger of falling to his skilful shooting. In Version 2 (Figure 3a), the Indian is less stereotyped: he is clothed, but bare-footed and he has a single feather in his hair. Again, he is successful in his hunting, despite the open terrain: two birds have been shot.

In the second, hunting situation, again this statement of success is clear. In both Version 1 and 2 (Figure 4a), the hunter, this time with a gun, has made a kill. However, it is not just the gun which distinguishes this scene from the previous one. The man is well dressed for the hunt, wearing boots and a hat. Because of this, he can hunt in difficult terrain where there is more cover. Not only can he kill from a longer distance because of the gun, but also the birds that have been shot, even if they have fallen to ground out of sight, can now be found and retrieved by his gun-dog – an animal which has been reared and trained specifically for this purpose.

In the third hunting situation (Figure 5: the first picture for which there is not a copy of the Brennand version), a cat is toying with two mice. It is a powerful and menacing picture revealing the dominance of the cat and the powerlessness of the mice.

Application

According to Brown, 'the next three discussions refine the concept of culture and raise the question of how culture is transmitted to younger generations'. Freire indicates that the debate is initiated by distinguishing in the situation what belongs to nature and what belongs to culture, anticipating the response that the bow, the arrows and the feathered headdress are all part of culture. The feathers were part of nature, while they were on a living bird, but they have been used now to make clothing and are hence a part of culture.

And how did the Indian learn such skill, hunting, tracking, making bows and arrows, making clothing? The discussion considers the transmission of learning through a non-literate culture, from father to son, mother to daughter. Then it moves on to suggest that the Indian, viewed from within his own culture, strictly should not be described as illiterate. *Illiteracy* derives its meaning only within a literate culture. This is an important point for the educator to clarify, for it is essential that the members of the group are led to contrast their situation with that of the Indian. 'By distinguishing the historical-cultural period of the hunter from their own, the participants arrive at the perception of what constitutes an *unlettered culture*.' This perception, Freire admits, might be dramatic for some participants because they perceive 'immediately that to be illiterate is to belong to an unlettered culture and to fail to dominate the techniques of reading and writing'.

It is exactly this domination that the hunter of the fourth situation has achieved. Brown puts it starkly: the second hunter is using a tool so complex in its construction that directions for making it must be recorded, and only those who can read can learn to make it. That is not all. In the culture to which the man with the gun belongs 'only those who can read can earn enough money to buy guns, so access to their use is controlled by the literate members of this culture'.

Clearly there are many differences between the Indian and the man with the gun. There is the difference in the technologies represented by the bow and arrow and by the gun. The latter is seen as an advance in technology because it gives the hunter 'growing possibilities for transforming the world'. This is therefore the point where the group again returns to the twin themes of 'education for technological development' and 'education for transforming the world'. The first theme centres on the result of man's increasing opportunity, his work and his creative spirit. The second has meaning only to the extent that it contributes to the humanization of people and is employed towards their liberation.

This idea is refined through the use of the fifth picture. The participants discuss the fundamental differences between human beings and animals. In the sequence of pictures, all three are hunters, but not all 'create' culture. The cat is not a hunter (caçador) but a pursuer (persequidor): the cat does not make tools with which to hunt, but acts only through instinct. The development of this debate produces, according to Freire, a wealth of observations about 'men and animals, about creative power, freedom, intelligence, instinct, education and training'.

Commentary

The three situations, all ostensibly around the theme of hunting, develop a very Cartesian epistemology. Human beings are distinguished from the animal world by the way in which not only do they *know* (that is they are self-directed by knowledge rather than by instinct) but they also *know that they know*. A human being is a conscious being (*corpo consciente*): it is not simply 'I think, therefore I am', but 'I know what I think, therefore I am'. It is in the way in which they know, in their awareness of what they think, that individuals become authentic.

It is towards this awareness that the three situations are directed, but the achievement of such an objective can be realized only through the neglect of other questions and interpretations. For example Freire offers a wholly pacifist and utopian analysis of the scene. Leaving aside the obvious fact that the man with the gun is, at least pictorially, no more successful than the man with the bow and arrow, and neither is more successful than the cat, there is the simple question of the 'culture of weapons', of how human beings use either guns or arrows.

There is a naive view that such weapons are for hunting. Evidently this is not untrue, but it does avoid the equally obvious use of weapons – for invasion, control, and domination. The arrow, like the gun, is an artifact of war. Both are means for transforming the world but there is no categorical imperative that such transformation should 'contribute to the humanization of man'. On the contrary, there is perhaps more evidence that the gun and the arrow have been one of the main expressions of man's inhumanity. There is indeed the expression of *playing or toying* with someone 'like a cat with a mouse'. This describes a relationship of oppression, the control of an Object by someone who has power: it is the very opposite of a dialogic relationship.

What is interesting is why Freire should have chosen the image of the cat. Perhaps more than any other household animal, the cat has been 'domesticated', accepting a life of control and possession as a means, albeit not self-chosen, of survival. The life as household pet may be unauthentic, but it is a way of staying alive.

Perhaps the illiterate peasant, oppressed and domesticated (the very image of Freire's concept of banking education) has more in common with the cat than with either of the hunters. However, Freire would not have tolerated a self-identification with the cat: he would not even have accepted an identification with the Indian, although perhaps culturally, economically and socially, many peasants could see themselves represented in that picture. The essential message of this Codification is not the personalized picture of the Indian, but the idea of the fundamental necessity of hunting: people need to hunt in order to live. It is this idea that makes possible the analogy that people need to be able to read in order to live.

It is, of course, unwarranted to go so far as to suggest that the three pictures support the analogy that the hunter searching in the wild is like a literate person in a non-literate society. However, it is not unreasonable to argue that they do support the analogy, or that they are intended to support the analogy, that the man with the gun is different from the Indian and the cat precisely because he is a symbol of the power of literacy. Freire wanted the Culture Circles to identify with the man with the gun. It is this latter instrument, like the book in the earlier pictures, which has the value of symbolizing what it means to be literate. At its most simple, it is argued that the use of guns (and therefore of the power that accompanies them) is controlled by those who are literate. Although there is a limited sense in which this might be true, there are sufficient examples of non-literate people having guns and ammunition to suggest that, here, Freire is special pleading. The peasant farmers knew that even the Indians had guns. Ah, but of course, the Indians were not literate.

This is the subterfuge which the co-ordinators used to exit from this dilemma. The Indian lives in an *unlettered culture*, in which strictly speaking, one cannot talk of being illiterate. The whole concept of illiteracy or non-literacy (there is a subtle difference of emphasis and of values in the two terms) has meaning only in the context of a *literate or lettered culture*. The group appreciate this through distinguishing the historical-cultural period of the Indian from their own. Freire wants to stress here his Cartesian analysis of pure-knowledge which is ultimately power-knowledge. The gun represents a particular competency which is attributed to those who are literate, through which they have power and control. In a sense, literacy is intended to give to the non-literates the ammunition with which to enforce a redistribution of this power.

This is where the force of the discovery about literacy arises. It comes not from the obvious comparing of the world of the animal with the world of humans, and not from comparing the world of the Indian with that of the peasant, but from the discovery that, if one lives in what is a lettered culture and yet one cannot 'dominate the techniques of reading and writing', then one is truly *illiterate*. The group is forced to give a currency value to a new coin, the heads and tails of which are that, on the one side, they are aware that they cannot read or write, and on the other side (and inextricably related) they are aware that they are dominated and oppressed by those who can read and write.

This is a rewriting of Graff's (1987b) literacy myth that gains its value not through re-affirming the myth of the savage Indian but through insinuating the myth of the sophisticated literate who can wield the power and control which is a product of being literate. This retexturing of the myth is achieved through the assertion that such power and control, such application of the values of literacy, 'only has meaning in that it contributes to the humanization of man'. The evidence is against Freire on this point, and his constant insistence on some other reality amounts indeed either to special pleading or to some unexpressed view that there is an almost 'magical' content which adheres to the concept of the Book and the ability to read it or write it.

There is much that is hidden in this sequence of pictures. The initial scenes that were so redolent of the Garden of Eden are now replaced by the realities of life on earth – survival, the need for food, the natural cycle of the hunter and the hunted. Following the analogy, reading is as basic and important as eating. The assumption is, of course, that human beings hunt out of necessity. It is perhaps not part of the culture of Brazil, and certainly not part of Freire's world view, that hunting can simply be for pleasure and entertainment. He would not accept that hunting should be considered a pastime.

This is not necessarily a moral judgement on the role of hunting in an affluent society. The point is rather that the co-ordinators of the Culture Circles cannot afford a discussion on the rights or wrongs of hunting as a pastime. That would be to dilute and weaken the analogy: hunting for pleasure rather than necessity would be like reading for pleasure, and it is not within the objectives of the literacy programme to attribute such a marginal importance to the need to read and write.

Freire suggests that the three pictures are primarily about the distinction between nature and culture. However, although presented in this guise, the underlying debate is actually about literacy and power. The major themes of the *Pedagogy of the Oppressed*, namely the identification of those who are oppressed with those who are not literate and the centrality of literacy as a means of liberating the oppressed, are reasserted here both overtly and covertly.

Freire asserts frequently that literacy is not simply the mechanical process of reading and writing letters. It is more fundamentally the process of conscientization and a necessary means of liberating people from the culture of silence in which they have been oppressed. Through these three pictures, with the dominant image of the gun playing the same totemic role as that of the book in the first scenes, the debate is led to the discussion of literacy and power. Literacy seems to be offered as the key to regaining power and one can easily imagine and explain the reactions of the dominant classes in Brazil in 1964, if this was all that they knew of the discussion of the Culture Circles.

What is not offered in these three hunting situations is any clear correlation either between literacy and humanization, or between the language of personal or social development and the language of power. What we then have to ask is: what other images have the co-ordinators got, what other convincing argument does Freire want to offer the Culture Circles, so that they will be motivated to continue with their quest for literacy? If it is evident by the end of the fifth situation that *illiteracy* is about *powerlessness*, what is the counter-argument to show that, while *literacy* is about *empowerment*, it is also about an empowerment, personally and collectively, which is more than the *replacement of one oppression* by another? The remaining five situations should provide an answer.

Figure 6a

**Sixth to seventh situations: Man transforms the material of nature by his work
A vase, the product of man's work upon the material of nature**

The situations (Figures 6 and 7)

Version 1 of Situation 6 offers a direct and simple picture of two men working at a potter's wheel. One man is engraving or decorating a pot while the other, who is sitting at the wheel and moving it with his feet, is making a pot. The scene is 'framed' by two large, potted trees with splendid fruit, possibly lemons or pomegranates. One of these pots is signed with the initials of Francisco Brennand. Version 2 (Figure 6a) shows the more obvious context of a

Figure 7a

workshop where the two men are again working, one modelling, the other decorating. Behind and to the side, there is a range of pots and earthenware jars, from the small and ornamental to the large and practical. In the foreground, near two substantial jars, is the written signature of Vincente de Abreu.

Both artists picture a vase of flowers for the seventh Situation. The vase in Version 2 (Figure 7a) is well decorated in symmetrical patterns that offset the shapes of the flowers. Version 1 has a cascade of flowers that droop down each side.

Version 1, however, shows one important visual difference. The vase is actually decorated in the centre and at the top rim with drawings of flowers. There is therefore a double representation: a picture of a vase of flowers on which there are graphic symbols of two different kinds of flowers.

106

Application

These two situations serve to move the discussion on from a general discussion of culture referring to other places (countryside) and time (Indian pre-literate culture) to the discovery for members of the group that they themselves are makers of culture. They recognize 'their brothers from the people making clay pots' and they realize that clay pots are as much culture as the work of a great sculptor.

Both Freire and Brown quote from comments made in the Culture Circles:

'They are working with clay,' all the participants answer. 'They are changing the materials of nature with work,' many answer.
'I make shoes,' said one participant, 'and I now discover that I have as much value as a professor who makes books.'

Freire intended here that there should be a discussion and analysis of work. The co-ordinator is able to ask whether the work represented in this situation will result in an object of culture. The expected answer is 'Yes. A vase. A pot. A jug, etc.'

In this sense, the main axis for an interpretation of culture is that of aesthetics rather than utility. The clay, which is nature, is transformed into culture by work, just as the flower, which is nature, is used for decoration – which is culture. The inherent values of culture are then reinforced by the use of the flowers and vase of V1. Effectively, the co-ordinators, who may have had copies only of Version 2, would have to make the point verbally here that the original version was significantly different. Version 1 illustrates, through the use of a graphic symbol, how ideas can be drawn, can be written. The flowers in the vase are represented by a drawing of them on the clay of the vase. Brown's comment is more than indicative: 'Nature, transformed into culture, has been transformed once again into a written symbol'.

The foundation is thereby laid for the use of Situation 8 – the written poem. That, at least, is the more obvious progression. Less obviously, Freire intended to make the transition through the use of the 'aesthetic dimension'. These two situations, he suggests, have awakened the ideas of aesthetics: these can now be discussed fully in the next situation when *culture is analysed on the level of spiritual necessity*.

Commentary

The severity of the previous discussion about power and domination seems to have been tempered in these two situations through the leading of the debate into questions of aesthetics and culture. This may have come about as an instinctive reaction that sought to control the revolutionable ideas about change and the use of literacy to challenge or to supplement the power of the gun. One could envisage the kind of Culture Circle where such argument would arise naturally in the course of discussion about Codifications 3–5. But that is not part of Freire's agenda. He wants to make the connection between literacy and culture rather than between literacy and revolution.

He is able to do this through a sleight of hand, a refinement of the argument

107

about *culture*. He has in effect created a confused middle term, CULTURE, but then the Culture Circles were not meant to revel in the finer points of logic. That is a very patronizing comment, but it is made in order to expose the patronage and directiveness that seeks to lead by misleading which is what, in a sense, Freire is attempting to do.

In the earlier discussion, *Culture* was contrasted with *Nature*; what was given (some would say 'God given') was nature: what was man-made was culture. Now, in these two scenes from the potters' workshop, culture is not simply what was man-made. It is rather those things which are man-made *and* which have an aesthetic value. The examples that will be selected here are pottery, flower-arranging, drawing/painting, poetry and, by extension, literacy. The unspoken conclusion from the premises expressed is that to be literate is to be cultured. There is a perceptible move away from the distinction between nature and culture towards the distinction between being, on the one hand, illiterate and, on the other hand, Cultured (with all the social and aesthetic values which lie hidden in the use of the majuscule).

This parenthesis is itself a product of the processes of literacy, but it exemplifies the degree of reorientation which Freire is seeking in the use of these two pictures. It is a form of expression that is essentially literate rather than oral. However, the point is not to create a semantic or linguistic diversion. It is an attempt to grapple with what is essentially a written rather than an oral use of language and to illustrate the degree of 'literateness' which Freire has imported into the discussion. His objective of discussing Culture (that is with the values of the capital C) is actually infused with his values realized through his own literacy. They are, by definition, not the values of those who are illiterate.

What the ensuing discussion of these two situations demands, therefore, is the very thing which Freire was at pains to deny for himself and to criticize in Banking Education, that is cultural invasion. For these discussions to be successful, in the short term in providing the generative words for the final three situations, and in the long term in providing a base of achievement and motivation for the rest of the literacy programme, Freire and his co-ordinators must impose their values of literacy. To do this, he offers the participants in the Culture Circle not the possibility of power and an ensuing liberation but the possibility of Culture and an ensuing *assimilation* into the ranks of those who have 'dominated the techniques of reading and writing'.

The very concept of assimilation, like that of cultural invasion, was so much the butt of Freire's criticism (see *Extension or Communication*: ch. 2) that it is all the more extraordinary to sense here the same processes in the style and content of his directing of the discussion towards his particular view of Culture. One may even pause to consider why he was at such pains to insist that the 'learning circles' should in fact be called Culture Circles. The naming of the groups in this way creates almost a predisposition for accepting the imposed debate about Culture. It serves as the unspoken rule of the group as much as it activates the hidden curriculum of the learning process.

Yet how is Freire able to do that, to achieve the manipulation of the discussion verbally from culture to Culture, in a way analogous to the written transition from *c* to *C* which would be immediately obvious to a reader. How can the verbal transition therefore go undetected?

The key lies again not so much in what is said as in what is not said. Freire's own guideline suggests 'after a series of analyses of work (some participants even speak of the pleasure of making beautiful things), the co-ordinator asks whether the work represented in the situation will result in an object of culture. They answer Yes.'

Within the debate as constructed by the co-ordinators, the answer has to be Yes. Freire himself records that, while everyone could look at the pictures and see that the men were working with clay, not all could answer immediately that the men were 'changing the materials of nature with work'. That is a learnt response, arising from the discussion, just as their final affirmative response is learnt within the group, 'after a series of analyses of work'. We are not told what this series of analyses contains, but it is clear what they do not contain: they are not centred on an economic analysis or on the nature of unproductive work.

As with the debate about the role and function both of the gun in the hunting situations, and of the book in the initial, farming situations, the discussion and analysis of work removes the reality of employment, market forces and exploitation from its known context. The Culture Circles could look at the two pictures and say:

> The picture of the flowers is irrelevant to our lives. We are more concerned with surviving, with finding food to eat. The realities of our poverty are not concealed beneath the cosmetics of flower arranging. The picture of the two men working is our reality: they have to work many hours a day, and while pots and jars are a necessity, they are a necessity for only part of the population. The rich do not buy clay pots for their dinner tables. The potters, having paid for their clay, their glazes and the wood for the kiln, can only charge for their wares what the poor can afford to pay.

Freire was either unaware of the real dimensions of social poverty (as opposed to cultural poverty) or he chose to exclude this debate from the analysis. Not all work results in an object of culture: not everyone who works has the 'pleasure of making beautiful things'. In the day-to-day necessity for production, few artisans can pause to lavish attention on their vase, at the risk of prejudicing the economic viability of the product.

There is within these two pictures the double bind of value systems that have their origin in Christian work values and/or in non-working class social values. The experience of the poor and the oppressed is that they are most exploited through their work, and that manual labour does not bring job satisfaction or pleasure. Additionally, there is the echo of the illusion of the enlightened savage of the hunting scenes, but this time offered as the illusion of the contented craftsman. Poor, illiterate he may be, but he can still 'make culture', can still contribute to society something that is beautiful. There is no discussion of the possibility of work as paid employment, of the oppression of the employers and landowners, or of the difficulties of being self-employed, without sickness insurance, pensions or other social security benefits.

On the contrary, the myth is reinforced by the silent approval of the statement that the person who makes shoes has as much value as the professor who makes books. This assertion is left unchallenged. Yet in what society is this true? How do the co-ordinators relate this kind of statement to the realities of the lives of the participants who are shoemakers, potters and farmers? In a utopian sense, there is an acceptable truth to the statement, but it reflects more a world of what should be than the world as it is.

Or does it? What happens if the illusion is reversed, if the values and hierarchies of the crypto-literate are rejected? It clearly suits Freire and his co-ordinators that the participants of the Culture Circles should themselves assert the literacy hierarchy within which all are inferior to the academic professor, the writer of books *par excellence*. This is an illusion, but an important illusion. The group cannot be encouraged to accept or even to admit the possibility of another reality where it is easier, for example, to live without books than it is to live without shoes, where the shoemaker actually has more social value than the professor. One has only to look at the pictures of bare-footed peasants, let alone know of the status which someone in a Third World society can gain through owning a pair of shoes, to be convinced that it could be wholly reasonable and possible for any critically active Culture Circle to challenge and ultimately to reject this illusion.

The fact that they do not do so, or that there is no evidence that they have ever done so, speaks more of the degree of 'mind-guarding' in the groups which has been a feature also of the earlier discussions. It is also helped by the fact that the co-ordinators are meant to channel the discussion away from the sketch of the workshop (Figure 6) towards the graphic representations of Figure 7.

The group is initially intended to discuss the difference between the flowers in the field, which are *Nature*, and the flowers in the vase, which is *Culture*. This distinction, which is suggested to a literate person visually by a change in print, has to be communicated to the group orally by the co-ordinators. There is an additional, but more complex, discussion about the validity of this distinction which becomes particularly clear when one asks 'What is natural and what is cultural?' rather than 'What is the difference between Nature and Culture?', but that is not the intended focus of the discussion here.

The more important point to draw out here, as noted explicitly by Brown, is that 'a graphic signal is introduced for the first time in this picture. The flowers in the vase are represented by a drawing of them on the clay of the vase'. The co-ordinators who had only V2 would have some difficulty in making this point and one wonders, if this point was so significant, why de Abreu was not advised to include an equivalent graphic form in his version.

None the less, the importance of the graphic signal is not whether it appears either in Version 1 or in Version 2. The real significance of Brown's comment is that it is not true. Obviously she intended using the written symbol of the flower as the starting point for a discussion of graphic (that is written) forms of literacy, in order to widen the approach to literacy so that it includes writing as well as reading. This is not invalid in itself, but it does illustrate the selectivity of the literacy tutor and the ways in which the whole discussion of these situations has been orchestrated to present a learning schedule where graphic symbols are introduced with Figure 7.

What then are we to make of the two major graphic symbols in Figure 6? In both versions of the pictures, the artists have writ large their signatures or initials. What do they represent and for what were they intended? In all the Brennand pictures, his initials are towards the bottom or to the side of the drawing and represent the normal marks of authorship and possession. In Figures 1–4 and 9–10 (Figures 5 and 8 are from de Abreu), the signing can be ignored: it is wholly incidental. However, in Figure 7, but particularly in Figure 6, the signature is in sharper focus and is clearly intended to be seen. It is a signal from the artist to the viewer. A picture it may be, one among a series, but the *viewer* (that person in the Culture Circle who will shortly be the *reader* and the *writer*) should be aware that Francisco Brennand has written his name.

Of all the visual images which the group could recognize in all the pictures, and which they could be expected to 'name', it could have been anticipated that any genuine but non-directive application of the Freirean method would have produced the question 'what is that in the box or the plant pot under the tree?' The constant question which underlies the methodology is 'What do you see?' Yet it appears here that nobody has seen what is there clamouring to be expressed – the artist's own signature. The only explanation can be that the co-ordinators were in fact working to their own agenda and not to the freely generated discussion which would have reflected the more immediate searchings of the group.

Despite his rejection of a literacy *Primer*, Freire has actually created a paradigm for the group discussions which serves exactly the same purpose, the establishing of certain common norms and ideas. Brown argues that Freire and his co-ordinators avoided the use of primers 'on the grounds that they were mechanical and did not lend themselves to much flexibility in the discussion. Furthermore, primers discourage people from expressing and writing their own ideas and words'. However, it is one thing to suggest in principle that the choice of words, questions, or ideas should be jointly undertaken by the non-literate adults and by the co-ordinators, when the realities even of time and resources (the Culture Circles often comprised some 25–30 non-literate participants, and the ten picture situations were intended to be discussed in as little as two hours) demand a highly structured and directed agenda.

If the graphic symbolism noted by Brown was such an important feature of Figure 7, then that detail should have been reproduced in the de Abreu version. Evidently it is not, even though de Abreu may well have had copies of the original slides. What is then all the more significant is that de Abreu has not copied the 'graphic signal' in Figure 7, but he has *signed* his own version of Figure 6 with exactly the same clarity and force as Brennand's Figure 6.

This has to be more than coincidence. Of all the de Abreu pictures, only Figures 2, 6 and 10 are signed, whereas all ten of Brennand are initialled. It is as though he alone has actually read Brennand's graphic signal on the plant pot, and reproduced the picture (two men working in the pottery workshop) *and* the graphic fuse which Brennand had left waiting to be lit.

In assuming that the written word is the only form of literacy, and in implicitly ascribing to literacy a value system created around their own cultural norms, the co-ordinators had misread, or not read at all, one of the most important cues in the whole sequence of pictures. Brennand and de Abreu, consciously or not, had *written their name*. They had given the lie to the claims of the literacy campaigners that writing one's name, naming one's world, was always going to be part of the process of collective liberation and personal recognition achieved through becoming literate. The educators themselves were not sufficiently aware of the very process taking place in front of their eyes. Sadly what seems to have caused this desensitizing lack of critical consciousness was their unquestioning acceptance of the importance of their own culture, the presumed culture of literacy.

In denial of the philosophy and the principles of his method, there is an elitism inherent in Freire's use of these pictures. It would have been possible to look at the work of the potter and to consider the social and cultural relevance of such work. It would then have been possible to suggest some practical reasons why someone like that who cannot read or write should become literate, thus grounding the discussion in the realities of the daily lives of the participants of the Culture Circles and showing them just what literacy has got to offer them.

Surprisingly, Freire does not take that line. On the contrary, he continues with his analysis of Culture and his argument based on aesthetics. He wants to move the discussion on to an analysis of Culture as a spiritual necessity. The reasons for this, and its effect, we shall now have to examine.

Eighth situation: Poetry

The situation (Figure 8)

The picture shows a large, open book. On one page, there is a short, two-verse poem *A Bomba*, and on the other, a representation of people and trees. The script of the poem is hand-written, rather than printed, but all the writing is in capital letters. Despite that simplicity, the text does not forgo the need to include accents and a hyphen, but it does take a modern, poetic licence to exclude commas and full stops. The actual text of the poem is

A BOMBA

A TERRIVEL BOMBA ATÔMICA	The awful, atomic bomb,
E A RADIO-ATIVIDADE	With its radioactivity,
SIGNIFICAM TERROR	Presages terror,
RUINA E CALAMIDADE	Ruin and disaster.
SE ACABASSEM COM A GUERRA	If all war were ended,
E TUDO FICASSE UNIDO	And all things united,
O NOSSO MUNDO DE HOJE	Then our world today
NÃO SERIA DESTRUIDO	Would not be destroyed.

Application

From Freire's own notes, it is not immediately clear where the emphasis of this situation lies. His directions are that the co-ordinator first reads the projected text slowly. This is accepted as a 'poem of the people', and there is then an ensuing discussion about whether such a poem is culture. In comparing the production of the vase, from the previous situations, and the production of a poem, the participants are intended to 'perceive, in critical terms, that poetic expression, whose material is not the same, responds to a different necessity'. There follows a discussion on the difference between popular and erudite artistic expression in various fields, and then a rereading by the co-ordinator of the poem.

Brown has more practical objectives. Building on her identification of the graphic signal of the flowers in the previous situation, she wants to use the picture of the poem as the next step in 'graphic representation'. Her theme is that 'words known by and put together by non-literate people can be written down and are as much poetry as poems by educated people'. When the co-ordinator reads the words of the text, the participants are able to recognize that they are the words of a song which they all know. The seed is sown for a later understanding that all and everything that can be sung or said can be written. Brown suggests that this discovery is highly exciting to non-literates because it shows them 'that they can learn to read the words and songs they already know'.

This latter point is significant because it underlies the whole framework of the Freirean method. The idea of 'generating words' and then decoding them syllabically, is based on the principle that the adult learners will be recognizing the written forms of words which they already know and use without any problem. It is in that sense that it has been suggested that no one is verbally illiterate: a non-literate person is simply someone who is as yet unable to master the techniques of reading or writing the words which they already know.

Commentary

It does appear that Freire and Brown are using this situation in very different ways, or at least with very different emphases. Given the high level of correspondence between the two over the presentation and interpretation of the previous situations, this divergence here needs to be explained. We need to question whether the differences lie simply in the prioritizing of ideas or whether there is a more fundamental, methodological difference. For one, the situation has been selected in order to give rise to a discussion on poetry and Culture: for the other, it is a means of establishing a practical confidence in the processes of word recognition.

It is possible to see Brown's approach as being product centred, focusing on certain selected outcomes, while that of Freire is more process centred, seeing the scene as part of the complex unveiling of critical consciousness. Pedagogically, one is skills based, the other is more theoretical. One is concerned with the content of literacy, the mechanics of word recognition, the other with the wider, cultural context.

Schematically, the difference can be summarized as follows:

Freire	*Brown*
process centred	product centred
theoretical	practical
the context of literacy	the content of literacy
literate Culture	literate culture

Presented in this almost traditional, binary system, the difference between the two educators is profound, representing a divergence both of method and orientation. It might therefore be logical to explore how effective either approach might be and to try to explain each in the light of their related personal philosophies and professional experience.

However interesting that might be, it would none the less distract from a more important question. While focusing, as do most discussions on the philosophy or practice of education, on the philosophers and the practitioners themselves, it would ignore the effect that such differences of method or emphasis might have on the learners, on the consumers of the method. So it would be better here to try to understand the role and position of the adult learner faced with this particular situation and Freire's and Brown's interpretation of it.

There is little to be gained from a simplistic 'cause and effect' analysis, which is more appropriate to Banking Education and the refinements of models of operant conditioning. What we need to look at is what actually occurs within the brain, or within the person, that impedes or facilitates *a learning moment*, that point in time when one appreciates that one now knows something which one did not know previously. It may be called revelation, or awareness or perception, or learning: it is always an acceptance of having changed.

This is the final objective of all education and one overtly pursued by Freire. Learning becomes a multi-threaded concept, the product of perception, memory, analysis and transference. For him, a learner needs to be able to perceive a learning need, to relate that need to other learning or knowledge, analyse what is the issue or problem to be solved, and to transfer then that accumulated learning to the new situation or event.

Through the 'problematization' of Figure 8, how can these principles be put into practice? Is such learning the most likely outcome for the participants of the Culture Circles?

The guiding criteria which would be relevant to such a judgement can be found in a key text of educational psychology, of which there was a Spanish edition and which Freire knew well: Koffka's (1935) *Principles of Gestalt Psychology*. It is suggested that there are two, interdependent laws of learning – the law of proximity and the law of closure. In essence, learning is facilitated where we can see the relationship, the correlation or unitary nature of several 'perceptions', in such a way that we are able to construct a new, composite piece of information. In the strict sense of the words, we *make sense* of possibly disparate or divergent information, we look for *coherence*. When we say something or somebody is 'coherent', we understand that to mean that they are intelligible. Hence the value of Koffka's laws: the nearer we are to an event or learning situation, or, more accurately, the nearer a learning situation is to us and our accumulated learning, memory and perceptions, either in actual physical, spatial or temporal proximity (*the law of proximity*), or the more intrinsically coherent the event or stimulus is (*the law of closure*), then the more likely are we to construct a meaningful understanding of it.

We can then ask whether the use of Figure 8 by either Freire or Brown does proximate to the experiences of the people in the Culture Circle, whether it enters their 'zone of proximate development' (to borrow Vygotsky's useful term), and whether their exposition of this situation is coherent both in itself and in relation to the other, preceding pictures? The degree to which the answer to either of these questions is found to be negative would create a measure against which we could assess the level of 'cultural invasion' required to implement this programme. That would be a value judgement over and above the more neutral assessment that, even within Koffka's laws, the educator has an instrumental role *vis-à-vis* the learner, the bridging of the gap between the learner's experience of perception and the relevance of the new learning stimulus. This would hold true even where the learning objectives have been created by, or agreed with, the learning group. Even when the educator accepts to work from a learner-centred agenda, the reality is that each leap of understanding, each new step towards learning, has to be facilitated. The learner is, by definition, the person who says 'How can I, unless someone helps me?'

Most learning theory (which perhaps, more accurately, we should call teaching theory) concentrates on this latter apodosis, on the way in which the teacher/educator can assist the learner or the learning process. This is what Freire had attempted to criticize in his analysis of Banking Education. He himself wants to reverse this view, to concentrate on the *I*, on the learner who is saying 'how can *I*?' He demands that we ask 'Who is the learner, who is the *me* who will say "I have learnt"?'

To concentrate on the individual, the person who is the learner, requires a movement away from the traditional behaviourist and cognitive theories of learning which are the hallmark of Banking Education, and the espousal of a theory and method which is truly 'learner-centred', that concentrates on creating learning which (in Koffka's terms) is so *proximate* that it is experienced as being directly and personally relevant.

Leaving for the moment the debate about how instrumental a teacher can be or ought to be, we can look at the criteria for assessing proximate learning:

1 It is the teacher who formulates the units or packages of learning
2 ideally in some 'developmental sequence'
3 that accommodates the cultural and social background of the learner.

The first two criteria need not detain us. Clearly the literacy programme has been created *by* experts *for the use* of co-ordinators and Culture Circles. Obviously, non-literate groups do not have the capacity to become 'self-taught'.

Reading and writing is not an innate skill, and it is not surprising that the learning sequence should be prepared by the educators.

The question of a learning sequence which is also developmental we shall leave until the end of the programme and then review the ten pictures/situations. That leaves the question of the relevance of this Codification to the learners, given their cultural and social background.

According to Brown, the poem is meant to be sung. In North-east Brazil, as in many other parts of the non-literate world, there is a strong tradition of spreading news, telling stories and giving information in song. Like the 'griots', their counterparts in Africa, individuals or groups in South America travel from town to town, singing the news, and entertaining the people. Clearly the structure of the poem, like the structure of the twelve bar blues in other cultures, would have been known to the Culture Circles. Freire notes that, after the poem had been read by the co-ordinator, the group would say 'This is a poem' and would describe it as popular, and would describe its author as 'a simple man of the people'.

Criticism from afar is always dangerous, if not always difficult, and at this point one may have to admit to a degree of cultural distance or alienation. None the less, it is still important to ask whether such 'simple men of the people' actually did go around singing songs against the atomic bomb. The simple poem actually carries a very complex, political message, the origins of which are uncertain. Brown suggest that the non-literates would be highly excited because this picture would show them that they can learn to read the words and songs that they already know. One possible source of the song/poem may have been as a reaction or popular comment to the Bay of Pigs incident, the narrowly avoided conflict between Cuba and the United States during the Kennedy presidency.

However, neither Brown nor Freire is concerned with the actual content of the poem, interesting as it might be. For Brown, it is a means of facilitating word recognition: the group 'sees' the visual image, the written words, of the song which they all know. It is a useful visual aid that is pertinent to the daily lives of the learners. For Freire, this utility is almost seen as a weakness because he prefers to insist on the debate about whether or not this poem is or is not culture. Yes, it must be culture because, like the vase, it is produced by people in response to a certain necessity – in this case, spreading the news. But no, it is not erudite, it is not artistic. Freire himself sets the agenda for the co-ordinators by making the distinction between popular and erudite artistic expression. It is his way of reasserting the difference between culture and Culture.

The point is subtly but powerfully made, for it is not a casual distinction. It is part of Freire's hidden agenda that the translation of culture to Culture is achieved through literacy. He makes this point, not through what is said by the co-ordinators or within the general discussion, but through the subliminal message of the visual image of the poem *in the book*.

In explaining their use of this situation, neither Freire nor Brown seems to be aware of the profound significance that the picture of the poem is actually a 'picture of a book in which is written the poem' under discussion, although their reactions implicitly make that observation. Brown says 'the words of

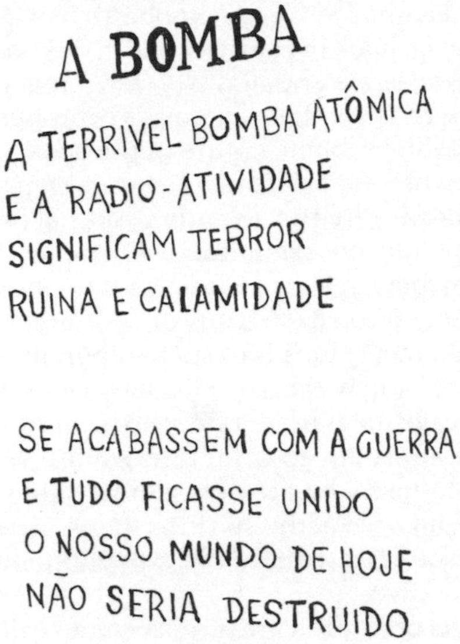

A BOMBA

A TERRIVEL BOMBA ATÔMICA
E A RADIO-ATIVIDADE
SIGNIFICAM TERROR
RUINA E CALAMIDADE

SE ACABASSEM COM A GUERRA
E TUDO FICASSE UNIDO
O NOSSO MUNDO DE HOJE
NÃO SERIA DESTRUIDO

Figure 8a

non-literate people can be written down and are as much poetry as poems by educated people'. This superimposes on the concept of poetry, which normally is taken to be an oral medium, the primacy of the written word. It is that which makes it cultural, in the value laden term which Freire uses. For him, the poem is culture – but it becomes Culture through being written in the book. The book enfolds the poem, just as it enfolds the whole world, – *osso mundo de hoje*, the pictorial image of which is on the page opposite the poem. The simple picture of the poem, which Freire could have used (Figure 8a) is markedly enhanced by the setting of the poem in the book. The power of the book, and thereby the power of literacy, is such that it can encompass the whole world, even the atomic bomb. It has the power to create, just as the bomb has the power to destroy. The picture is no longer a representation of a poem or song, but rather a picture of a poem-in-a-book, a page from a poetry book. That this bibliocentrism is subliminal only renders it the more powerful.

So the debate can be seen to be less about the bookish nature of poetry and more about the bookish nature of literacy. Brown confronts the Culture Circle with the *text* of words which they already know. Freire confronts them with *Culture*. Both are foreign to the group, both represent a high level of cultural invasion. The degree of proximate learning, in Koffka's terms, is simply an illusion. The members of the Culture Circles are no more textually competent than they are culturally competent.

Freire does not explain how the poem, which is essentially about oral communication, is any different for being written down. However, there is an implied hierarchy of culture, rising from the oral (the original song) to the visual (the representation projected on to the wall of the classroom) to the written (the book). Figure 8 serves to emphasize covertly the primacy of the written form. Unlike the book in Figures 1 and 2, this book is decontextualized: it is not held by anyone, nor associated with anything. It is simply The Book.

A *text* without a *context* is normally taken as a contradiction in terms, but here it serves to emphasize the sublime nature of the book, of literacy itself. That is what Freire meant when he said, at the end of Figure 7, that the aesthetic values which had been raised in the discussion about the vase, would be 'discussed fully in the following situation, *when culture is analysed on the level of spiritual necessity*'. Nowhere in Figure 8 does he actually discuss spiritual necess-ity, but what has been projected on that wall, writ large, is not the poem but the unspoken value of literacy which is of such importance to the life of human-kind that one can legitimately call it a 'spiritual necessity'.

Where does that leave the non-literate who is confronted by this picture, by these values which appertain to a literate world? Does it not represent a damning criticism of those who are non-literate? They cannot read or write, and apparently have no need of this spiritual necessity which is engendered by literacy. They are a sub-class, cultured in a populist and simple way, but not artistic, erudite, or creative.

So again, the impact of cultural invasion becomes evident. The non-literates are presented with a set of values which are not their own but which must replace their own, if they are to become literate. Figure 8 is an invitation for them to begin the process of assimilation into the world of literate culture, the world represented in the picture of the book.

Freire sounds like a missionary of old, seeking conversion on the basis of spiritual necessity. What in fact he has created through this invasion of non-literate culture is not a pedagogy of liberation but a pedagogy of assimilation, enculturation. As a model of change, both for individuals and for society, that is the complete antithesis of *Pedagogy of the Oppressed*. How interesting then that his book, *Reading the Word, Reading the World* encapsulates, in its title, the two processes required in this picture: on the one page, there is the Word, the Text, while, on the other page, there is the World. Both symbolically represent that world from which non-literates are excluded and by which they are oppressed.

In this picture, the book which is the world of literacy is open for them to see. It is an invitation, an opportunity. What then must they do to ensure that this book will not again become closed to them? Unnervingly, Freire, who has allowed the real text of this picture to be read in silence, has already prepared a response to that question. In anticipation that the Culture Circle may have correctly interpreted the unconscious message of Figure 8, he has prepared Figure 9 and a discussion of resistence to change.

Ninth situation: Patterns of behaviour

The situation (Figure 9)

This Codification shows two men: one is a *gaucho* from the South of Brazil, and the other is a cowboy from the North-east. They are dressed in clothes which

Figure 9a

are typical of the two areas. Version 1 shows the differences more clearly than Version 2: there is a marked contrast between the boots, trousers, jackets and hats of the two men. The first man is warmly dressed in wool – he comes from a largely sheep-rearing area in the colder South. The second man, from the cattle country of the North-east, wears clothes made from the leather which is both readily available and a useful protection against the cacti which are found throughout the scrubland.

In both versions, behind the men, there is one horse, perhaps symbolically representing the fact that both are cowboys. Version 1 might indicate a simple situation where the two men have met and, standing a little apart, are having a conversation. In Version 2 (Figure 9a), it is more difficult to recognize the difference in clothing and styles. At least to the unlearned eye, they seem to be dressed in a very similar fashion. The background of spiky plants suggest the scrubland of the North-east.

However, despite the similarities, the men are intended to be different, not so much in clothing but because one of the men is holding a book and seems to be reading it to his companion. Structurally, the picture is an exact echo of that used in Figure 2 where the relationship between two people is mediated again by the presence of The Book.

Application

Neither Freire nor Brown alludes to this significant feature in the picture. Rather, Freire intended the picture to be used to 'analyse patterns of behaviour as a cultural manifestation, in order subsequently to discuss resistance to change'. By analysing the two traditions, North and South, shown here as differences of clothing, the discussion can move on to consider differences in other forms of behaviour. A comment, first noted in a Culture Circle in the South, is used to guide the other groups: 'traditions are formed as a response to need. Sometimes the need passes, but the tradition goes on'.

Another context in which to view this picture is Freire's remark (1967b: 25) about the enforced isolation of the regions in Brazil under colonial rule. 'Such relations, if permitted would have provided an indispensable exchange of experiences by which human groups, through mutual observation, correct and improve themselves'. It is interesting that the potential of this scene to create political discussion is not mentioned by Freire in his commentary, preferring as he does to emphasize the nature of culture and behaviour.

Brown has a slightly wider use for the picture, intending as she does to 'expand the notion of culture by showing that clothes and ways of behaving are also part of culture'. She notes that sometimes (but, evidently, not always), the picture leads to a discussion of people's resistance to change.

Commentary

This is the weakest of the sequence of pictures, not only because there is no great clarity about the focus or use of the picture, but also because it is presenting no information that has not already featured in the programme. The picture could be removed from the set, without loss to the overall theme or to the required development of ideas.

What is required here is an extreme degree of orchestration of the discussion. It is not immediately obvious from the Codification that the different fashions in clothing are meant, almost metonomically, to represent the differing modes of behaviour/traditions in different parts of the country. It may, at best, support a discussion that looks at the broader definitions of 'culture', but there is a leap of logic required to channel that debate towards the notion of resistance to change.

The extended syllogism must run as follows: In the case that

(a) Culture (e.g. clothing and behaviour) is created out of Necessity,

and (b) Tradition (= continuous Culture) implies a continuation of the original Necessity,

but (c) Tradition may also continue beyond the original Necessity (= unnecessary Culture),

and (d) Unnecessary Culture implies resistance to Change,

then it is also the case that

(e) *Culture is created either out of necessity or as a reaction against change.*

Brown concentrates on premises (b) and (c), Freire on (a) and (d). Neither has an evident logic, nor do the discussions which they suggest sound like the authentic voice of people from within the Culture Circles. The objectives for this picture require that the coordinators manipulate the discussion around the confused middle term of *tradition*, shown above in premises (b) and (c).

Neither Freire nor Brown pauses to recognize that Culture is also a confused middle term, and both fail to draw the more obvious conclusion which arises from their intended premises which is that 'Culture is a reaction to change, either to create it or to deny it'. Not only would this have provided Freire with a base on which to explain the Culture of Silence (that reactionary culture which exists beyond the need) but also he could have begun to explain or explore what were the contemporary needs of the group that would have led them to redefine their culture, what in other contexts Freire would have called 'naming their world'.

This is what he singularly fails to do, almost as if he had in mind some other picture or some other debate. It does seem to be the case that the discussion which he was seeking here is only marginally supported by the picture, while, on the other hand, what is actually in the picture he does not use.

What is missing is any comment or reference on his part to the presence of the book. This is the more remarkable, given the incongruity of a picture of two cowboys reading a book, a scene which could not have been part of the everyday life of the members of the Culture Circles. How can this be explained?

A first response would be that Freire was again seeking, through a kind of subliminal advertising, to emphasize the totemic value of The Book, that prime symbol of literacy. He seems to know instinctively that the whole impact of such advertising is enhanced by silence, that it ceases to be subliminally effective once the targeted individuals or group become consciously aware of it. As such, it represents a very powerful form of cultural invasion.

However, it is more than that. The very totemic value of the book reveals, in an encoded way, the personal value system which Freire has for identifying or asserting the importance of literacy. Although he has elsewhere spoken of the centrality, within the process of conscientization, of that very active process which he called 'naming the world', the evidence from these pictures suggests that, in practice, he offered a pedagogy that required a more passive response on the part of the learners. Literacy would enable them to read the word, that is, to read the world. They would be assimilated into the world of the coordinators. That was the role-model which was presented when the co-ordinators read the poem in Figure 8, although it was stated that this was a popular song already known to the group. There would then have been an opportunity, if so required, for the group themselves to 'read' the poem.

But this was not required. The constant image of the sequence of pictures is that of the *literate person who is a READER*, and this is the role-model which is affirmed and reaffirmed in Figures 1, 2, 7, 8 and 10. Nowhere in any of the ten pictures is anyone seen to be *writing*, yet it is writing, rather than reading, which is more symptomatic of dialogic learning. It is in writing that we come closest to actually 'naming our world'.

This is not simply to assert the primacy of writing, of the written over the oral, in some Derridean fashion. It is to draw attention to the important fact, which Freire has here neglected, that, unless it is clearly and symbiotically related to Writing, Reading, like the voice of the educator, can so easily be another mode of Banking Education: it is the educator who writes, but the student who reads. It is the sound, says the old Zen master, of one hand clapping. This is an incongruous image, the epitome of non-dialogue, yet it is an apt way of describing both the sight of the book in Figure 9 and the sound of the silence occasioned by Freire's lack of attention to it.

The paradox of this figure is that, while ostensibly it portrays two men who have stopped to have a conversation (a dialogue), it actually reveals the presence of a book which may be anti-dialogic. The scene itself, representing a meeting of two men from the North and from the South, is perhaps a little out of the ordinary, but at least the men are ordinary, recognizable to their peers in the Culture Circle. What is extra-ordinary is the unspoken fact that the men are quite different from the participants of the Culture Circle for they are (or at least one of them is) *el hombre nuevo*, revolutionized, conscientized and literate.

The men in this picture inhabit two different worlds, within which their cultural differences from the North or from the South are insignificant. Each man might inhabit a different culture, but both men live in the world of The Book. De Abreu has named this world visually: his picture does not just speak the book, but does, in the full sense of the common expression 'speak volumes'.

Even when they have been using de Abreu's version, both Freire and Brown retreat behind the simplicity of Brennand's visually more simple picture. They could project the former (V2) on to the wall of the Culture Circle, but it is around the latter (V1) that they both direct the discussion. For them to achieve their objectives in the session, it is essential that the group are led, encouraged, or directed to discuss what is *not* in the picture in front of them (the obvious cultural differences between the two men) while disregarding what is actually there, the presence of The Book.

What is it then about The Book in this picture which forces Freire into such a blatantly false pedagogy, into contradicting the very principles of his own method of 'decoding' critically what people can actually see? In the context of these pictures, there may be the germ of an answer or explanation.

It may be that Freire has never fully come to terms with the powerful dualism or Manicheism of which he often spoke and which is inherent in the Catholicism that has so clearly influenced his personal and professional life. This we have already noted in the constant, binary nature of much of his thought, where there is always a polarity between good and bad, rich and poor, oppressed and oppressors, teachers and taught. Nothing can be simply good or bad: virtue and hope and loving are always contaminated with the possibility of sin, despair and non-loving. The most bigoted oppressor or the most enculturally silenced of the oppressed still retain a spark of being 'something other', of being humanized, for even in the darkness of oppression there is always the possibility of humble, positive, creative change.

We have noted earlier in the Second Situation the implied context of a Garden of Eden, and the representative figures of the man and the woman as the Adam and Eve of humanizing literacy. There it was the woman bringing the Book of Life, here it is the cowboy, but the implied choice is the same. The parallels between the two pictures, even pictorially, are clear (Figure 9b), but whereas Freire's use of Figure 2 was positive and generative, his use of Figure 9 is guarded and selective, almost as if, like the Adam figure, he first wanted to refuse what was offered. This is because the tree of life is also the tree of the Knowledge of Good *and* Evil. Its benefits are not unalloyed.

Without sharing his disquiet with the Culture Circles, Freire has had to confront his ambivalence towards issues of literacy and power, and towards the real content of what is contained in the book. On the one hand, he is wanting to assert the positive aspects of literacy, of naming the world, of creating one's own history and of being liberated. On the other hand, he is not wanting to explain why it is that those who are literate are more likely to be the oppressors, why the book, like the gun, is not necessarily dialogic, why being able to read the word does not automatically enable a person to read the world. The book may reveal the possibility of change, but it equally shows up resistance to change. The book both gives and demands a bifocal, even Manichean, perspective of the world. Freire perhaps unconsciously knew that, and tried to say so, not only in overlooking the presence of the book, but also in insisting that the discussion, against the evidence, was not so much about cultural habits and fashions but about *resistance to change*.

This ninth Codification is not truly a part of the sequence of learning for the Culture Circles because primarily its content is not directed towards the learner participants. It provides rather the focus for a discussion among the educators and co-ordinators about their approach to literacy, about their reluctance to forgo the methods and styles of Banking Education and about a fear of that very change which they are in the process of facilitating. The question is not whether they understand or respect the various cultures of the people in the North or the South, although it is hard to assert such respect and still go ahead with the cultural invasion which this picture demands. The fundamental question is even more demanding and threatening: given the culture of the people, are they really prepared to accept that the people should be in possession of the book in the way that is proclaimed in this picture?

Figure 9b

124

Figure 10a

From their refusal to see the book, and from their orientation of the discussion, the evidence suggests that, despite the rhetoric, Freire and the co-ordinators were inhibited by their own resistance to change from acknowledging that the people had the right to unrestrained access to the book. They had refused to see the book, to countenance this possibility, and, as a result, the members of Culture Circles had been disabled from reading the picture correctly. The co-ordinators, like the God in Paradise, had said: if truly you could eat of the tree of Life (if truly you were literate, without need of us), then you would be like us.

Is Figure 9 therefore really about resistance to change on the part of the co-ordinators, or is it more about the obverse, their fear of being the same as

Figure 10b

the people of the Culture Circles? Or is its hidden agenda more positively altruistic and more about tuning the speed or the quality of change which is occasioned by literacy to the life style and capacities of the group so that, in the longer term, the full, liberating effects of literacy can be realized? Is Figure 9 about Banking Education, benign paternalism, or the offer of radical, dialogic learning? The intended summary of Figure 10 may finally provide an answer.

Tenth situation: A Culture Circle in Action: synthesis of the previous discussions

The situation (Figure 10)

There is a high level of consistency between the two versions of this Codification (Figure 10a). Both show a group which is recognizable as a Culture Circle discussing one of the projected pictures of these introductory lessons, the pot of flowers. The Brennand picture, V1, is obviously a copy of his own earlier picture. Abreu has not copied his own, but has done a drawing which closely resembles Brennand's, perhaps indicating that he had a print to hand from which to make the new slides (Figure 10b).

Both versions show the small projector on which the presentation depends. In Version 1, the group is quite small, some ten people among whom there appears to be only one woman. In Version 2, there is a larger group, 25 or more, of whom three or four are women.

In neither version is the group sitting in a circle. On the contrary, the pictures reveal a very traditional, classroom situation, with the 'pupils' all turned to face the board or projected picture. In Version 2, the male co-ordinator is pointing to the picture with a stick, perhaps eliciting a question or clarifying a point. In Version 1, the co-ordinator, again male, is not using his stick but is pointing to the picture with his hand. Both are very directive gestures and, even within the freeze-frame of the pictures, it seems clear that it is the co-ordinator, standing at the side of the picture and in front of the class, who is speaking at the time and leading the discussion.

At the bottom right side of the picture, each artist has signed or initialled his name.

Application

This final Codification is intended as a structured reflection where, according to Brown, the 'group can look at itself and reflect on its own activity. The function of the circle of culture is examined by everyone, what the experience has meant, what dialogue is, and what it means to raise one's consciousness'. Freire says the same, but with a different intensity: 'The participants analyse the functioning of the Culture Circle, its dynamic significance, the creative power of dialogue and the clarification of consciousness'.

This is, however, not a simply discursive review of the previous situations. Brown's stage direction sets the tone: 'The co-ordinator introduces the phrase *"democratisation of culture"* to be discussed in the light of what has been happening in the circle of culture' (Brown 1974: 29). It is intended that the discussion of democracy and culture be set within the more general context of fundamental democratization. The end product of this evidently complex discussion is that 'the participants have regained enormous confidence in themselves, pride in their culture and a desire to learn to read'. So the base is laid for the next stage of the literacy process.

Commentary

This tenth drawing is not intended as an idealization of the principle of Culture Circles, nor as a portrait of a successful group that would serve as publicity material in the programme prospectus. It is essentially a photo-drawing of a situation which the participants of the groups would easily recognize. It makes no pretence to be more than is claimed in its title: A Culture Circle in Action. Its value is that it is correct in detail. The participants can recognize the projected picture as that which they have already discussed, they can see the little projector, perhaps recognize the co-ordinator who may have taught them and, most importantly, begin to recognize themselves as the participants in the picture.

Consequently, while there are no detailed, written, process recordings available of what actually happened in the groups, this pictorial record has particular significance. The details of the picture can be confirmed to such a degree that there is no doubt that this is a 'Culture Circle'.

When, in 1963, Freire was appointed as Director of the National Literacy programme, he spearheaded the design and organization of a National Development Plan. He planned that this would involve some 2 million people, who would be enrolled in the Culture Circles. Clearly he was influenced both by the success of such groups within the trade union movement in Brazil in the 1920s, and particularly encouraged by the experience of the Cuban Literacy experiment which had been completed the year before.

The relative size of the illiteracy problem in Cuba may well have been greater than that in Brazil. Kozol records that, in 1953, the year of the last official census prior to Castro's speech, 1,032,849 adults were illiterate, approximately one in four of the adult population. None the less, Cuban educators were convinced that conventional, educational methods (by which they meant a teacher working with a class of pupils) would not confront this problem. Instead, they were looking for a normative teacher/pupil ratio of 1:2, but were accepting of a higher ratio of 1:4 in exceptional circumstances.

Freire followed much of the structure of the Cuban programme, but differs markedly from it on this point. Nowhere has he explained this major divergence of teaching method. It may be that it was simply an acceptance of the financial and political reality where he could enrol only a small and limited number of educators in his programme and where the enormous resource of the Cuban *brigadistas* (which Castro had obtained by closing all the schools and enrolling teachers and secondary school pupils) was not available to him.

Instead he opted for large group teaching, justifying this choice in part on unit costings. Although there is a divergence in the actual figures which he has quoted, there is no doubt that the overall expenditure for the programme was cost efficient. He notes (1976b: 53) that 'in a period of six to eight weeks, we could leave a group of 25 persons reading newspapers, writing notes and simple letters, and discussing problems of local and national interest'. The Polish-made projector, of which the Education Ministry imported 35,000, cost $13 and, because they did not have their own laboratory, a film-strip cost

$7–$8. Three years later, in 'Education for Awareness', he recalls that the Polish projectors cost $2.50 and the film/slides cost $1, and that, on the basis of a group of twenty-five, each initial cycle of the programme would cost $5–$7 per group/Culture Circle (1970n: 14).

This is the evidence (the size of the group, the projector and the projected picture) which clearly supports the conclusion that Figure 10 represents a Freirean Culture Circle. It is, as Brown notes, a picture which 'shows a circle of culture functioning: participants can easily recognize it as representing themselves'. What the observer sees, however, is not just the participants but also the pedagogy, the *functioning* of the group. It is here that some major contradictions are exposed.

The most obvious is the overtly directive manner of the teaching. There is no hint here of a learning partnership, of a dialogue between equals. Rather, what is evident is the clear distinction between the teacher and the taught. Figure 10 actually presents an image of that Banking Education which Freire had so rejected in *Pedagogy of the Oppressed*:

A careful analysis of the teacher–student relationship, inside or outside school, reveals its fundamentally *narrative* character. This relationship involves a narrating Subject (the teacher) and patient, listening objects (the students). Narrative Education turns students into 'containers', into receptacles to be filled by the teacher. The more completely he fills the receptacles, the better a teacher he is. (1982: 45)

There is nothing in Figure 10, in either version, to suggest that the teacher–student contradiction has been resolved, although Freire insists that Education must begin with the reconciling of these two poles so that both teacher and students are 'simultaneously teachers *and* students'. On the contrary, the picture reveals the central, controlling role of the co-ordinator who must, for this picture as for the earlier pictures, direct the discussion to preset learning objectives. It is the co-ordinator who introduces the phrase 'the democratization of culture' which is a theme which the group is unlikely to come to unaided.

The democratization of culture, however, is not the democratization of learning, that is the possibility that learning outcomes could be controlled by the learners. Brown and Freire are already assured of the outcome of the discussions: for the former, it is that the participants would have regained enormous self-confidence, pride in their culture and a desire to learn to read. For the latter, it is that there is a foundation for the literacy programme.

This foundation, a prerequisite for the continuation of the programme, has been created in just two sessions, possibly in two hours, so that, on the third night, the literacy programme can begin. The actual statement by Freire here needs careful analysis:

The preceding situations are discussed in two sessions, strongly motivating the group to begin on the third night their literacy programme, which they now see as a key to written communication. (1976b: 81)

It is evident that, with only two sessions, the co-ordinators would have to control the content of the discussions. To actually consider all the pictures, the agenda setting picture of Figure 1 through to the summary and conclusions of Figure 10, a high degree of manipulation and direction is required on the part of the co-ordinator. Certain themes which lie outside the experience of the group have to be introduced: other questions or issues, which would be thrown up in the light of the experience of the group, have to be avoided.

Taking just three of the symptoms by which Freire identifies the attitudes and practices of Banking Education (1982: 46), we see in this Figure 10, and indeed throughout the programme, that it is

- the teacher who chooses and enforces his choice, and the students who comply
- the teacher who acts and the students who have the illusion of acting through the action of the teacher
- the teacher who chooses the programme content, and students (who were not consulted) who adapt to it.

There is a subtle, but important, nuance in the difference between students being self-motivated to begin their literacy programme, and the fact that it is 'the preceding situations (the discussion of the ten pictures) which strongly motivates the group'. The participants of the group are led to a position where they can *express* a need for literacy rather than to a position where there is an awareness in the group of their own *felt* needs. This is because the essential content of Figure 10 is educator-centred rather than student-centred. The *real* personal need, therefore, for literacy is required to give place to a kind of superficial, reactive need which is normally voiced, in other contexts, by a consumer to a supplier. The illusion is that the need, the demand for literacy, is created by the consumer and that it is the supplier who must respond by providing the learning programme. In reality, it is the supplier/educator who has created the need, and the level of demand has been controlled so that the consumer will ask only for that which is currently available.

This dichotomy or inversion of the outcomes of critical consciousness is encouraged in this Figure 10 through the unconcealed implication that there is a difference between the processes of literacy and the processes of conscientization. The discussions of the ten pictures may have contributed to the latter, but they serve only as an introduction to the former. It is stated that it is only on the third night, that is after the discussion of the pictures, that the participants *begin* their literacy programme. The discussions, however valuable or essential, are clearly intended to be distinct from the actual literacy programme.

This two-stage introduction to literacy also reveals a modular programme of learning that was not previously apparent. For the non-literates, there is a first stage of learning to read the word, but that in itself is still only a key, an introduction to stage two: writing the word.

The critical second stage, which is the prerequisite of writing the world and righting the world, has actually been avoided by Freire. Throughout the pictures, there has been very little emphasis on writing. On the contrary, the main themes have been about reading, reading the word and reading the world. There has been no analysis of the processes by which words are written, no reflection on the technologies of writing, no consideration of script as culture. At best there has been the refrain, the reinforcement of the view that literacy is about 'dominating the techniques of reading and writing' (Figure 3).

Thus a further difference within the literacy process is identified: that learning to read is a key to learning to write. Literacy is not simply a composite of both skills, a reading-and-writing skill. It is instead a hierarchy of skills concealed within a single term (literacy) that has two related but different definitions.

In the first instance, literacy might mean 'the mastery of the skill of *reading* and the mastery of the book'. In the second instance, literacy means 'mastery of the skills of *reading AND writing* and the mastery of the pen'. The content of each of these skills is left vague: Freire simply asserts a correlation between the two, although for many of the participants of the Culture Circles this may not be obvious. They would almost certainly know of people who could read but who could not write, just as they would know of people who could read but who were still oppressed.

The importance of this confusion is that, having said that literacy is a key to written communication, Freire then asserts that

> Literacy makes sense only in these terms . . . literacy which is not external to people but becomes a part of them, comes as a creation from within them. I see validity only in a literacy programme in which people understand words in their true significance: as a force to transform the world. (1976b: 81)

What is thereby left unsaid is that literacy, without the ability to write, cannot transform the world because literacy, if that means only the ability to read, is not dialogic. At this late stage of the discussion, Freire might want to assert the critical role of Writing and the primacy of the written. As an image, it is as if he were saying that it is not the person with the book who can change the world, but the person with the pen. But the rhetoric fails the reality. Throughout the sequence of pictures, no mention has been made of the pen, no hint has been given as to this hierarchy of influence. On the contrary, the participants have been encouraged, motivated to start their literacy programme only because it will enable them *to read*.

This is a severe accusation of the Freirean methodology and philosophy for such literacy has, as its objective, to enable people to conform to their world rather than to transform it. It succours the oppressed with the balm of assimilation. It is not a pedagogy *of* the oppressed: it is a pedagogy *for* the oppressed.

Freire ends by saying

> Learning to read and write has meaning in that, by requiring men to reflect about themselves and about the world they are in and with, it makes them discover that the world is also theirs, that their work is not the price for being men but rather a way of loving – and of helping the world to be a better place. (Freire 1976b: 81)

Such is the utopianism, the claim that literacy makes sense only in these terms, which so many critics have noted in Freire. The reader of Freire has to consider the evidence of the whole of Freire's philosophy, and a detailed analysis of his method. The question then left to be asked is whether this sequence of ten pictures, so often offered uncritically in praise of Freire, is consistent with his pedagogy or whether, by exposing the contradictions, it actually denies it.

SIX

A reconstruction of literacy

Redefining the obvious

The final picture used in Freire's literacy programme clearly highlights the essential interaction between the teacher and the learner, the literate and the non-literate, bringing into question the viability of a truly dialogic process of attaining literacy. Across the divide between teacher and learner there lies the double problem of a form of education which is anti-dialogic, Banking Education, and the very notion of a pedagogy of, for, the 'oppressed'.

Many critics have noted that Freire has never defined what he means by 'oppressed', and that it is not clear whether the collective noun refers to the working classes, to those who are non-literate, to the socially deprived, or to those who feel themselves, for whatever reasons, to be oppressed. This is an important criticism, but one that might be answered by the simple response that it is only of academic interest. The oppressed know who they are: only the non-oppressed have need to pose the question which, if it is at all genuine, is really the obverse of the more personally threatening question: who are the oppressors?

What is more detrimental to Freire's argument, however, is not the lack of clarity about the obvious term 'oppressed' but the lack of explanation of the more critical, underlying term 'literacy'. Besides saying that the oppressed cannot read or write, and that this is unjust, Freire has never disclosed what he means by literacy. There is only the implied understanding that 'You, the reader, will know what I mean (because, by definition, that is what it means to be a READER)'.

The assumption, based on the innate sense of superiority of literate cultures, is that literacy is self-explanatory. This accounts for the fact that, in so many studies of literacy and not least in Freire, this fundamental question is never posed. Graff (1987b: 18) notes that 'It is depressing but instructive to note how rarely debates and discussions about literacy levels pause to consider what is meant by reference to literacy', but he excuses that in part by saying that the question of definition is at once an insolubly complex problem and a deceptively simple issue.

Graff's own solution is to define literacy primarily as a technology of communication used for decoding and reproducing written and printed materials, in the broadest sense of the term. While this may be generally helpful and particularly useful as a lens to review Freire's approach to literacy, it remains descriptive and does not confront the underlying value judgements on which the idea of literacy is constructed.

It is here that we see that literacy has been 'gravely undertheorized' (Giroux 1989: 150) and that it has been accepted, as a consquence either of ideology or of pragmatism, following one theory or another, as desirable for certain social or cultural settings, compulsory for education, advisable for employment or obligatory for economic development. Yet all these approaches conceal diverse, even mutually exclusive, theories of literacy.

An explanation that confronted these inherent contradictions would enhance this immediate study of Freirean literacy. It would also serve to clarify other key concepts which are necessarily included in any literacy discussion, for example the idea of *orality* and *illiteracy*, which underlies Freire's use of the terms 'lettered' and 'unlettered'. Illiteracy is not to be taken as the converse of literacy, nor orality as its obverse. There is no simple continuum

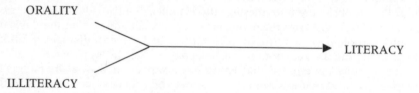

ORALITY

LITERACY

ILLITERACY

nor is there any automatic correlation between orality and illiteracy.

The point is worth making strongly because many projects which claim to be 'Literacy Campaigns' are couched in terms of combating or eradicating *illiteracy*. The now classic campaigns in Cuba and Nicaragua (Kozol 1978; Cardenal and Miller 1981) which became models of similar campaigns in Africa and Asia, are good examples of this literacy inversion. Here one is not simply playing with words: frequently the motivation for literacy teaching, the adequate resourcing and effective support for such activities politically, financially, practically, and the evaluation of identifiable outcomes depends on how and why one has drawn the distinction between 'illiteracy' and 'non-illiteracy'.[1] It also depends on how one draws the distinction between literacy as a PROCESS and literacy as a MEDIUM.

In considering literacy as process, as the *content* of teaching/learning to read and write, we could consider what actually happens when someone learns to read and write, what theories of linguistics or theory of knowledge explain the process, what pedagogical exchange takes place, what books are used, what script is produced, what changes individually or socially are directly attributable to this 'literacy event', the passage from a non-literate state to literacy, etc.

Literacy as a *medium* is recognizably different, not least because it immediately provokes the question: Of what is literacy a medium? It would reveal the difference between 'being literate and behaving as literate' (Heath 1986: 282), where literacy objectives are actually more about 'literateness' than about reading or writing. 'Being literate' clearly represents a certain range of social and personal values, and in certain settings and relationships it is important to be 'seen to be literate'. It is frequently said to be the case that people who are not literate can conceal their illiteracy: by appropriate imitation of acceptable, literate behaviour, they can 'hide their deficiency'.

Even a casual reading of the aims and objectives of certain literacy projects, national or local campaigns, reveals that a priority is placed on the teaching of literacy precisely because it serves as a medium for group and social control, correct thinking, correct behaviour, citizenship, or cultural integration. This is more than the application to literacy of Bourdieu's theory of education and cultural reproduction. It is the enactment through literacy education and training of the value in Olson's statement (1977: 257) that 'Speech makes us human and *literacy makes us civilised*'.

This distinction between the processes of literacy learning and the outcomes or consequences of such learning, takes us back to the question: 'What do we mean by *literate* and *illiterate*?'

The prime meaning of literate describes a person who 'has some acquaintance with literature'. To be literate is to be well educated, cultured, able to think and speak in a particular way, to be 'well read', learned as well as wise, able to appreciate the finer things of life, attuned, as Freire would say, to literacy as a spiritual necessity.

Paradoxically, in the more modern times of mass literacy, this maximal view of literacy has received little attention. Heath (1985) makes the same point:

> It is unfashionable, except in certain narrow circles, to discuss what being literate means or to take up topics that ring with elitism. The term 'literate' smacks of exclusivity and values traditionally tied to the leisured upper classes; it is often used synonymously with being intellectual. (Heath 1985: 2)

The focus of contemporary literacy debates is less directed to looking up to cultural literacy, to the 'upper' classes and to the great heights of knowledge and learning, than to looking down (and the social and political connotations of the expression are not to be missed) to functional literacy, the basic, minimal skills of 'being able to read and write' and, some would add, 'the ability to count'.

The possible confusion then in describing someone as literate is evident, but that is not the end of the difficulties. Even when 'literate' is reduced to what Freire would call the mechanical skills of being able to read and write, a further reduction is possible. 'Literate' can mean simply 'the ability to read'. Many literacy projects, schooling curricula and educational policies concentrate on reading, and very little attention is given to writing. In common parlance, a person who cannot write but who can read will be counted as literate.

Who then is illiterate? Given the usage of 'literate', a person may be illiterate who

1 cannot read or write,
2 cannot write but can read, or
3 can read and write but not 'properly', that is not reflecting the level of cultural literacy as defined by the dominant classes.

This latter category of person may appropriately be classed as 'semi-literate', even though in a different assessment where literacy was not the dominant value, it would be just as true to say that they were 'semi-cultured'. (It is a quite a separate issue whether Society then regards this group as literate but 'uncouth'.) What then of the other two categories of 'illiterates'? A useful distinction can be made in French, in part in Spanish, but not in English, that confronts this difficulty and may help in finding appropriate English terms.

In French and Spanish, one can speak of those non-literates who have had no direct exposure to literacy, whose discourse and patterns of communication are founded in modes of orality: these are *les analphabètes, los analfabetos*, those who have never been 'alphabetized'. In relation to the First or the Third World, one can speak of a literacy programme as a *campana de alfabetizacion*, and of areas of illiteracy, for example, as *poches d'analphabétisme*.[2]

On the other hand, *illettrisme*,[3] a concept which translates only with difficulty into Spanish or English, specifically denotes those who inhabit a literate culture, who have been through formal schooling but who either, despite that experience, have never learnt to read and write, or who achieved such a low level of competency in reading and writing that they have regressed to a state of non-literacy or sub-literacy.

'Illettré' in this sense approximates to what I have called 'semi-literate', rather than 'illiterate' in the broad English sense. As an idea, it serves to highlight the necessity of distinguishing this from other forms of non-literacy, particularly in the case where, given the fact that the construct of illiteracy only pertains to a literate society, the use of the term 'illiterate' to describe people in an oral culture may indeed be a form of intellectual colonization. This is exactly the issue raised in Freire's third Codification.

In the strict sense of the term, people who live in an oral society are *non-literate*: literacy is simply not a construct that is meaningful or relevant to them in the context of their individual lives and collective culture. However, people who are members of an otherwise literate society but who cannot read and write are more precisely il-literate. They may be aware that they are outwith the cultural norms of the society and may be seeking to remedy that situation through learning to read and write; they may be unaware of any particular problems arising from their illiteracy; or they may be aware of particular problems, but none the less have chosen to remain illiterate. It is always possible that the costs of acquiring literacy skills outweigh the possible, future advantages or may even result in the loss of certain present benefits.

The English expressions, therefore, of *illiterate* and *illiteracy* have too broad a connotation, referring as they do to both non-literacy and sub-literacy. This creates a major problem in translating Freire for, in the different settings of his pedagogy, in the First and the Third World, this distinction would be critical to the proper understanding of his work. Would be, that is, if Freire himself made that distinction. Yet nowhere does he adjust his method, nowhere does he adapt the content of the Codifications, nowhere does he seem to be aware that the participants of the Culture Circles may be semi-literate. He prefers the undifferentiated, naive distinction between being literate and being other, and it is this, perhaps above all, which has confused so many of his readers.

It is still instructive, none the less, to try to use the greater clarity of these differentiated terms to focus on the actual terrain of literacy teaching.

Literacy is now accepted as a universal social paradigm (Chartier and Hébrard 1989). Reading is omnipresent, at one and the same time a functional necessity, a legitimate pastime, and a never-ending task. 'One never finishes learning to read.' The importance of their argument is not that it imposes on the world of education a Cassandra-like pessimism, but that, on the contrary, it provokes a social optimism in that it situates universal literacy alongside universal suffrage.

There are those indeed who consider literacy as a fundamental human right, an implied term in, for example, the United Nations Charter on Human Rights. Article 26 states that

> Everyone has the right to education. Education shall be free, at least in the elementary and fundamental stages. Elementary education shall be compulsory. Education shall be directed to the full development of the human personality.

The first obvious problem arises in deciding whether the terrain of literacy teaching is located within this general right to education. If literacy is a right, might it not also be an obligation? If schooling is itself compulsory, that is obligatory at least at elementary level, does one have the right not to be the literate? Can one claim the right to be literate by the end of elementary schooling? Must all education be literate education?[4]

The cultural and economic dominance of the Literate Societies encourages the view that literacy is essential for the proper development of the individual and of the society but rests short of saying clearly that literacy is a basic human right.

The linguistic anthropologist will, of course, say that to insist on literacy as a right, as *the* means of development, personally or socially, devalues other societies, particularly those which are not literate. As we cannot consider such societies as sub-human, as there is no social imperative to be literate, we may assert that literacy is highly desirable, but we cannot assert that it is a fundamental right.

Freire is close to this argument at least to the degree that he argues his case on the basis of literacy as a spiritual necessity. Only through the influence of Cabral did he see also that it was an economic necessity, but even here he has never been prepared to insist on literacy as an economic or social right. The reason why this might be the case exposes the wider context, the real rather than the theoretical terrain of literacy, in which Freire, and all other educators, have been obliged to work.

Oppressive literacy: a new definition

In redefining literacy, we need to uncover two forms of oppression which lie hidden both in the general use of the word and in the texts of Freire. The first is that, in looking at the terrain of literacy through the twin focal points of power and knowledge, or dominance and ignorance, it becomes evident that this represents a singularly male perspective. It appears as a fact that sexism is inherent in the prefabricated structures which define the relationship between language, literacy and power itself. In that sense, Freire is both typical of his own culture and typical of most cultures of literacy.

What would be required, if literacy were genuinely to be accepted as a human right, would be a complete restructuring both of the discourse and of the functions of literacy. Yet, as Rockhill (1987) has pointed out

> With rare exception, discourses about literacy, whether about power, skills or social relations, are strangely silent on the questions of gender or of women – especially strange since women are the primary participants of literacy programmes. (Rockhill 1987: 7)

Nearly 70 per cent of women are non-literate. None the less, the criteria for assessing the Experimental World Literacy Programme were based on the judgement that functional literacy should bring about a 'change for the better, on condition that it is associated with a process of genuine innovation (of a political, social, or technical nature) in which participants are themselves involved' (Unesco 1976: 160).

What Unesco was unable to contemplate was that, for many women, its campaign of functional literacy was dysfunctional. The way in which women live literacy or illiteracy, as the way in which they live patriarchy, politics, society and technology, means that they cannot profit from literacy policies or programmes which are predominantly designed by men for men.

That is why the objectives of functional literacy programmes are a non-sense to many women. What they are directed towards is not in their interests and does not reflect their needs. Rather, traditional objectives are directed towards a male role-model, for example the man who will get a job and work outside the home, who will drive a car or a lorry, who will complete tax returns for himself and for his wife. It is he who will read the public notices, and it will be his voice that is heard in local politics.

It is one of the paradoxes of literacy, but one ignored totally by Freire, that many non-literate or semi-literate women are more *literate* than their male counterparts. However, it is the male definition of literacy which is validated, forged as it is in the public economy of the workplace and tempered as it is with cultural and social patriarchy. Women's literacy is devalued because it belongs to the home, to the care of children and to the maintenance of private life.

The terrain of teaching and learning literacy is peopled primarily by women.

Therefore, to the degree that either the concept or the practice of literacy lack a predominantly female construct, to that degree will they fail in their objectives to promote creativity, equality, and liberation. If literacy is a human right, it cannot be a right only for men.

The difficulty of accepting the above conclusion is that literacy could be a means of dismantling the world of patriarchy which underpins most oppression and exploitation. In that sense, Freire's pedagogy would be truly revolutionable. There is, however, another sense in which Freire provokes a reinterpretation of the myth of literacy.

We started by asserting that literacy is social because primarily it is about the means of communication: the literate person requires a societal context in which to express and communicate his or her literacy. Might it not be more true to say, however, that Society requires literacy (which is literacy rather than a literate person) because in the power–knowledge relationship of the modern world, literacy defines who controls the means of production, that is the means to produce wealth (industry) and the means to reproduce knowledge (education).

If this is true, then the very nature of literacy has changed and we are forced to consider the possibility that literacy cannot combat oppression, precisely because it is literacy which gives Oppression its voice. When we consider the interface, the 'between', which is created either when two people try to communicate or when an individual reflects on his or her role in the larger society, what is the role of literacy? The communicative, humanizing view of literacy offered by Freire would see literacy as the thread that spins the web of human relationships in what Arendt calls the 'space of appearance', the context in which we encounter one another, are seen and are heard (Arendt 1958: 180).

Each person, as Subject, is free to communicate orally or in writing with another Subject. They recognize, with Freire, that the human word is not just vocabulary, it is word-and-action.

> As such it is a primordial human right and not a privilege of the few. Speaking the word is not a true act if it is not at the same time associated with the right of self-expression and world expression, of creating and recreating, of deciding and choosing and ultimately participating in society's historical process. (Freire 1970h: 212)

Within this co-operative relation, literacy enables individuals and communities to name their world, to speak their Word. But as a means of combating oppression, of overcoming domination, what kind of power does literacy actually have? Two points need to be noted here.

First, educationalists talk easily of that 'symbolic violence' which is the prerequisite for cultural reproduction (Bourdieu and Passeron 1970), often hoping perhaps that, if something is only a symbol, it lacks efficacy. They scarcely pause to consider the contradictions of 'Compulsory Education'. On the one hand, what is the content of the compulsion? No one can be compelled to learn: they can be compelled only to attend schooling. On the other hand, what is the content of education? What the system of education compels people towards is not learning and erudition, but rather to 'finding their place in society', particularly through finding a place in the labour market. So Bowles and Gintis (1976: 94) identify the two interrelated aims of education: there is the acquiring of cognitive capacities and concrete technical and operational skills, including literacy skills; then there is the development of certain personality traits (for example, motivation, perseverance and docility), *plus* certain behavioural traits (self-presentation, dress, good manners, style of speech, encultured 'social distance'), all of which are included in the assessment of 'literate behaviour'.

Second, sociologists will talk of social stratification and even of structural inequality, but they rarely consider that there is no stratification of caste or class, rich or poor, male or female, young or old, which is not structured through some element of literacy and which does not contribute something to the archaeology of literacy.

What gives strength to both these is the *Voice*, the Word contributed by literacy. The oppressed and many educators know that Speech is helpless when confronted by Violence: hence Freire's 'culture of silence'. But what is mostly ignored is that 'Violence itself is incapable of speech' (Arendt 1985: 19) and that it is literacy, which is both the ability to write and to think as a writer, and the ability to read and to think as an interpreter, that is the co-author, along with economics, of oppression and violence. That is why the same literacy cannot be, at one and the same time, the means of giving voice to domination and the means of liberating those who are dominated.

Literacy is not an independent, moral personage: it has no existence outwith the atmosphere of human communication. Of its essence it is social, founded in History, and it cannot be idealized, like Justice, Truth, or its sister Beauty. Yet sometimes this is implied, as when we speak of 'the effects of literacy', 'the myth of literacy' or 'the right to literacy'.

In that demythologized view, there is no such thing as 'critical literacy' or 'emancipatory literacy': there are only *people* who are *critically literate*, people who can *engage in a literate way* in their own emancipation, just as there are *people* who are *non-literate or illiterate*. Literacy is an attribute, first of a society and, only by extension, is it taken to be an attribute of an individual.

One might reject this point because it appears to confuse the experiences of a Society with some superordinate element called 'literacy'. However, the argument is intended to illustrate that our current perceptions of the individual, the individual in community, community and the wider society, and society and the State, no matter what period or what culture we might be considering, are so impregnated by literacy and the effects of literacy that we cannot think otherwise. As literates, we cannot begin even to imagine a society which is decontaminated of all trace of literacy. To think 'society' at all is to think, consciously or not, 'literate society'. We are condemned to never being able to get behind literacy to reinvent orality or an oral society.

None the less, in order to assess Freire's pedagogy, we do need some understanding of the starting-point of a learner who has not inhabited our literate world. We do know, for example, that Oral Culture is performance rather than information centred, and knowledge is conveyed, through the drama of epic, narrative and folklore from one generation to the next. Children learn by experience and by practice, not by theory and abstraction. Teaching is task oriented, for only useful knowledge is considered to be proper knowledge. Communication is authentic because all discourse has the immediacy of presence, and because there is no dichotomy between word and action. People in an oral culture have a pictorial view of their world, yet within that they can encompass, and even explain, contradictions, uncertainties and not-knowing. Often there is a directive fatalism that softens or accounts for what otherwise would be the sadness of things. Given that, and because culturally people can live only in the present (there being no Past, only Narrative) those who live in an oral society may live hopefully (full of hope) but they cannot live optimistically. The present world is the best of all possible worlds because it is the only possible world.[5]

This is not to say that hegemony and oppression never existed before literacy: oral cultures have never been thought of, even by the most romantic, as ideal societies somehow marked by the principles of advanced democracy, equality, and social or economic parity. Elitism and segregation, dominance and subservience are factors of both orality and literacy. The difference is that literacy can structure the inequalities which orality could only organize. In a textualized world, power over land, money, life, marriage, over faith, freedom, over government and administration, over individuality and even over memory, all have gained an objectivity and security because each could be justified: Look, here is the written evidence as proof.[6]

In an oral society, force, even where it existed, could only be imposed: it could never be legitimized, or justified. Force was always violence, a violation of the society and/or of the individual. In a literate society, force does not need to be justified: it is written into the very fabric of society by the structures which literacy creates for its own support and protection. The evidence is that there is now no social, economic, political or religious institution that could exist without it.

Freire was presenting this scenario in the Culture Circles: to pretend otherwise is to reinvent literacy, to idealize it. This did not prevent him, however, from disguising this reality in the language of utopianism. He presents the aesthetic values of literacy as part of a bibliocentric culture and spiritual necessity through the very concept of liberating literacy.

If literacy is the means of conscientization, and of the breaking out of the culture of silence, transforming the world and the individual, it is no less than a means of Social Salvation. The image is deliberate, using one of Scribner's (1984) metaphors of literacy. Literacy is deemed to enfold a certain piety, in the religious and classical sense of the word: one has a duty, a responsibility to be cultured, to be educated. In a civilized society, the Book is culturally sacred (Steiner 1972) which is why it is held that the burning of books for political or other ends, for example, is equivalent to a crime against humanity.

The bookish nature of Salvation we have already seen. Freire holds up *The Book* as the symbol of the new world. It represents all that the non-literate is not for, in the eyes of those who are literate, non-literates inhabit a deficit culture. The dominant literate community justifies its sense of superiority by claiming that non-literates are, by definition, intellectually deficient – a view that is still frequently and publicly stated (Penichaut 1990; Olson 1982), despite the increasing evidence to the contrary.

> The notion that literacy per se creates a great divide in intellectual abilities between those who have and those who have not mastered written language is deeply entrenched in the educational circles of industrialized countries. (Scribner 1984: 14)

But if the difference is not cognitive or intellectual, what is the real difference? The answer, cynically, lies in the differential quality of salvation. Although everyone has a universal right to be saved (to be literate), the dominant classes are saved economically and culturally, while the oppressed classes are saved functionally.

The functionality of functional literacy

The root idea of functional literacy has developed with that of Adult Basic Education around the apparent logic that (a) all adults have a right to a basic education, and that (b) literacy is functional. Universal suffrage and pragmatism meld in mutual convenience.

No one would deny the right to functional literacy, without appearing churlish, superior or oppressive. But that itself creates a difficulty: what is basic is deemed to be of value, to be essential, while what is functional is deemed to work or to be effective. The very language around *functional literacy* discourages a critical analysis, and this is shown by the largely unquestioned acceptance of the term.

It was first used by the US Army in the Second World War to categorize those recruits who were 'less than fully literate', that is *illiterates* as defined by 'persons who are incapable of understanding the kinds of written instructions that are needed for carrying out basic military functions or tasks' (Harman 1970: 227). It is not certain, however, whether this really refers to literacy competence or literate performance, the ability to write and read or the ability to behave like literates. One cannot ignore the fact that three to eight years' schooling – the main criteria for assessing literacy levels (Harman 1970; Levine 1982) – also comprises certain behavioural and attitudinal development which might also be essential for the Army.

What should be noted is that, contrary to Harman, schooling and literacy have never been solely about reading and writing. No one has ever learnt to read or write just so that they could read or write: such skills have always served specific functions. In that sense, as a technology of culture and of communication, literacy has only ever been functional. What the expression *functional literacy* draws attention to is not its literateness but its *functionality*. The obvious question which then arises is 'Of what is literacy a function?'

One response is contained in the very definitions which Harman and Levine use without comment. While *illiteracy* is defined as 'the ability to read, write and compute at or above the minimum level of competence', *literacy* is defined

142

as 'the ability to hold a decent job to support self and family, to lead a life of dignity and pride' (Harman 1970).

To the degree that decency, dignity and pride are social values, they illustrate how the map of literacy is drawn by tracing over the values of any given society. Postman (1970) demonstrates this effectively with his allegations that, if you cannot read, you cannot be a 'good citizen'. First, if you cannot read forms, regulations, notices, signs, etc., you cannot be governed, you cannot be an obedient citizen. Second, you cannot be a good consumer, because you are immune to so much advertising and product information. Third, you cannot be a loyal citizen, perhaps the most disturbing allegation, because you will not be sufficiently well read to have imbibed the myths and superstitions of your society. Reading serves the important function of making political and historical myths accessible to students (Postman 1970: 246).

That literacy should be twinned with Citizenship is, of course, not a modern phenomenon, and it underlies the problem which confronted Plato in the *Republic*: how does one decide between the conflicting interests of universal or selective literacy and universal or selective franchise, especially where the former is used to define or control the latter. Citizenship requires that the person is a consumer, politically and economically: citizens consume the products of the market place (for which they need to be literate), plus they consume what governments produce, that is laws and regulations (for which equally they need to be literate).

That is exactly the principle which was defined in Gray's influential report for Unesco (Gray 1956: 24) which was widely accepted as the bench-mark of, and justification for, literacy. A person is functionally literate who 'has acquired the knowledge and skills in reading and writing which enables him or her to engage in all those activities in which literacy is normally assumed in his/her culture or group'.

The 'normally assumed', however, is bi-focal. It is taken as applying to the individual but it actually applies, in the first instance, to the culture or society. It is the society that requires a certain level of literate functioning, that 'assumes' or 'presumes' a given level of literacy. Therefore, in order to find their place in that society, its members need to function in a way that is commensurate with those literate expectations which reflect the societal norms.

These norms are reaffirmed in other ways, as the later development of the idea of functional literacy shows. While the principle of adequate functioning was argued initially during the Second World War in the US Army, it had an immediate, international application after the war as the primary criteria of employability. It became associated with the idea of *Human Capital* which replaced *Knowledge Capital* in the jargon of education and training. It provided the justification for investment both in adult education and in primary/ secondary schooling, because the product of such outlay, in terms of skills, attitudes and behaviour, would result in greater economic profits.[7] It represented a centrifugal force, pushing literacy out from the centre to the margins of society, and was explained in terms of initiatives aimed at integration, reinsertion and rehabilitation.

The effect of this redefining of functional literacy from the centre is not just a reaffirmation of literacy in terms of holding down a job and living with dignity and pride. It acts as a device for defining only the *minimum competencies* required of an individual (that is the individual as worker and citizen) in a print society. In Kozol's words (1985: 185), it is 'mean minded' because it concentrates on coping, on survival. It prefers an inhumane, subsistence literacy to that creative literacy which would enable people to discover, express and develop their humanness.

On the other hand, the aesthetic or more than minimum literacy that Kozol seeks has never been part of mass literacy. Despite the fact that functional literacy is seen as a target standard for both educational and economic development in the Developed World but particularly in the Third World, experience has shown that the more it moves beyond defining the criteria for employment towards defining the criteria for the quality of human life, then the more it is used to assess social and life skills, health education, the family, the community environment, health and nutrition.[8] In other words, functional literacy is used to create discrimination and division: literacy does not function to produce greater democratization, freedom of expression, or a more genuine realization of the power of citizenship. On the contrary, it encourages a move towards the readjusting of the hierarchies of literacy, a realigning of the 'positional economy' which hinges upon literacy.

The positional economy (Hirsch 1977) is based upon the maintenance of differentials, the process of contrived inflation that occurs in a situation where a once scarce resource becomes common and hence devalued. Thus, in the situation where mass literacy or functional literacy becomes the norm, those with more than the basic competencies seek to revalue their own skills, diplomas and qualifications.[9]

Functional literacy provides the base line on which is built the pyramid of literacy that ultimately defines the various echelons of power in a society. That is the true 'legacy of literacy', that 'stresses behaviours and attitudes appropriate to good citizenship and moral behaviour, largely as these are perceived by the elites of the society'.

> Literacy has been used, in age after age, to solidify the social hierarchy, empower elites, and ensure that people lower in the hierarchy accept the values, norms and beliefs of the elites, even when it is not in their self interest (or class interest) to do so. (Gee 1988: 204)

This is more than a Labovian conditioning of what is acceptable language. It is the functioning of literacy as an expression of hegemony. Like subsistence poverty, with which it has much in common, functional literacy is a relative concept, but relative not primarily to the experience of total poverty or destitution, but to the experience of the difference between being 'really wealthy' and being 'comfortable'.[10] As there are those who are *rich*, 'less well off', and *poor*, so there are those who are *highly literate*, functionally literate and *illiterate*. But, as shown by that relativity in the first diagram, functional literacy is a category of literacy and not of illiteracy and is therefore located above the axis of superiority, the social cleavage of illiteracy (Esperandieu 1984: 102).

This, at least, is the conclusion that is to be drawn from the rhetoric which surrounds functional literacy and the objectives which are directed to the integrated functioning of an individual in his or her society.

the very wealthy	the very literate
the less well off	the functionally literate

(the axis of superiority)

the poor	the illiterates

However, if we move beyond the discourse analysis of idealism to an analysis of the *functions* incorporated in functional literacy, then we uncover the reversal of its significance and find what can only be called *symbolic literacy*. This results not from a play on words but from a real relocation of the axis of power, schematically shown in the second diagram.

the very wealthy	the very literate

(the axis of superiority)

the less well off	the functionally literate
the poor	the illiterates

Symbolic literacy then becomes an uncoded term which signifies that functional literacy is actually dysfunctional for illiterates or non-literates but functional for those who are more highly literate. It is this latter group who, because of their position in the economy and because of their cultural superiority, are able literally to define the principles, socially, morally and economically, which those wanting to function in a literate society must accept.

The evidence for this claim is not just the general fact that functional literacy has rarely lived up to the claims made for it, for example in terms of employability, social relations or national, economic development. There is the further, specific argument that, within functional literacy, WRITING has only a minor and very limited role.

The project REALISTIC is not untypical in its prioritizing of *RE*ading, *LIS*tening and arithme*TIC* (Sticht 1972). The influential programme 'Right to Read' in the United States (Allen 1970) which spawned many other functional literacy initiatives in the 1970s and 1980s, clearly also made the diagnosis that the dysfunctioning of the society was related to the large numbers of people who could not read. It was not considered necessary for them to be able to write:

A person is functionally literate when he has command of reading skills that permit him to go about his daily activities successfully on the job, or to move about society normally with comprehension of the usual printed

145

expressions and messages he encounters. (British Association of Settlements 1974: 5)

The inherent sexism in this quotation, noted by Levine (1982: 256) only emphasizes the point already made that functional literacy is doubly dysfunctional for women.

Functional literacy concentrates on Reading because it is in reading the word that one creates the possibility of consensus or convergence. Yet it is only Writing which can create the possibility of dissent. *If I can read, I can follow what you want to say to me. But if I can write, you can read what I want to say to you.* Writing alone raises contradiction – the possibility that something can be 'said against'. This is more than mere disagreement, which obviously can result from reading: it is the creating of a response which is counter-hegemonic. The paradox of Writing, which is one of the most refined symbolic systems created by humankind, is that it has the potential to be anti-symbolic: it is fundamentally iconoclastic.

For the elites, iconoclasm creates the challenge which is experienced by all orthodoxies in that it encourages heresy, even deviance. For them, a literacy which produces a writing of, or a rewriting of, the relationship between knowledge and power becomes dysfunctional for it does not educate the citizen into orthodoxy, into that governability, even that vulnerability to governance and to media and myth, which are the signs of an 'educated person'. In Freire's terms, Reading is the currency of Banking Education, Writing is the currency of Dialogue. The former creates imitation, the latter innovation.

For Freire functional literacy is a contradiction in terms. It creates the silence of the passive reader, the silent receiver who has found their place in society, who has been given entry into the elite's library of knowledge and who therefore may be seen there, but who cannot, or must not, be heard. This is neither the society nor the culture into which he was wanting to introduce the non-literates, for finally and paradoxically, it is this functional literacy which creates the Culture of Silence from which the non-literates are trying to escape.

Literacy, Freire has always said, is about reading the word and the world. Perhaps he should have said that it was about 'Writing the Wor(l)d'. That one lies within the other is now obvious, but this does not explain why, in redefining the obvious, 'writing the word' and 'reading the world' remains the ultimate contradiction of Freire's pedagogy.

Conclusion

Freire's pedagogy has enabled us to deconstruct the dialectic relationship between the Power of Literacy and the Literacy of Power. It is not possible today to live in other than a textualized world: neither Power nor Literacy can be dis-invented. What is possible is to imagine a different con-text within which a different literate text could be written and where Literacy would serve to create a new world, to liberate and not to domesticate. It is a pedagogy which is hopeful, in the strict sense of the word, full of hope. It is also full of contradiction.

'To contradict' does not always mean 'to criticize negatively, to argue against, to put down'. It can also mean 'to put the other side of, to see a contrary view, to affirm by posing the opposite'. In this positive sense, it is a privilege to be able to contradict and to be contradicted, for contradiction widens horizons, permits other perspectives, and creates the possibility of difference. The pedagogy of the oppressed, the *oppressed's pedagogy*, expressed in the narrative of the learners and not in the discourse of the teachers (Ellsworth 1989) thrives on contradiction, exploits it as the ruptural principle which engenders change.

Thus we have seen that conscientization does not bring about literacy, any more than literacy results in conscientization. The one can be used to *describe* the other, but neither can *prescribe* the consequences of critical consciousness. The paradox (the Greek form of contradiction) is that we have to be able to think and speak in a literate way *before* we can become 'literate'. 'Although the fact of writing historically follows the fact of speech, nonetheless the idea of speech depends upon the idea of writing' (Harland 1987: 129). To speak the word, name the world, in Freire's usage, is to be already literate.

We have seen how the very idea of writing the word, reading the word are not two sides of the same literate coin. They represent such antithetical skills and competencies that any attempt to forge a synthesis results in blatant contradiction. What else is Functional Literacy? In this latter case, we found that Literacy was dysfunctional for non-literates and for those becoming literate precisely because Literacy is both the author of the status quo within which the dominant classes are the literate classes, and controller of the means by which those classes express their superiority over those who are non-literate or illiterate.

We have had to ask: does Freire's Method enable the learners of the Culture Circles to become authors, Subjects who name and create their own world? Or does it enable them only to achieve a sufficient level of literacy so that they could be assimilated into their Society, the new generation of *assimilados*? Despite their enthusiasm and capacity to create their own self-preparation for this new citizenship, has their involvement in the literacy campaign already defused, culturally and politically, any real potential movement towards fundamental, social change? Is it not the case that no radical change has ever been ushered in through the ballot box just because the person who made his or her mark on the ballot-sheet was literate?

We have seen that Freire had codified the oppressed culture of the learners, but he seems never to have codified the oppressive culture of the literate educators, except through the one important image of Banking Education. If the reciprocity of dialogue is to be respected, should there not have been some opportunity for the participants of the Culture Circle to ask that the educators reveal a picture-codification which is typical of their lives and culture and that they declare what generative words they use to decode their world?

In the absence of that equilibrating disclosure, more threatening even than the invitation to the educator to undertake class suicide, we have seen how the analysis of Freire's literacy programme shows that the rhetoric which announced the importance of dialogue, engagement, and equality, and denounced silence, massification and oppression, did not match in practice the subliminal messages and modes of a Banking System of education. Albeit benign, Freire's approach differs only in degree, but not in kind, from the system which he so eloquently criticizes.

The genuine difference between the two systems is one of intention, and here Freire's sincerity and personal commitment is not in doubt. This does not disguise the fact, however, that he is at heart a very traditional pedagogue. We have seen how he repossessed the traditional philosophic and religious roots of European education in order to find a language in which he could re-state his own pedagogy. Because of (or in spite of) that, he remains the classic teacher who loves his classroom, even though he professes not to need it (1989: 12). The learner is not just someone who needs to learn: he or she is also someone who needs to be taught. Freire's faith in humankind, perhaps like all faith, prevented him from looking objectively at this fact, but helped him to find what he wanted to find – an enlightened learner who could 'name his or her own world' through dialogue with an enlightened teacher.

The tendency to think of Freire as an abstruse, Latin American educator who was propelled by events to the world stage of education but who there found himself out of his depth, unable to communicate with anyone other than his own North-eastern compatriots, is wholly contradicted by the events. Freire has occupied a pivotal place in the formulation of education campaigns throughout the Third World, and his influence on other European and North American educators has been considerable.

He is an educator of a world-wide university, yet he was, and still is, fiercely Brazilian. The scars of exile will always be there, but he is now, more than a decade later, firmly reintegrated into Brazilian society. He has taken a new lease on life and has begun to place the various texts relating to his own history and his own achievements in a clearer context or perspective. On the face of it, he does not have, and has never had, the profile of a radical, revolutionary educator. Born into a middle-class family, he took the career path through Law, bypassed politics, but continued with little direction until influenced by his wife and by fate to exploit his evident aptitude for teaching. Then he found himself upon the road to Literacy that has brought him, by diverse routes, to his destination as one of the most creative Pedagogues of the twentieth century.

There then emerged, as it were between the lines of his texts and bio-texts, the 'método Paulo Freire' and a problematizing of the obvious: a method, with the genius of simplicity, that actually works but which is deceptive in appearance. Too many people have considered Freire as a purveyor of literacy, whereas in fact he is a politician of pre-literacy. What he may not have admitted to himself is that, while he offered 'Literacy in Thirty Hours' to meet certain felt needs on the part of the peasants and the oppressed, what he was actually doing was confronting the underlying real needs of those individuals and of society. The educator in Freire is not neutral: he has always denied that teachers have the right to self-absolution by claiming such impartiality. But he is not just a pedagogue of the oppressed: he is that most subversive of social radicals, a crypto-politician.

In that sense, his pedagogy is revolutionable, a learning iceberg where what is most important is invisible to the eye. It is what cannot be seen that contradicts the obvious. So Freire's final contradiction is that the pedagogy of this 'Vagabond of the Obvious', as he liked to call himself, is not primarily about literacy, but rather about pre-literacy. It is a pedagogy which places the presence of oppression before the absence of literacy but which also, against the popular logic, insists on treating the effect in order to remedy the cause.

Freire can be easily dismissed for comfortable idealism, utopianism, other-wordly mysticism and irrelevance. Yet beneath that, beneath the Banking system which he has diverted into a Co-operative Banking system, there is a pedagogy of contradiction, which is contradictory because it creates another reality, a critical, practical awareness, an 'I now know where I am in this world-ness' that presages action. It is disturbing, deranging, uncompromising and irreverent. A homeopathic medicine it might be, but its side-effects are considerable.

To want to write the word (pre-literacy) and so learn to read the word (passive literacy) and then to write it (active Literacy) is the goal of Freire's pedagogy. He may not have put it that way, but neither would he now deny it. In reviewing the Texts of Freire, that might not appear to be the case at first glance. That this might emerge only through the intense analysis of this kind of study which has tried 'not just to consume ideas, but to create and recreate them' (1985a: 4) is Freire's way of proving his point and of gainsaying, contradicting his critics. In the end, the fact that many of Literacy's contradictions are now unveiled is Freire's ultimate success. At least now the right questions can be asked.

There is no greater accolade that can be bestowed upon a pedagogue. If the reader of the word and the world can now return to reading the diverse texts of Freire, a new *Dialogue with Freire* can be written. That next volume of the writing of the wor(l)d will not just be another text to be read: together, we can make it a further chapter in the righting of oppression.

Notes

Introduction: the textualizing and contextualizing of Freire

1 It is important to note that these tributes come from other, recognized educators: I. Illich (undated) *Yesterday I Could Not Sleep Because Yesterday I Wrote My Name*, Centre for the Study of Democratic Institutions, Santa Barbara, California, audio-tape; Ohliger (1971: 7); Lovett (1975: 15); McLaren (1986: 394).

2 To appreciate the force of these criticisms, the reader would need to place them in their original contexts: see Jerez and Hernandez-Pico (1971); Knudson (1971); Boston (1972); Colins (1972); Griffith (1974); Egerton (1975); O'Neill (1973); Barndt (1980); R. Mackie (1980); Kidd and Byram (1982).

3 This important point on adjusting the biographical lens owes much to Skinner (1969), whose caution about parochialism, that is 'misdescribing, by a process of historical foreshortening, both the sense and the intended reference of a given work' should also be noted.

4 A useful explanation of the nature of historical understanding (*verstehen*) as an epistemological problem is contained in Hitzler and Keller (1989). Rabinowitz (1977) proposes that one best understands a writer not by examining the authored text (which seeks to identify the author's intentions) but by considering the con-texts, the audiences implicit or explicit in the text.

5 The *emics* and *etics* analysis does not create two standpoints which are dichotomic, but rather two elements which compose a stereographic picture. None the less, this study has emphasized the construction of an *etic* perspective. The method, still little known, has enormous potential in the analysis of textuality. For the definition and application of the *emic/etic* distinction, see Hymes (1964); Headland (1990).

6 The Adult Learning Project in Gorgie-Dalry in Edinburgh is one of the few learning programmes in the United Kingdom which has been committed to putting Freire's ideas into practice. A documented review of their experiences is given in Kirkwood and Kirkwood (1989).

7 Three books by Boal are worth following up to see how Freire's initial insight can be

applied to other forms of teaching/learning: *Theatre of the Oppressed, Stop, its Magic* and *The Rainbow of Desire*.

1 A biographical sketch

1 In Brazil, although there were institutes of higher education from 1808, in Medicine and Law, and a widespread growth in the 1920s of technical colleges and polytechnics which were judged to be essential for economic development, the first universities were founded only in 1934 (São Paulo) and 1935 (Rio de Janeiro). The new *Faculdade de Filosofia, Ciências e Letras* at São Paulo was seen, academically and politically, to be the cornerstone of the university. Its first director, Teodoro Ramos, was sent to Europe to recruit an eminent cadre of professors/academics in the Social Sciences. Eight of the ten were French; the French government contributed to the scheme sufficient books to form the basic libraries in each of the departments (Philosophy, Social Sciences, History, Geography and Humanities). The visiting professors, individually and collectively, had an enormous influence on intellectual life in Brazil. They included Roger Bastide, Claude Lévi-Strauss, Fernand Braudel, Lucien Febvre, Gérard Lebrun and Michel Foucault. See Capelato and Prado (1989).

2 *Pedagogy of the Oppressed* is currently in its eighteenth, twentieth and thirty-fifth editions in Portuguese, English and Spanish respectively.

3 Freyre's *The Masters and the Slaves* first appeared in Portuguese as *Casa-grande e Senzala* in 1933 but was the last of Freyre's major works to be translated into English (1970). Two other important studies, which equally clarify the context of Freire's work at that time, had already been translated: *The Mansions and the Shanties* (1963), and 'The Patriarchal Basis of Brazilian Society', in J. M. Maier (ed.) (1964) *The Politics of Change in Latin America*, New York, Praeger.

4 An outline of the work and function of the *Comunidades Eclesiales de Base* can be found in Ferndandes (1985). Behind these changes can be heard the powerful voices of Jacques Maritain and Gustavo Gutierrez whose works were well known to Freire. For a useful summary of the emergence of Latin American social or liberation theology, see Chopp (1986).

5 The practice of small group, community-based learning is so widespread that its origins are difficult to trace. Brookfield (1984: 90) traces the existence of such groups, prior to their widespread use in the US labour movement of the 1920s, to the Juntos proposed by Franklin in 1727, the Lyceum Movement in the 1820s and the Settlements in England in the 1880s. Hall (1978) finds Workers' Circles well established in St Petersburg in 1887, and Study Circles in Sweden effective from the turn of the century. Spies-Bong (1989) highlights the key role of the Learning Circle in Petersen's 1927 'Iena Plan'.

6 There is some confusion over this doctorate. Jerez and Hernandez-Pico (1971: 499), who are right on other details, say that Freire was awarded a doctorate *Honoris Causa* from the university because of the success of his education programme, and that it was this doctorate that enabled Freire to teach in the university: 'Cuando su filosofía y sus programas educacionales le habían hecho ya famoso en gran parte de Brasil, la Universidad de Recife le otorgó el grado de Doctor Honoris Causa en Pedagogía. Desde entonces enseño filosofía de la educacíon en dicha universidad.'

7 For an absorbing and enthusiastic account of the Cuban Literacy Programme which captures the excitement and achievement of what it means to become literate, see Kozol (1978).

8 More than a quarter of a century later, the level of schooling in Brazil is still a major problem. Braslavsky (1988) suggests that 30 per cent of all children aged 7–14

(7,553,741) are not receiving a full-time education, a figure confirmed by Freire in his recent role as Secretary for Education (1991: 17).

9 It is difficult to reproduce in English the power of the expression *tomada de consciencia*. As in the French *prise de conscience*, the verb is as important as the noun: conscience, consciousness or awareness. *Tomar* and *prendre* have that added sense of 'taking, taking seriously, taking possession of' which signifies both a conscious, responsible act and an identifiable result or consequence.

10 It is interesting to note that, later, immediately after the successful, US-backed coup against Allende, General Pinochet declared Freire *persona non grata* in Chile (R. Mackie 1980).

11 The influence of his current work, through teaching and through directing post-graduate studies, is explicit in Braslavsky (1988) and in the review by Francisco Gomes de Matos (1989) of eight recent, Brazilian publications on literacy.

12 Interesting, for the point of authorship versus status, is the fact that the book is commonly attributed to Freire, although the copyright actually belongs to Shor.

13 This is the book cited twice in Freire (1987b: 62, 114). Although a footnote is numbered in the text, no reference is actually given.

14 Araujo Freire, Ana Maria (1989) *Analfabetismo no Brasil*, Cortex Editora, INEP.

2 Backgrounds and borrowings: a review of selected sources and influences

1 The English text gives no reference: the French text quotes an English version of Goldman's (1969) *The Human Sciences and Philosophy*, but nuances 'mechanistic change' by translating it 'la transformation de la réalité peut s'opérer auto-matiquement'. Freire (1985a: 32) again refers to Goldman's transition of consciousness, but quotes an undated Spanish translation: *Las Ciencias humanas y la filosofia*.

2 See Petersen (1965). A more recent résumé of the main points of the Plan, plus a synthesis of other of Petersen's writings, is to be found in Spies-Bong (1989).

3 This affirmation has to be placed within the traditional teaching of the Church on social issues. On the condition of the working classes, the Papal Encyclical *Rerum Novarum* (May 1891) had stated: 'The transference of property from private individuals to the community is emphatically unjust' (para 3). This argument had been used to deny land reforms in Brazil and the breaking up of the large *latifundia*. Forty years later, *Quadragesimo Anno* (1931) reaffirmed these principles and made it clear that 'no catholic could subscribe even to moderate Socialism'. Even as late as 1961, *Mater et Magistra: New Light on Social Problems [sic]* was stating that 'The permanent validity of the Catholic Church's social teaching admits of no doubt' (para 218).

The Catholic Church was far from the position of liberal Protestantism as evidenced by Paul Tillich: 'First and foremost I owe to Marx an insight into the ideological character not only of idealism but also of all systems of thought, religious and secular which serve power structures and thus prevent . . . a more just organisation of reality' (Tillich 1973).

4 While this expression clearly echoes Teilhard, it is actually a reference to Mounier's *Be Not Afraid*, here quoted from an English version (1954). Earlier (p. 12), Freire refers to a French edition of 'Le christianisme et la notion de progrès' in *La Petite Peur du XX Siècle*.

It is interesting to note the re-emergence of a *leitmotif* which lies deep in Freire's psyche and which is reflected in a short bibliography of his references: Mounier's *Be not Afraid*, Tillich's *The Courage To Be*, Fromm's *The Fear of Freedom* and *To Have and To Be*, and Sartre's *Being and Nothingness*.

5 De Kadt (1970: 90ff) details Mounier's influence on the Church and on Brazilian intellectuals. Mounier stressed the importance of interpersonal relations, and brought a Christian–Marxist analysis to bear on society and injustice. However, he saw change primarily as a process which concerned the individual and he made little analysis of institutions of power and oppression. None the less, his demand for authenticity had to imply some measure of social change, simply because a society could not be authentic if the poor and the marginalized remained oppressed.

A Portuguese translation of Mounier's *Le Personalisme* was available from 1964: *O personalisme*, Lisbon, trans. Joåo Bénard da Costa.

6 It is the whole fabric and concept of *Pedagogy of the Oppressed* which is rooted in Personalism, although it is easy to find particular quotations which sound like direct translations. For example, 'The movement of enquiry must be directed towards humanization – our historical vocation' (Freire 1982: 58). 'Dialogue (Engagement) involves critical thinking, thinking which discerns an indivisible solidarity between the world and humankind admitting no dichotomy between them' (1982: 64). 'Intervention in reality – historical awareness itself – thus represents a step forward from emergence' (1982: 81).

7 The quotation also highlights the problem of translation. The English edition of *Pedagogy of the Oppressed* carries the footnote 'in English, the terms *to live* and *to exist* have assumed implications opposite to their etymological origins. As used here, *live* is the more basic term, implying only survival; *exist* implies a deeper involvement in the process of *becoming*.' The footnote does not appear in the Portuguese or French editions. Exactly the same footnote had already been used in the English edition of *Education: The Practice of Freedom*.

The problem lies in the use of *viver* and *exister* in Portuguese, *estar* and *ser* in Spanish, *sein* and *leben* in German, the contrary use of *to be* and *to exist* in English, and the confused use of *être* and *exister* in French. There is therefore a double process of interpretation underpinning the translation of Freire into English which also operated when Freire was trying to understand, for example, Heidegger's concept of *in-der-welt-Sein* through an English translation.

8 Teilhard de Chardin played an important role in shaping Catholic intellectualism in the early 1960s, particularly prior to the Vatican Council. His central tenet, as a scientist and palaeontologist, was that humankind is progressing to its goal, its Omega point, of complete socialization (1965: 334). As such, we are all in a state of becoming (p. 13), incomplete human beings seeking out our own personalization or humanization (p. 192).

A Spanish edition of his major work, *El Fenómeno humano*, Madrid, Taurus, was available in Brazil from 1963. It is this text which Freire quotes in 'Notes on Humanization and its Educational Implications' (1970m).

9 Freire to some extent demystifies Teilhard, preferring in this case to speak of encircling proximity as *limit situations*, 'the real boundaries where all possibilities begin' (Freire 1982: 71). *Thinking the world* is analogous both to *naming the world*, speaking the word to transform reality (Freire 1970h: 213) and to the process whereby 'There is no longer "I think" but "We think". The object is not the end of the act of thinking, but the mediator of communication' (Freire 1976b: 135). The *process of complexification* is exactly the applied technique of *problematizing*: 'If education is the relation between Subjects in the knowing process, then it must be *problem posing*' (Freire 1976b: 150).

10 Kosik was one of the few survivors of the Czech Resistance during the Second World War. He was arrested by the Gestapo and deported to a concentration camp. After

the liberation, he completed his studies at Prague and later at Leningrad but re-turned to Prague to take up a post from 1962 as Professor of Philosophy. After his dismissal from the university in 1968, his house was raided by the police and much of his private work, notes and lecture materials were confiscated.

11 Perhaps because Kosik is not given as a reference to clarify this expression, the translation of this text in *The Politics of Education* misses Kosik's (and Freire's) point about the symbiotic nature of action and reflection. Therefore, 'Like our presence in the world, our consciousness transforms knowledge, *acting on and thinking about what enables us to reach the stage of reflection*' (1985a: 100, my emphasis added) is ultimately an inadequate translation.

12 Freire's references to C. Wright Mills date from this period and may well have come through Kosik (see Freire 1982: 83; 1985a: 4). The method which Freire en-couraged the field investigators to use their collecting of generative themes, namely registering every detail in notebooks, is a technique proposed by Wright Mills in his *Sociological Imagination*. This source is acknowledged by Freire in the French and Portuguese versions of the *Pedagogy*, but the reference both in the text and as a footnote is missing from the English version.

13 This is Freire's underlying model of the relationship between oppressor and op-pressed (1982: 16, 26, 46). Confirmation of Freire's possible encounter with Hegel's *Phenomenology* in 1967 is that *Education: The Practice of Freedom*, which was written early in 1967, also contains the important image of master–slave. Here, however, the theme is taken from Gilberto Freyre's detailed, historical study (1963) *The Mansion and the Shanties* (see Freire 1976b: 25) and not from Hegel's intellectualizing.

3 Education and liberation: the means and ends of Dialogue and Conscientization

1 Berger (1975: 34, 35) is dismissive of the arrogance of Conscientization as 'con-sciousness raising'. This is a 'project of higher class individuals directed at a lower class population who are in need of enlightenment. Put differently, the concept allocates different levels to "them" and to "us", and it assigns to "us" the task of raising "them" to the higher level.' For Berger, 'a better term would be conversion, and anyone claiming to raise the consciousness of other people should be seen as a missionary'.

2 The Church's failure to distinguish Marxism from atheistic communism has vit-iated this debate which was only gradually opened up by South American theo-logians and intellectuals who needed, more and more, an alternative paradigm with which to analyse society, to reconstruct a valid, historical and sociological per-spective, and to explore new political options. Chopp (1986: 16) offers a useful résumé which does not diminish the felt risk and threat to the Church in those first steps into the Christian–Marxist dialogue: 'Marxism is as much a general attitude emphasising the historical and transformative nature of all actions and reflection as it is a specific political structure or set of philosophical assumptions'.

3 Although Freire knew Heidegger's *Sein und Zeit*, he does not exploit the concept of *in der welt sein* which would have clarified the social and temporal, and therefore historical, construct of our existence. Instead, Freire is still confined by his vision of that other-worldliness offered by Christianity, and by the believers' compromise between being 'in the world but not of it'.

4 This is an assertion which has evaded many of Freire's critics and followers alike. Ewert (1981) is perhaps typical of many: 'Unlike many of his colleagues, Freire has

explicitly addressed the problem of exploitative social structures: his educative strategy amounts to a call for revolution'.

4 The 'Método Paulo Freire': generative words and generating literacy

1 Fernandes (1985) illustrates how these groups were used by the CEB for political goals. 'The political consciousness-raising of the CEBs has contributed to a significant increase in the strength of popular grass roots movements. The CEBs strengthen internal democratic participation that values each human being and brings forth his or her full potential as an agent of change.'

2 Ewert (1981) says that, in his experience, the co-ordinators were often forced to adopt a parent–child relationship simply because they were considered to be there in order to solve the communities' problems. Nevertheless, Ewert is clear that 'Freire's concept of codifications has tremendous conceptual power for transforming perspectives and providing hope in the face of dominance' (1981: 32).

3 *Mangue*, which appears in two lists, illustrates the problem of taking the read word out of the context in which it was written. It has both an agricultural and an urban connotation, giving at least two possible decodings in a Culture Circle: it is a swamp or marsh, but it also refers to the 'red light' district of the city of Rio (Sanders 1968).

4 Le Men (1985) raises a parallel point in questioning the use of alphabetic learning: '*Seeing* letters is an obstacle to reading. The Alphabet is not made for reading but for being heard and spoken'. She contrasts synthetic literacy, that builds up words from individual syllables which in themselves have no meaning, and analytic literacy which is based on recognition of whole words which are given meaning by the reader.

5 Le Men (1985) argues that this analytic method of whole word recognition, which was current even in the fifteenth and sixteenth centuries, found little favour among educationalists because it is based more on intuition and memory rather than on logic and repetitive learning. It is not without significance that the latter are more controllable and examinable than the former.

6 A reconstruction of literacy

1 Reflecting this disparity of approach, Nickerson (1985) notes that the lack of significant progress towards literacy has not been the result of lack of attention. Quoting Weber (1975), he points out that, in the United States, some ten major federal agencies were authorized by nearly thirty laws to teach reading to adults, while more than six hundred non-governmental agencies were engaged in adult basic education. In a national guide to literacy facilities, Kadavy *et al.* (1983) lists thirty-nine national literacy programmes and several thousand state-level resources.

2 For an example of French and Spanish usage of these terms, see Jerez and Hernandez-Pico (1971); Roman (1990).

3 The word seems to have first been used by the ATD-Quart monde in the 1960s, and passed into widespread usage in the 1980s. See Fondet (1990). *Le Robert* Dictionary quotes a 1983 usage of *illettrisme*: 'état de ceux qui sont illettrés', and defines *illettré* as 'qui est *partiellement* incapable de lire et d'écrire'. It is worth noting that in current French usage *lettré* retains the high cultural values of 'literate' in English: 'qui a des lettres, de la culture, du savoir', for which the synonyms given are *cultivé* and *érudit*.

4 In his review of the proceedings of the International Symposium for Literacy which was held at Persepolis, Iran, Bataille (1976) confirms Unesco's commitment to literacy as a universal, human right. Its programme *Education for All* (1984) was

modelled on a similarly argued programme within the World Health Organization (WHO), *Health for All*. The WHO had proposed, following its conference on primary health care in Alma Ata (USSR), in 1978, a programme of basic health care to achieve 'a more equitable distribution of health resources throughout the world'. Unesco aimed to achieve a more equitable distribution of educational resources, and both programmes state as their aim 'to enable all people to lead a life which was socially and economically productive'.

See Organisation Mondiale de la Santé (1987) *Evaluation de la stratégie de la santé pour tous d'ici à 2000* Vol. 1, OMS, Genève; Unesco (1984) *Projet de plan à moyen terme, 1984–1989*, Programme II.1, Généralisation de l'Intensification de la lutte contra l'analphabétisme, Paris, Unesco.

5 This summary of the main traits of Orality that echoes of the anthropological approach of Lévi-Strauss and Malinowski with which Freire was familiar. Obviously the main source is Ong (1988). It is to be hoped that the summary is not a total injustice to his influential book.

6 A detailed exposé of all these elements can be found in Goody (1986), albeit that he considers literacy primarily from a technological rather than a teleological perspective, with little analysis of literacy as Power-Force.

7 For a detailed, economic development of this point, see Becker (1975) and Blaug (1966).

8 'Framework for Action', Appendix 2 of the Final Report (1990) *Education for All*, Jomtien, New York, Unicef, p. 54.

9 An interesting study of 'qualification inflation' can be found in Dore (1976) where he shows how the social justifications for schooling changed through the process which related quantitatively measurable educational achievement to both social mobility and employability.

10 The correlation between poverty and illiteracy is made explicitly in the report of ATD Quart-Monde (1980) *Données sur l'illetrisme: le cas français*, Paris, Pierrelaye.

Bibliography: Part A

Selected works of Paulo Freire

1959   *Educacåo e Actualidade Brasileira*. Doctoral Dissertation, Récifé University, Récifé.

1961 a: *A Propósito de Uma Administracåo*. Imprensa Universitaria, Récifé.

      b: 'Escola Primaria para o Brasil', *Revista Brasileira de Estudios Pedagogicos* 35: 82, 15–33.

1964   'Conscientizacåo e Alfabetizacåo', *Estudos Universitarios*, 4, 5–24.

1965   'Alfabetizacíon de Adultos y Conscientizacíon', *Mensaje*, 142, 494–501.

1967   *Educação como Prática de Liberdade*. Paz e Terra, Rio de Janeiro.

1968 a: *Educação e Conscientização: Extensionismo Rural*. CIDOC, Cuernavaca.

      b: 'Contribucíon al Processo de Conscientizacíon en America Latina', *Cristianismo Y Sociedad*, Suplémento.

      c: *Cultural Action and Conscientization*. Santiago, Unesco.

      d: 'La Concepcíon bancaria de la educacíon y la dehumanizacíon: la concepcíon problematizadora de la educacíon y la humanizacíon, *Seminario ISAL*, May, Document No 3.

      e: 'La Méthode d'alphabetisation des adultes', *Communautés*, 23, 13–29.

      f: *La alfabetizacíon funcional en Chile*. Paris, Unesco.

1969 a: 'Consideracíones criticas en torno el acto de estudiar', *Pastoral Popular*, 110, 41–8.

      b: *Sobre la Accion Cultural*. Santiago, ICIRA.

      c: *1968 Annual Report: Agrarian Reform Training and Research Institute*. Santiago, ICIRA.

      d: 'Accion Cultural Liberadora', *Vispera*, 10, 23–8.

      e: *Extensíon y Communicacíon*. Santiago, ICIRA.

1970 a: *Pedagogy of the Oppressed*. New York, Herder & Herder.

      b: 'Cultural Freedom in Latin America', in L. M. Colonnese (ed.) *Human Rights and Liberation of Man in the Americas*. Notre Dame, Notre Dame University Press.

      c: *Cultural Action and Conscientizacåo*. Washington, Catholic Inter American Cooperation Programme.

d: *The Real Meaning of Cultural Action*. Lecture at CIDOC, Cuernavaca, Mexico, January, CIDOC, Doc. 70/216.

e: 'Education as Cultural Action', in L. M. Colonnese (ed.) *Conscientization for Liberation*. Washington, USCC.

f: *Cultural Action: A Dialectic Analysis*, Cuernavaca, CIDOC.

g: 'Witness to Liberation', in *Seeing Education Whole*. Geneva, World Council of Churches.

h: 'The Adult Literacy Process as Cultural Action for Freedom', *Harvard Educational Review*, 40: 3, 205–25.

i: 'Cultural Action and Conscientization', *Harvard Educational Review*, 40: 3, 452–77.

j: *Cultural Action for Freedom*. Cambridge, Mass., *Harvard Educational Review* Monograph.

k: 'Development and Educational Demands', *World Christian Education*, 3, 125–6.

l: 'Politische Alphabetisierung: Einführung ins Konzept einer humanisierenden Bildung', *Lutherische Monatshefte*, October.

m: 'Notes on Humanization and its Educational Implications', from the seminar *Tomorrow Began Yesterday*, Rome, Education International.

n: 'Education for Awareness', *Risk*, 6: 4, 7–19.

o: 'Letter to a Young Theology Student', *Perspectivas de Dialogo*, December.

1971 a: 'A Few Notions about the Word Conscientization', *Hard Cheese*, 1, 23–8.

b: 'To the Co-ordinator of a Cultural Circle', *Convergence*, 4: 1, 61–2.

c: 'Conscientizar para Liberar', *Contacto* 8: 1, 42–52.

d: 'Conscientizing as a Way of Liberating', LADOC, II, 29a, April.

e: *Knowledge is a Critical Appraisal of the World*, CERES, *FAO Review*, 4: 3, 46–55.

f: 'By Learning They can Teach', *Studies in Adult Education*, No 2, University of Dar Es Salaam.

1972 a: *Cultural Action for Freedom*, Harmondsworth, Penguin.

b: 'Education: Domestication or Liberation', *Prospects*, 2: 2, 173–81 (see also 1975b).

c: 'The Role of the Church in Latin America', LADOC III.

1973 a: 'Education, Liberation and the Church', *Study Encounter*, 9: 1.

b: 'Conscientization and Liberation'. Interview at the Institute of Cultural Action, Geneva, IDAC, Doc. 1.

1974 a: 'Research methods', *Literacy Discussion*, 5: 1, 133–42.

b: 'The Adult Literacy Process as Cultural Action for Freedom', *Literacy Discussion*, 5: 1, 63–92.

c: Transcript of lecture at the *Consultations* at Cartigny, Switzerland, 28 October, World Council of Churches, Geneva.

d: *Education for Critical Consciousness*. London, Sheed & Ward.

e: 'Conscientization and Liberation', *Communio Viatorum*, 3, 110–22.

1975 a: 'The Pedagogy of Liberation', in J. M. Rich (ed.) *Innovations in Education: Reformers and their Critics*. Boston, Mass., Allyn & Bacon.

b: 'Education: Domestication or Liberation', in I. Lister (ed.), *Deschooling*, Cambridge University Press (see also 1972b).

c: 'Education for Liberation', *One World*, July.

d: *Are Adult Literacy Programmes Neutral?*, International Symposium for Literacy, Persepolis, 3–8 September. Ref. Eng/SIPA/10.

e: *An Invitation to Conscientization and Deschooling*. Geneva, World Council of Churches.

1976 a: 'Literacy and the Possible Dream', *Prospects*, 6: 1, 68–71.

b: *Education: The Practice of Freedom*. London, Writers and Readers Co-operative.

c: 'Notions about the Word "Conscientisation"', in R. Dale (ed.) *Schooling and Capitalism*. Milton Keynes, Open University Press, 224–7.

1978   *Pedagogy in Process: The Letters to Guinea-Bissau*. London, Writers and Readers Co-operative.

1979   'To Know and To Be', *Indian Journal of Youth Affairs*, June.

1980   'Letters to a Young Nation'. Extract from a Handbook for Literacy Workers, Co-ordinating Commission of the Popular Culture Circles of the Republic of São Tomé and Princípe.

1981   'The People Speak Their Word Learning to Read and Write in São Tomé and Príncipe, *Harvard Educational Review*, 51: 1, 27–30.

1982   *Pedagogy of the Oppressed*, Harmondsworth, Penguin, from the 1972 edition, translated by Myra Bergman Ramos.

1983 a: 'You have the Third World inside You', *Convergence*, 16: 4, 32–7.

b: *A propos of Education*. Rio de Janeiro, Paz e Terra, co-written with Sergio Guimaroes.

1985 a: *The Politics of Education: Culture, Power and Liberation*. London, Macmillan. Translated by Donaldo Macedo with an introduction by Henry Giroux.

b: *Essa escola chamada vida*, co-written with Frei Betto.

1987 a: *A Pedagogy of Liberation: Dialogues on Transforming Education*. London, Macmillan, co-written with Ira Shor.

b: *Literacy: Reading and Word and the World*. South Hadley, Mass., Bergin & Garvey, co-written with Donaldo Macedo.

1988   *Pedagogia do Oprimido*. Rio de Janeiro, Paz e Terra, 18a edicão.

1989   *Learning to Question: A Pedagogy of Liberation*. New York, Continuum, co-written with Antonio Faundez.

1990   'I Momenti della Pratica Educativa' *La Scuola*, Universita di Bologna, febbraio/marzo.

1991   *L'Education dans la ville*. Paris, Païdeia.

Bibliography: Part B

Bibliographic references

Alinsky, S. (1973) *Rules for Radicals*. New York, Vintage Press
Allen, J. E. (1970) 'Right to read: Target for the 1970s', *School and Society*, 98, 82–4.
Althusser, L. (1969) *For Marx*. London, Allen Lane.
Andrade, M. de (1980) 'Introduction', in A. Cabral, *Unity and Struggle*. London, Heinemann, African Writers Series.
Araujo Freire, A.-M. (1989) *Analfabetismo no Brasil*. Cortez Editora, INEP.
Arendt, H. (1958) *The Human Condition*. Chicago, University of Chicago Press.
Arendt, H. (1970) *On Violence*. New York, Harcourt-Brace.
Arendt, H. (1985) *On Revolution*. Harmondsworth, Penguin.
Armstrong, K. (1977) *Masters of their Own Destiny: A Comparison of the Thought of Coady and Freire*. Vancouver, University of British Columbia, Occasional Papers, 13.
ATD Quart-Monde (1980) *Données sur l'illettrisme: le cas français*. Paris, Pierralaye.
Bakhtin, M. (1981) *The Dialogic Imagination*. Austin, University of Texas Press.
Barndt, D. (1980) *Education and Social Change: A Photographic Study of Peru*. Iowa, Kendall Hunt.
Barthes, R. (1960) 'Histoires et littérature: à propos de Racine', *Annales*, 15, 524–37.
Bataille, L. (1976) *A Turning Point for Literacy*. Oxford, Pergamon Press.
Becker, G. S. (1975) *Human Capital*. New York, Columbia University Press.
Bee, B. (1980) 'The politics of literacy', in R. Mackie (ed.), *Literacy and Revolution: The Pedagogy of Paulo Freire*. London, Pluto Press.
Berger, P. L. (1975) 'The false consciousness of consciousness raising', *Worldview*, 33–8.
Bernstein, B. (1970) 'Education cannot compensate for society', *New Society*, 26 February.
Berthoff, A. (1987) 'Foreword', in P. Freire and D. Macedo, *Literacy: Reading the Word and the World*. South Hadley, Mass., Bergin & Garvey.
Betto, F. (1981) *¿O Que é Comunidade de base?* São Paulo, Editora Brasiliense.
Blaug, M. (1966) 'Literacy and economic development', *School Review*, 74, 393–418.
Boal, A. (1980a) *Théâtre de l'opprimé*. Paris, Maspero.
Boal, A. (1980b) *Stop! C'est magique*. Paris, Hachette.

Boal, A. (1990) *La méthode Boal de théâtre et de thérapie: l'arc en ciel du désir*. Paris, Ramsay.

Boston, B. (1972) 'Notes of a loving critic', in S. Grabowski (ed.), *Paulo Freire: A Revolutionary Dilemma for the Adult Educator*. New York, ERIC Clearing House.

Bourdieu, P. (1971) 'Systems of education and systems of thought', in M. F. D. Young, *Knowledge and Control*. London, Macmillan.

Bourdieu, P. (1984) *Questions de sociologie*. Paris, Editions de Minuit.

Bourdieu, P. and Passeron, C. (1970) *La Réproduction*. Paris, Editions de Minuit.

Bowers, C. A. (1985) *Elements of a Post-Liberal Theory of Education*. New York, Teachers College Press.

Bowles, S. and Gintis, S. (1976) *Schooling in Capitalist America*. London, Routledge & Kegan Paul.

Braslavsky, C. (1988) *Alternativas de alfabetización en América Latina y el Caribe*. Santiago, Unesco-OREALC.

British Association of Settlements (1974) *A Right to Read*. London, Author.

Brookfield, S. (1984) *Adult Learners, Adult Education and the Community*. Milton Keynes, Open University Press.

Brookfield, S. (1986) 'Media power and the development of media literacy: An adult educational interpretation', *Harvard Educational Review*, 56(2), 151–70.

Brown, C. (1974) 'Literacy in 30 hours: Paulo Freire's process in NE Brazil', *Social Policy*, 5(2), 25–32.

Cabral, A. (1975) *Unité et Lutte*, Vol.1. Paris, Gallimard, Cahiers Libres.

Cabral, A. (1980) *Unity and Struggle*. London, Heinemann, African Writers Series.

Camara, H. (1969) *The Church and Colonialism*. London, Sheed & Ward.

Capelato, M. and Prado, M. (1989) 'A l'origine de la collaboration universitaire franco-brésilienne', *Préfaces*, July, 100–5.

Cardenal, F. and Miller, V. (1981) 'Nicaragua 1980: the battle of the ABC's', *Harvard Educational Review*, 21(2), 163–75.

Carr, W. (1987) 'What is an educational practice?', *Journal of Philosophy of Education*, 21(2), 163–75.

Castro, J. de (1952) *The Geography of Hunger*. Boston, Little, Brown.

Castro, J. de (1969) *Death in the North-east*. New York, Vintage.

Catholic Bishops of Northeast Brazil (1973) *Eu Ouvi os Clamores do meu Povo*. Pastoral Letter, Salvador, Editora Beneditina, 6 May.

Chartier, A. and Hébrard, J. (1989) *Discours sur la lecture (1880–1980)*. Paris, Services des Etudes.

Chopp, R. (1986) *The Praxis of Suffering*. Maryknoll, New York, Orbis Press.

Claparède, E. (1973) *L'éducation fonctionnelle*. Neuchâtel, Delachaux et Niestlé.

Colins, C. (1972) 'Man names the world: A study of Freire's theory of knowledge and its relationship to adult literacy'. Unpublished paper, Toronto, Ontario Institute for Studies in Education.

Collins, D. (1977) *Paulo Freire: His Life, Works and Thought*. New York, Paulist Press.

Costigan, M. (1983) 'You have the Third World inside you: A conversation with Paulo Freire', *Convergence*, 16(4), 32–7.

Descartes, R. (1960) *Discourse on Method*. Harmondsworth, Penguin Classics.

Dore, R. (1976) *The Diploma Disease*. London, Unwin.

Drummond, T. (1975) *Using the Freire Method in Nutrition Education: An Experimental Plan for Community Action in Northeast Brazil*. New York, Cornell International Monograph Series.

Duiguid, L. H. (1970) 'Brazil wages two-pronged war on illiteracy', *Washington Post*, 20 December.

Dunn, E. (1971) *Economic and Social Development: A Process of Social Learning*. Baltimore, Johns Hopkins University Press.

Egerton, J. (1975) 'Searching for Freire' in J. M. Rich, *Innovations in Education: Reformers and their Critics*. Boston, Allyn and Bacon.

Elias, J. (1972) 'Adult literacy education in Brazil, 1961–1964: método Paulo Freire', Unpublished paper.

Elias, J. (1974) 'Social learning and Paulo Freire', *The Journal of Educational Thought*, 8(1), 5–14.

Elias, J. (1976a) 'Paulo Freire: Religious educator', *Religious Education*, 71(1), 40–56.

Elias, J. (1976b) *Conscientising and Deschooling*. Philadelphia, Westminster Press.

Ellsworth, E. (1989) 'Why doesn't this feel empowering? Working through the repressive myths of critical pedagogy', *Harvard Educational Review*, 59(5), 297–324.

Esperandieu, V. (1984) *Des illettrés en France*. Paris, Documentation française.

Ewert, D. E. (1981) 'Proverbs, parables and metaphors: Applying Freire's concept of codification to Africa', *Convergence*, 14(1), 32–42.

Fanon, F. (1965) *The Wretched of the Earth*. Harmondsworth, Penguin.

Fernandes, L. (1985) 'Basic Ecclesiastic communities in Brazil', *Harvard Educational Review*, 55(1), 76–85.

Fondet, C. (1990) *Vaincre l'illettrisme*. Paris, ATD Quart-Monde, Editions Science et Service.

Foucault, M. (1969) *L'archéologie du savoir*. Paris, Gallimard.

Foucault, M. (1970) *The Order of Things: An Archaeology of the Human Sciences*. London, Tavistock.

Freinet, C. (1968) *La méthode naturelle*. Neuchâtel, Delachaux.

Freyre, G. (1974) *Maîtres et esclaves: la formation de la société brésilienne*. Paris, Gallimard.

Fromm, E. (1978) *To Have and To Be*. London, Abacus.

Fromm, E. (1989) *The Fear of Freedom*. London, Arc-Routledge.

Fuglesang, A. (1973) *Applied Communication in Developing Countries*. Uppsala, The Dag Hammarskjöld Foundation.

Furtado, C. (1965) *Diagnosis of the Brazilian Crisis*. London, Cambridge University Press.

Furter, P. (1974) 'On the greatness of being utopian', *Literacy Discussions*, 5(1), 117–24.

Gee, J. P. (1988) 'The legacies of literacy: from Plato to Freire through Harvey Graff', *Harvard Educational Review*, 58(2), 195–212.

Gerassi, J. (ed.) (1971) *Camilo Torres, Revolutionary Priest*. Harmondsworth, Pelican Latin American Library.

Gerhardt, H. P. (1979) *Zur Theorie und Praxis Paulo Freires in Brasilien*. Frankfurt am Main, Gerhardt.

Gerhardt, H. P. (1989) 'Pourquoi l'alphabétisation? Pluralité des approches culturelles', *Perspectives*, 19(4), 535–51.

Giroux, H. (1989) *Schooling for Democracy: Critical Pedagogy in the Modern Age*. London, Routledge.

Goldman, L. (1969) *The Human Sciences and Philosophy*. London, Jonathan Cape.

Goody, J. (1986) *The Logic of Writing*. London, Cambridge University Press.

Grabowski, S. M. (ed.) (1972) *Paulo Freire: A Revolutionary Dilemma for the Adult Educator*. New York, ERIC Clearing House.

Graff, H. (1987a) *The Legacies of Literacy: Continuities and Contradictions in Western Culture and Society*. Bloomington, Indiana University Press.

Graff, H. (1987b) *The Labyrinths of Literacy*. London, Falmer Press.

Gray, W. S. (1956) *The Teaching of Reading and Writing*. Paris, Unesco.

Griffith, W. (1974) 'Paulo Freire: Utopian perspectives in literacy education for revolution', *Literacy Discussion*, 5(1), 93–116.

Habermas, J. (1970) 'Towards a theory of communicative competence', *Inquiry*, 13(4), 360–76.

Hall, B. L. (1978) 'Continuity in adult education', *Convergence*, 11(1), 8–14.

Harland, R. (1987) *Superstructuralism*. London, Methuen.
Harman, D. (1970) 'Illiteracy: An overview', *Harvard Educational Review*, 40(2), 226–43.
Harman, D. (1971) 'Methodology for revolution', *Saturday Review*, 19 June.
Haviland, R. (1973) 'An introduction to the writings of Paulo Freire', *Adult Education*, 45(5), 280–5.
Headland, T. (ed.) (1990) *Emics and Etics*. New York, Sage: Frontiers of Anthropology, 7.
Heath, S. B. (1985) 'Being literate in America: a socio-historical perspective', in J. Niles and R. Lalik (eds), *Issues in Literacy: A Research Perspective*. Rochester, New York, The National Reading Conference, Inc.
Heath, S. B. (1986) 'Literacy and language change' in D. Tannen (ed.), *Language and Linguistics*. Washington, Georgetown University Press.
Hegel, G. F. (1892) *Philosophy of History*. London, Dover Publications.
Hegel, G. F. (1967) *The Phenomenology of Mind*. London, Harper & Row.
Heidegger, M. (1978) *Being and Time*. Oxford, Blackwell.
Hirsch, F. (1977) *Social Limits to Growth*. London, Routledge & Kegan Paul.
Hitzler, R. and Keller, R. (1989) 'On sociological and common sense *Verstehen*', *Current Sociology*, 37(1), 91–101.
Hymes, D. (1964) 'Towards ethnographies of communication', *American Anthropology*, 66(6), 1–34.
Jerez, C. and Hernandez-Pico, J. (1971) 'Paulo Freire y la educacion: accion cultural liberadora', *Estudios Centro Americanos*, 26(274), 498–539.
Jesus, C. M. de (1970) *Beyond All Pity*. London, Panther Modern Society.
Kadavy, R., Moore, C. and Hunzeker, D. (1983) *Reducing Functional Illiteracy*. Lincoln, NE: Contact Literacy Center.
Kadt, E. de (1970) *Catholic Radicals in Brazil*. London, Oxford University Press.
Kelly, G. (1955) *The Psychology of Personal Constructs*. New York, Norton.
Kidd, R. and Byram, M. (1982) 'Demystifying pseudo Freirean development', *Community Development Journal*, 17(2), 91–105.
Kirkwood, G. and Kirkwood, C. (1989) *Living Adult Education*. Milton Keynes, Open University Press.
Knudson, R. (1971) 'Review of pedagogy of the oppressed', *Library Journal*, 96, April, 1261.
Koffka, K. (1935) *Principles of Gestalt Psychology*. New York, Harcourt Brace.
Kosik, K. (1988) *La dialectique du concret*. Paris, La Passion.
Kozol, J. (1978) 'A new look at the literacy campaign in Cuba', *Harvard Educational Review*, 48(3), 341–77.
Kozol, J. (1985) *Illiterate America*. New York, Doubleday
Leach, T. (1982) 'Paulo Freire: Dialogue, politics and relevance', *International Journal of Lifelong Education*, 1(3), 185–201.
Le Men, S. (1985) 'Les Abécédaires enseignaient-ils à lire', *Communication et langages*, 63(1), 31–47.
Levine, K. (1982) 'Functional literacy: Fond illusions and false economies', *Harvard Educational Review*, 52(3), 249–66.
Lévi-Strauss, C. (1958) *Anthropologie structurale*. Paris, Plon.
Lévi-Strauss, C. (1962) *La pensée sauvage*. Paris, Plon.
Lloyd, A. (1972) 'Freire, conscientisation and adult education', *Adult Education*, 23(1), 3–20.
Lovett, T. (1975) *Adult Education, Community Development and the Working Class*. London, Ward Lock,
McCarthy, T. (1978) *The Critical Theory of Jürgen Habermas*. London, Polity Press.
MacEoin, G. (1971) 'The new game plan for Latin America', *The National Catholic Reporter*, 19 February.

MacEoin, G. (1972) 'Conscientisation for the masses', *The National Catholic Reporter*, 17 March.

Mackie, K. (1983) *The Application of Learning Theory to Adult Learning*. Nottingham, Nottingham University.

Mackie, R. (ed.) (1980) *Literacy and Revolution: The Pedagogy of Paulo Freire*. London, Pluto Press.

McLaren, P. (1986) 'Postmodernity and the death of politics: A Brazilian reprieve', *Educational Theory*, 36(4), 389–401.

McLaren, P. (1988) 'Culture or canon? Critical pedagogy and the politics of literacy', *Harvard Educational Review*, 58(2), 213–34.

Marcuse, H. (1968) 'The affirmative character of culture', *Negations*. Harmondsworth, Penguin.

Maritain, J. (1957) *Existence and the Existent*. New York, Doubleday Image.

Marrero, G. (1971) 'Towards love and justice: conscientisation', *Church and Race*. New York, United Presbyterian Board of Mission, 5, 1–8.

Mashayekh, F. (1974) 'Freire, the man, his ideas and their implications', *Literacy Discussion*, 5(1), 1–62.

Matos, F. Gomes de (1989) 'L'alphabétisation au Brésil: huit ouvrages des années 80', *Perspectives*, 19(4), 676–81.

Memmi, A. (1973) *Portrait du Colonisateur*. Paris, Payot.

Mounier, E. (1951) *Be not Afraid: Studies in Personalist Sociology*. London, Rockliff.

Nickerson, R. (1985) 'Adult Literacy and technology', *Visible Language*, 19(3), 311–55.

Ohliger, J. (1971) *Lifelong Learning or Lifelong Schooling?* New York, Syracuse University.

Olson, D. R. (1977) 'From utterance to text: The bias of language in speech and writing', *Harvard Educational Review*, 47(3), 257–81.

Olson, D. R. (1982) 'What is said and what is meant in speech and writing', *Visible Language*, 16(2), 151–61.

O'Neill, P. (1973) 'A critical exposition of Paulo Freire's philosophy of education'. Unpublished MEd thesis, Trinity College Dublin

Ong, W. (1988) *Orality and Literacy: The Technologising of the Word*. London, Methuen.

Organisation Mondiale de la Sonté (1987) *Evaluation de la Stratégie de la Sonté pour tous d'ici à 2000*. OMS, Genève.

Otto, W. and Stallard, C. (1976) 'One hundred essential sight words', *Visible Language*, 10(3), 247–52.

Penichaut, N. (1990) 'Illettrisme: la méthode Renault', *Libération*, 22 May, 21–2.

Petersen, P. (1965) *Der Kleine Jena-Plan: einer freien allgemeinen Volksschule*. Weinheim, Julius Beltz.

Pomes, J.-C. (1989) 'Tâtonnement expérimental et environement informatique', in P. Clanché and J. Testanière, *Actualité de la pédagogie Freinet*. Bordeaux, Presses Universitaires de Bordeaux.

Postman, N. (1970) 'The politics of reading', *Harvard Educational Review*, 40(2), 244–52.

Rabinowitz, P. (1977) 'Truth in fiction: a reexamination of audiences', *Critical Enquiry*, 4, 121–42.

Reimer, E. (1970) 'Does the shoe fit? A background piece on the "silent majority"', *America*, 23(3), 69–70.

Reimer, E. (1971) *School is Dead*. Harmondsworth, Penguin Education Special.

Rockhill, K. (1987) 'Gender, language and the politics of literacy', *British Journal of Sociology of Education*, 8, 153–67.

Roman, J. (1990) 'La lecture, l'illettrisme', *Esprit*, 3/4, 142–5.

Sanders, T. G. (1968) 'The Paulo Freire method: Literacy training and conscientisation'. Manchester Student Christian Movement, roneo-text from the World Council of Churches, Geneva.

Sartre, J.-P. (1957) *Being and Nothingness: An Essay on Phenomenological Ontology.* London, Methuen.

Scribner, S. (1984) 'Literacy in three metaphors', *American Journal of Education,* 93(1), 6–21.

Secord, P. (1974) *Social Psychology.* London, Mcgraw Hill.

Shaull, R. (1982) 'Introduction' in *Pedagogy of the Oppressed.* Harmondsworth, Penguin.

Skidmore, T. (1967) *Politics in Brazil, 1930–1964: An Experiment in Democracy.* London, Oxford University Press.

Skinner, Q. (1969) 'Meaning and understanding in the history of ideas', *History and Theory,* 8(1), 3–53.

Spies-Bong, G. (1989) *Pour une pédagogie en communauté de vie: le petit plan d'Jena de Peter Petersen.* Paris, Editions Universitaires.

Stanley, M (1972) 'Literacy: the crisis of conventional wisdom', in S. Grabowski (ed.), *Paulo Freire: A Revolutionary Dilemma for the Adult Educator.* New York, ERIC Clearing House.

Steiner, G. (1972) 'After the book', *Visible Language,* 6(3), 197–210.

Sticht, T. (1972) 'Project realistic: Determination of adult functional literacy levels', *Reading Research Quarterly,* 7(3), 424–65.

Sturrock, J. (1974) 'Roland Barthes: A profile', *New Review,* 1(2), 13–21.

Szulc, T. (1960) Articles in the *New York Times,* 31 October; 1 November, quoted in Castro, J. de (1969) *Death in the Northeast.* New York, Vintage.

Teilhard, P. (1965) *The Phenomenon of Man.* London, Collins-Fontana.

Tillich, P. (1967) *The Courage To Be.* London, Fontana.

Tillich, P. (1973) *The Boundary of Our Being.* London, Fontana.

Unesco (1965) *Literacy as a Factor of Development.* Paris, Unesco Press.

Unesco (1976) *The Experimental World Literacy Programme: A Critical Assessment.* Paris, Unesco Press.

Unesco (1984) *Project de plan à moyen terme, 1984–1989,* Programme II.1, Généralisation d L'Intensification de la lutte contre l'analphábetisme. Paris, Unesco Press.

Unesco (1990) *World Declaration on Education for All.* New York, UNICEF House.

Vygotsky, L. S. (1978) *Mind in Society.* Cambridge, Mass., Harvard University Press.

Weber, R. M. (1975) 'Adult illiteracy in the United States', in J. Carroll and J. Chall (eds), *Towards a Literate Society.* New York, McGraw Hill.

Wilkinson, A. (1985) 'I communicate, therefore I am', *Education Review,* 37(1), 65–76.

Youngman, F. (1986) *Adult Education and Socialist Pedagogy.* London, Croom Helm.

Index